التوسل المتواصل

Continuous Calling

التوسل المتواصل

Continuous Calling

Papyra

Continuous Calling

Copyright © 2025 Papyra Pty Ltd. All rights reserved. No portion of this book may be reproduced in any form without written permission from the publisher or author, except as permitted by applicable copyright law.

Papyra Pty Ltd
Sydney, Australia
www.papyra.com.au

Paperback ISBN: 978-1-923486-02-7
Pocket Edition ISBN: 978-1-923486-03-4

Arabic texts are in the Public domain.

Quranic translations quoted, and at times adjusted, from The Qur'an with a Phrase-by-Phrase English Translation by Ali Quli Qarai. Copyright © Ali Quli Qarai. Used with respectful acknowledgement for educational and critical purposes.

بِسْمِ ٱللَّهِ ٱلرَّحْمَٰنِ ٱلرَّحِيمِ

يَٰٓأَيُّهَا ٱلَّذِينَ ءَامَنُوا۟ ٱذْكُرُوا۟ ٱللَّهَ ذِكْرًا كَثِيرًا ۝ وَسَبِّحُوهُ بُكْرَةً وَأَصِيلًا ۝ هُوَ ٱلَّذِى يُصَلِّى عَلَيْكُمْ وَمَلَٰٓئِكَتُهُۥ لِيُخْرِجَكُم مِّنَ ٱلظُّلُمَٰتِ إِلَى ٱلنُّورِ ۚ وَكَانَ بِٱلْمُؤْمِنِينَ رَحِيمًا ۝

Oh you who believe! Remember Allah with frequent remembrance, and glorify Him morning and evening.

It is He who blesses you—and so do His angels—that He may bring you out from darkness into light, and He is most merciful to the faithful.

Quran 33:41-43

Contents

Preface 1
Quranic Dua 2
Dua Ghareeq and the Etiquette of Dua 16
Dua Hujjah 18
Dua Faraj 19
Dua Ahd 21
Dua Nudbah 26
Dua Tawassul 48
Dua Kumayl 58
Dua Mashlool 75

Ziyarahs

Prophet Muhammad (saaw) 91
Imam Ali (as) 110
Sayedah Fatma (as) 147
Imam Hassan (as) 154
    Ziyarat Ameenullah 156
Imam Hussein (as) 161
    Ziyarat Ashura 186
Imam Zeinul Abideen (as) 195
Imam Baqir (as) 199
Imam Sadiq (as) 202
Imam Kadhem (as) 204
Imam Redha (as) 210
Imam Jawad (as) 218
Imam Hadi (as) 223
Imam Askari (as) 227
Imam Mahdi (as) 233
Ziyarat Jamia Kabeera 238

Preface

This book has been compiled not as a comprehensive guide to dua and ziyarah, but rather as a practical way to remain in constant conversation with Allah (swt). While all of the material here is available online, it is often difficult to find a way to dedicate a substantial portion of your time reading dua and ziyarah. Unless you know the name of the dua or ziyarah already, you may be unable to find a sufficiently long ziyarah, or you may be unaware of the existence of certain dua.

I've therefore included 33 Quranic dua to keep you in conversation with Allah (swt) throughout the day, 8 common dua for throughout the week, and 19 substantial ziyarahs to keep you in contact with the Ahlul Bayt throughout the year.

For the Quranic duas, I've included descriptions of the problems they solve. These should keep you in conversation with Allah (swt) throughout the day, with you constantly repeating your chosen dua until your problem is solved.

For the common duas, I've included information of when to read them, and if relevant, the source and recommendation for reciting it.

For the ziyarahs, I've included occasions to recite them in. I have chosen long and beautiful ziyarahs to allow you to dedicate a substantial length of time to conversation with Allah (swt) and the Ma'soom of that day and to connect with them strongly. The ziyarahs themselves are not necessarily the most recommended to recite. Rather, I have prioritised based on their eloquence and storytelling of the life of that Ma'soom.

Before each ziyarah, I've included a quote to show the love that Ma'soom has for us.

For some of them, I've needed to take Ziyarahs from multiple places to create a Ziyarah that is long enough to feel like you have given that Imam (as) an appropriate amount of time, as the existing Ziyarahs were too short individually.

The translations are as literal as possible and I have tried to keep translations consistent for similar words, this allows the reader to extract multiple meanings from the text, rather than the author simply choosing one.

For example, the word "sayyed" is always translated as "chief". This consistency allows the reader to understand this as "leader" or "best of" or even both, depending on context, rather than the translator choosing one or the other.

Quranic Dua

Surah Fatiha

In a golden chain from Imam Askari (as) through all the previous Imams (as) to Prophet Muhammad (saaw) who says:

"Allah, Mighty and Majestic said "I have divided the 'Opening of the Book' (Surah Al-Fatiha) between Myself and My servant. So half of it is for Me and half of it is for My servant, and for My servant is whatever he asks for." (Tafseer Noor Al-Thaqalayn)

Allah (swt) says when one recites Surah Al-Fatiha, He completes their affairs, blesses them, removes their afflictions, increase them in bounties, give them from His compassion and mercy, makes the Day of Judgement easier for them, overlooks their sins, increases rewards for their worship, rescues them from harsh conditions, holds their hands in days of difficulty, and guides them to the straight path while protecting them from His misguidance and anger.

In the name of Allah, the most Compassionate, the most Merciful	بِسْمِ اللَّهِ الرَّحْمَٰنِ الرَّحِيمِ
All praise belongs to Allah, Lord of all the worlds	الْحَمْدُ لِلَّهِ رَبِّ الْعَالَمِينَ
The most Compassionate, most Merciful	الرَّحْمَٰنِ الرَّحِيمِ
Master of the Day of Judgement	مَالِكِ يَوْمِ الدِّينِ
It is You alone who we worship and You alone who we ask for help	إِيَّاكَ نَعْبُدُ وَإِيَّاكَ نَسْتَعِينُ
Guide us to the Straight Path	اهْدِنَا الصِّرَاطَ الْمُسْتَقِيمَ
The Path of those You have blessed, rather than those You are angry with or those who are astray	صِرَاطَ الَّذِينَ أَنْعَمْتَ عَلَيْهِمْ غَيْرِ الْمَغْضُوبِ عَلَيْهِمْ وَلَا الضَّالِّينَ

Quranic Dua

Surah Baqarah

Quran 2:155-157

Allah (swt) promises:

> "We will surely test you with a measure of fear and hunger and loss of wealth, lives, and fruits; and give good news to the patient; those who, when an affliction visits them, say:

> "Indeed we belong to Allah and to Him we return."

إِنَّا لِلَّهِ وَإِنَّا إِلَيْهِ رَاجِعُونَ

> It is they who receive the blessings of their Lord and mercy, and it is they who are guided."

Constantly recite this dhikr when you are being tested and emotions are running high. Remembering that this world is nothing but a temporary test, and that Allah (swt) has something better for you, brings a calmness to the heart.

Quran 2:201

Allah (swt) tells us that there are some who ask for good in this world, but they will have no share in the next world. So instead ask:

> Our Lord! Grant us good in this world and good in the Hereafter, and protect us from the punishment of the Fire.

رَبَّنَآ ءَاتِنَا فِى ٱلدُّنْيَا حَسَنَةً وَفِى ٱلْءَاخِرَةِ حَسَنَةً وَقِنَا عَذَابَ ٱلنَّارِ

Then Allah (swt) will reward you with the fruits of your labour.

Quran 2:250

Talut's army was marching to face the much larger army of Goliath. Many of Talut's army failed the test at the river and were sent away. Some of those who remained believed all hope was lost. The army then recited the following:

> Our Lord! Pour down upon us patience, and make our steps firm, and help us against the disbelieving people

رَبَّنَآ أَفْرِغْ عَلَيْنَا صَبْرًا وَثَبِّتْ أَقْدَامَنَا وَٱنصُرْنَا عَلَى ٱلْقَوْمِ ٱلْكَافِرِينَ

By the permission of Allah (swt), Goliath was defeated. Recite this dua when you are facing a challenge beyond your capacity. Lose hope in your own strength and efforts, and place all your hope in Allah (swt) (Quran 12:87).

Continuous Calling

Quran 2:255

Ayatul Kursi is a verse which protects against every kind of problem in this life and the next. It is the peak of the Quran and a special gift given to no Prophet before Prophet Muhammad (saaw). The one who recites it while in Sajdah will never enter Hellfire. (Bihar al-Anwar vol 89, ch 30).

Allah! There is no god except Him, the Ever-Living, the Sustainer	اَللّٰهُ لَآ إِلٰهَ إِلَّا هُوَ ٱلْحَىُّ ٱلْقَيُّومُ
Neither drowsiness nor sleep overtakes Him	لَا تَأْخُذُهُ سِنَةٌ وَلَا نَوْمٌ
To Him belongs whatever is in the heavens and whatever is on the earth	لَهُ مَا فِى ٱلسَّمٰوٰتِ وَمَا فِى ٱلْأَرْضِ
Who can intercede with Him except with His permission?	مَن ذَا ٱلَّذِى يَشْفَعُ عِندَهُۥٓ إِلَّا بِإِذْنِهِۦ
He knows what is ahead of them and what is behind them,	يَعْلَمُ مَا بَيْنَ أَيْدِيهِمْ وَمَا خَلْفَهُمْ
And they do not comprehend anything of His knowledge, except what He wills	وَلَا يُحِيطُونَ بِشَىْءٍ مِّنْ عِلْمِهِۦٓ إِلَّا بِمَا شَآءَ
His seat encompasses the heavens and the earth,	وَسِعَ كُرْسِيُّهُ ٱلسَّمٰوٰتِ وَٱلْأَرْضَ
And their preservation does not tire Him	وَلَا يَـُٔودُهُۥ حِفْظُهُمَا
And He is the Exalted, the Great	وَهُوَ ٱلْعَلِىُّ ٱلْعَظِيمُ

Quran 2:286

Allah does not burden a soul beyond its capacity	لَا يُكَلِّفُ اللَّهُ نَفْسًا إِلَّا وُسْعَهَا
For it, is what it earns, and against it, is what it incurs	لَهَا مَا كَسَبَتْ وَعَلَيْهَا مَا اكْتَسَبَتْ
Our Lord! Take us not to blame if we forget or make mistakes	رَبَّنَا لَا تُؤَاخِذْنَا إِنْ نَسِينَا أَوْ أَخْطَأْنَا
Our Lord! Do not place on us a burden as You placed on those before us	رَبَّنَا وَلَا تَحْمِلْ عَلَيْنَا إِصْرًا كَمَا حَمَلْتَهُ عَلَى الَّذِينَ مِنْ قَبْلِنَا
Our Lord! Do not place on us what we have no strength to bear	رَبَّنَا وَلَا تُحَمِّلْنَا مَا لَا طَاقَةَ لَنَا بِهِ
And pardon us, and forgive us, and have mercy on us	وَاعْفُ عَنَّا وَاغْفِرْ لَنَا وَارْحَمْنَا
You are our Master, so help us against the disbelieving people	أَنْتَ مَوْلَانَا فَانْصُرْنَا عَلَى الْقَوْمِ الْكَافِرِينَ

Recite this for protection from suffering as those in history have suffered.

Surah Alee Imraan

Quran 3: 8-9

Our Lord! Do not deviate our hearts after You have guided us, and bestow on us from Your mercy. Indeed, You are the Bestower	رَبَّنَا لَا تُزِغْ قُلُوبَنَا بَعْدَ إِذْ هَدَيْتَنَا وَهَبْ لَنَا مِنْ لَدُنْكَ رَحْمَةً إِنَّكَ أَنْتَ الْوَهَّابُ
Our Lord! Indeed, You are the Gatherer of mankind for a Day in which there is no doubt. Indeed Allah does not break His promise	رَبَّنَا إِنَّكَ جَامِعُ النَّاسِ لِيَوْمٍ لَا رَيْبَ فِيهِ إِنَّ اللَّهَ لَا يُخْلِفُ الْمِيعَادَ

Recite this for protection from complacency and losing progress in religion. Imam Baqir (as) says that faith can be confiscated after having been deposited. (Quran 6:98, Tafseer al Ayashi).

Continuous Calling

Quran 3: 26-27

Say "Oh Allah! Master of the Kingdom!	قُلِ اللَّهُمَّ مالِكَ المُلكِ
You give sovereignty to whoever You will, and take sovereignty away from whoever You will!	تُؤتِي المُلكَ مَن تَشاءُ وَتَنزِعُ المُلكَ مِمَّن تَشاءُ
And You honour who You will and debase who You will	وَتُعِزُّ مَن تَشاءُ وَتُذِلُّ مَن تَشاءُ
In Your hand is goodness	بِيَدِكَ الخَيرُ
Indeed You have power over all things	إِنَّكَ عَلى كُلِّ شَيءٍ قَديرٌ
You pass the night into the day	تُولِجُ اللَّيلَ فِي النَّهارِ
And You pass the day into the night	وَتُولِجُ النَّهارَ فِي اللَّيلِ
And You bring out the living from the dead	وَتُخرِجُ الحَيَّ مِنَ المَيِّتِ
And You bring out the dead from the living	وَتُخرِجُ المَيِّتَ مِنَ الحَيِّ
And You provide for whoever You will without account"	وَتَرزُقُ مَن تَشاءُ بِغَيرِ حِسابٍ

This indicates that your situation is in Allah's (swt) hands, so make peace with it.

Quran 3:35

This was the dua of the mother of Sayedah Maryam (as).

My Lord! Indeed I vowed to You what is in my womb freely, so accept it from me. Indeed you are the Hearing, the Knowing	رَبِّ إِنِّى نَذَرتُ لَكَ ما فى بَطنى مُحَرَّرًا فَتَقَبَّل مِنّى إِنَّكَ أَنتَ السَّميعُ العَليمُ

For the sisters, recite while pregnant, dedicating your child to Allah (swt).

Quranic Dua

Quran 3:38

Nabi Zakariya (as) prayed for a child using this dua and Allah (swt) gave him Nabi Yahya (as).

My Lord! Grant me from You a good offspring. Indeed, You are the Hearer of supplications	رَبِّ هَبْ لِي مِن لَدُنكَ ذُرِّيَّةً طَيِّبَةً إِنَّكَ سَمِيعُ الدُّعَاءِ

Recite to ask for a good child.

Quran 3:191-194

"Those who remember Allah while standing, sitting, and lying on their sides, and reflect on the creation of the heavens and the earth.

Our Lord! You have not created this without purpose.	رَبَّنَا مَا خَلَقْتَ هَذَا بَاطِلًا
Glory be to You! Protect us from the punishment of the Fire"	سُبْحَانَكَ فَقِنَا عَذَابَ النَّارِ

Recite when you are in awe of the creation of Allah (swt). You can also continue with the below:

Our Lord! Whoever You make enter the Fire, surely You disgraced him	رَبَّنَا إِنَّكَ مَن تُدْخِلِ النَّارَ فَقَدْ أَخْزَيْتَهُ
And for the wrongdoers, there are no helpers	وَمَا لِلظَّالِمِينَ مِنْ أَنصَارٍ
Our Lord, indeed we heard a caller calling to faith, calling, "Believe in your Lord!" So we believed	رَبَّنَا إِنَّنَا سَمِعْنَا مُنَادِيًا يُنَادِي لِلْإِيمَانِ أَنْ آمِنُوا بِرَبِّكُمْ فَآمَنَّا
Our Lord! So forgive us our sins, and remove from us our misdeeds	رَبَّنَا فَاغْفِرْ لَنَا ذُنُوبَنَا وَكَفِّرْ عَنَّا سَيِّئَاتِنَا
And make us die with the righteous	وَتَوَفَّنَا مَعَ الْأَبْرَارِ
Our Lord! And grant us what You promised us through Your Messengers	رَبَّنَا وَآتِنَا مَا وَعَدتَّنَا عَلَى رُسُلِكَ

Surah Nisa

Quran 4:75

Our Lord! Bring us out of this town whose people are oppressors	رَبَّنا أَخرِجنا مِن هذِهِ القَريَةِ الظّالِمِ أَهلُها
And appoint for us a guardian from You	وَاجعَل لَنا مِن لَدُنكَ وَلِيًّا
And appoint for us a helper from You	وَاجعَل لَنا مِن لَدُنكَ نَصيرًا

Recite for relief from oppression in your hometown or assistance when migrating away from an oppressor.

Surah Maida

Quran 5:83

"And when they hear what has been sent down to the Messenger, you see their eyes overflowing with tears because of what they recognize of the Truth. They say:

Our Lord, we have believed, so record us among the witnesses	رَبَّنا آمَنّا فَاكتُبنا مَعَ الشّاهِدينَ
And why should we not believe in Allah and what has come to us of the truth?	وَما لَنا لا نُؤمِنُ بِاللَّهِ وَما جاءَنا مِنَ الحَقِّ
And we are eager for our Lord to admit us among the righteous people	وَنَطمَعُ أَن يُدخِلَنا رَبُّنا مَعَ القَومِ الصّالِحينَ

So Allah will reward them for what they said with Gardens under which rivers flow, to stay there forever. And that is the reward of the good-doers."

Recite when your heart is humbled to the signs of Allah (swt).

Quranic Dua

Surah An'am

Quran 6:78-79, 161-163

Based on these verses of the Quran, Imam Sadiq (as) recommended the following dua to be recited before the prayer (Al Ihtijaaj Vol 2, p307,):

I have turned my face towards the One Who has originated the heavens and the Earth	وَجَّهْتُ وَجْهِيَ لِلَّذِى فَطَرَ السَّمَاوَاتِ وَالْأَرْضَ
A Hanif and a Muslim	حَنِيفًا مُسْلِمًا
On the way of Ibrahim and the religion of Muhammad and the guidance of the commander of the faithful	عَلَى مِلَّةِ إِبْرَاهِيمَ وَدِينِ مُحَمَّدٍ وَهُدَى أَمِيرِ الْمُؤْمِنِينَ
And I am not of the polytheists	وَمَا أَنَا مِنَ الْمُشْرِكِينَ
Indeed, my prayers, my sacrifice, my life, and my death are for Allah, Lord of the worlds	إِنَّ صَلَاتِي وَنُسُكِي وَمَحْيَايَ وَمَمَاتِي لِلَّهِ رَبِّ الْعَالَمِينَ
No partner to Him	لَا شَرِيكَ لَهُ
And with that, I have been commanded	وَبِذَلِكَ أُمِرْتُ
And I am from the Muslims	وَأَنَا مِنَ الْمُسْلِمِينَ
Oh Allah! Make me from the Muslims	اللَّهُمَّ اجْعَلْنِي مِنَ الْمُسْلِمِينَ
I seek refuge in Allah, the Hearing, the Knowing	أَعُوذُ بِاللَّهِ السَّمِيعِ الْعَلِيمِ
From the expelled Satan	مِنَ الشَّيْطَانِ الرَّجِيمِ

Continuous Calling

Surah A'raf

Quran 7:23

This was the Dua of Nabi Adam (as) and Sayedah Hawwa (as) after they ate from the tree.

> Our Lord, we have wronged ourselves, and if You do not forgive us and have mercy upon us, we will surely be among the losers

رَبَّنَا ظَلَمْنَا أَنفُسَنَا وَإِن لَمْ تَغْفِرْ لَنَا وَتَرْحَمْنَا لَنَكُونَنَّ مِنَ الْخَاسِرِينَ

Allah (swt) forgave them but warned them not to let Shaytan deceive them again. It should be noted the eating from the tree was not a sin.

Recite when you've been deceived by Shaytan into committing a sin, and avoid repeating the sin afterwards.

Surah Tawba

Quran 9:58-59

"There are some of them who are critical of your distribution of alms. If they are given some of it they are pleased, but if not they are enraged. If only they had been content with what Allah and His Messenger had given them and said,

> Allah is sufficient for us; Allah and His Messenger will give to us out of His grace. Indeed to Allah we are eager"

حَسْبُنَا ٱللَّهُ سَيُؤْتِينَا ٱللَّهُ مِن فَضْلِهِ وَرَسُولُهُ إِنَّا إِلَى ٱللَّهِ رَاغِبُونَ

Recite when you feel stinginess in your heart.

Quran 9:128-129

"A Messenger has come to you from among yourselves. He is grieved by your suffering, and concerned about you, and kind and merciful to the believers. But if they turn back, then say:

> Allah is sufficient for me, there is no god but He; on Him do I rely, and He is the Lord of Great Throne."

حَسْبِيَ ٱللَّهُ لَا إِلَٰهَ إِلَّا هُوَ عَلَيْهِ تَوَكَّلْتُ وَهُوَ رَبُّ ٱلْعَرْشِ ٱلْعَظِيمِ

Recite when you are frustrated by people ignoring the religion of Allah (swt).

Quranic Dua

Surah Ibrahim

Quran 14:40-41

My Lord! Make me an establisher of prayer, and from my descendants	رَبِّ اجعَلني مُقيمَ الصَّلاةِ وَمِن ذُرِّيَّتي
Our Lord! And accept my supplication	رَبَّنا وَتَقَبَّل دُعاءِ
Our Lord! Forgive me and my parents, and the believers, on the day when the reckoning is held	رَبَّنَا اغفِر لى وَلِوالِدَىَّ وَلِلمُؤمِنينَ يَومَ يَقومُ الحِسابُ

Surah Israa

Quran 17:24

For our parents Allah (swt) tells us to lower the wings of humility and say:

My Lord! Have mercy on them both as they raised me when I was little	رَبِّ ارحَمهُما كَما رَبَّيانى صَغيرًا

Recite to show gratitude to your parents for being the avenue by which Allah (swt) cared for you.

Quran 17:80

My Lord! Admit me with a worthy entrance, and bring me out with a worthy departure	رَبِّ أَدخِلنى مُدخَلَ صِدقٍ وَأَخرِجنى مُخرَجَ صِدقٍ
And grant me from You a supporting authority to assist	وَاجعَل لى مِن لَدنكَ سُلطانًا نَصيرًا

Recite when you enter into something you fear. (Tafseer Hub-e-Ali).

Surah Kahf

Quran 18:23-24

Do not say that you will do something tomorrow without saying:

If Allah wills	إِنْ شَاءَ اللَّهُ

If you forget to say it, then whenever you remember, you should say it, no matter how long it has been. This is a dua, asking Allah (swt) to assist you in and not prevent you from what you intend to do.

Surah Ta-Ha

Quran 20:25-28

My Lord! Expand for me my breast	رَبِّ اشْرَحْ لِي صَدْرِي
And make my task easy for me	وَيَسِّرْ لِي أَمْرِي
And untie the knot from my tongue	وَاحْلُلْ عُقْدَةً مِنْ لِسَانِي
So they may understand my speech	يَفْقَهُوا قَوْلِي

Recite before speaking to a person/people about any important matter.

Quran 20:114

My Lord! Increase me in knowledge	رَبِّ زِدْنِي عِلْمًا

Recite before, during, and after any task where you are seeking knowledge.

Surah Anbiya

Quran 21:83-84

Nabi Ayyub (as) was very wealthy, had many children, a wife, and good health. Allah (swt) tested Nabi Ayyub (as) by the death of his children, the loss of his wealth, poor health, and finally with the desperation of his wife. Then he recited the following dua:

My Lord! Indeed distress has touched me, and You are the most Merciful of the merciful	رَبِّ أَنِّي مَسَّنِيَ الضُّرُّ وَأَنْتَ أَرْحَمُ الرَّاحِمِينَ

Allah (swt) returned to him his wealth and health, then revived his children, removing all distress from him.

Quranic Dua

Quran 21:87-88

Nabi Yunus (as) went away from his people angry, and Allah (swt) caused the fish to swallow him. His situation was hopeless, he was in the darkness of the belly of the fish, in the darkness of the sea, in the darkness of the night. He called out:

| There is no god but You. Glory be to You! Indeed, I was among the wrongdoers | لَا إِلَهَ إِلَّا أَنْتَ سُبْحَانَكَ إِنِّي كُنْتُ مِنَ الظَّالِمِينَ |

Allah (swt) rescued him from the fish, and similarly He responds to and rescues the believers from their hopeless situations when they call out to him.

Quran 21:89

Nabi Zakariya (as) and his wife had grown old and not had any children, so he called out:

| My Lord! Do not leave me alone, and You are the best of inheritors | رَبِّ لَا تَذَرْنِي فَرْدًا وَأَنْتَ خَيْرُ الْوَارِثِينَ |

Allah (swt) answered his dua and gave him Nabi Yahya (as) as a son.

Surah Furqan
Quran 25:74

Imam Sadiq (as) tells us to make this dua in the following form (Tafseer Hub-a-Ali):

| Our Lord, grant us from our spouses and our descendants a comfort for our eyes, and make for us an Imam from among the righteous | رَبَّنَا هَبْ لَنَا مِنْ أَزْوَاجِنَا وَذُرِّيَّاتِنَا قُرَّةَ أَعْيُنٍ وَاجْعَلْ لَنَا مِنَ الْمُتَّقِينَ إِمَامًا |

Recite for a wife, children, and to enter into the wilayah of your Imam (afs).

Surah A-Shura
Quran 26:169

Nabi Lut's (as) community began engaging in widespread homosexuality and other forms of degeneracy and oppression. Nabi Lut (as) prayed:

| My Lord! Deliver me and my family from what they do | رَبِّ نَجِّنِي وَأَهْلِي مِمَّا يَعْمَلُونَ |

Allah (swt) rescued the believers of his family from that community. Recite when you are in fear of degeneracy invading your family.

Surah Qasas

Quran 28:24

Nabi Musa (as) had lost everything. Exiled from his country, wanted for murder, with no food, he asked Allah (swt) for food by saying:

My Lord! I am indeed in need of any good You may send down to me	رَبِّ إِنِّي لِمَا أَنْزَلْتَ إِلَيَّ مِنْ خَيْرٍ فَقِيرٌ

Allah (swt) immediately gave him a job, a mentor, a wife, a home, and corrected all his affairs.

Surah Az-Zumar

Quran 39:46

Oh Allah! Originator of the heavens and the earth! Knower of the unseen and the seen! You judge between Your servants concerning that over which they used to differ	اللَّهُمَّ فَاطِرَ السَّمَاوَاتِ وَالْأَرْضِ عَالِمَ الْغَيْبِ وَالشَّهَادَةِ أَنْتَ تَحْكُمُ بَيْنَ عِبَادِكَ فِي مَا كَانُوا فِيهِ يَخْتَلِفُونَ

Surah Al-Hashr

Quran 59:10

Our Lord, forgive us and our brothers who preceded us in faith	رَبَّنَا اغْفِرْ لَنَا وَلِإِخْوَانِنَا الَّذِينَ سَبَقُونَا بِالْإِيمَانِ
And do not put any resentment in our hearts toward those who believed	وَلَا تَجْعَلْ فِي قُلُوبِنَا غِلًّا لِلَّذِينَ آمَنُوا
Our Lord, indeed You are Kind and Merciful	رَبَّنَا إِنَّكَ رَءُوفٌ رَحِيمٌ

Recite when you feel jealousy for your believing brothers.

Quranic Dua

Surah Al-Falaq

In the name of Allah, the most Compassionate, the most Merciful	بِسْمِ اللَّهِ الرَّحْمَٰنِ الرَّحِيمِ
Say, I seek refuge in the Lord of the Al-Falaq (Pit in Hell)	قُلْ أَعُوذُ بِرَبِّ الْفَلَقِ
From the evil of what He has created	مِن شَرِّ مَا خَلَقَ
And from the evil of darkness when it covers	وَمِن شَرِّ غَاسِقٍ إِذَا وَقَبَ
And from the evil of the blowers in knots	وَمِن شَرِّ النَّفَّاثَاتِ فِي الْعُقَدِ
And from the evil of an envier when he envies	وَمِن شَرِّ حَاسِدٍ إِذَا حَسَدَ

Recite for protection from every evil, especially the darkness of the night, black magic, and the envious eye.

Surah An-Nas

In the name of Allah, the most Compassionate, the most Merciful	بِسْمِ اللَّهِ الرَّحْمَٰنِ الرَّحِيمِ
Say, I seek refuge in the Lord of Mankind	قُلْ أَعُوذُ بِرَبِّ النَّاسِ
King of Mankind	مَلِكِ النَّاسِ
God of Mankind	إِلَٰهِ النَّاسِ
From the evil of the devious whisperer	مِن شَرِّ الْوَسْوَاسِ الْخَنَّاسِ
Who whispers into the chests of Mankind	الَّذِي يُوَسْوِسُ فِي صُدُورِ النَّاسِ
From among the Jinn and Mankind	مِنَ الْجِنَّةِ وَالنَّاسِ

Recite for protection from every evil, especially the whispers of the Devils.

Continuous Calling

Dua Ghareeq and the Etiquette of Dua

Imam Sadiq (as) says "After this, a time will come when you will not be able to see the Imam of the time. In that period no one will be saved except the one who recites "Dua Ghareeq"". The narrator asked about what Dua Ghareeq is. Imam Sadiq (as) replied:

Oh Allah, oh the most Compassionate, oh the most Merciful	يَا أَللَّهُ يَا رَحْمْنُ يَا رَحِيمُ
Oh Turner of hearts	يَا مُقَلِّبَ ٱلْقُلُوبِ
Make my heart firm upon Your religion	ثَبِّتْ قَلْبِي عَلَى دِينِكَ

The narrator repeated the dua but he added "Turner of hearts and visions". The Imam said "Indeed God is the Turner of hearts and visions but only say Turner of hearts". (Kamaaluddin, Sayyid Rizvi translation, page 363)

This narration indicates to us that each supplication contains a deeper reality. Every word plays a role within the dua, and even a couple of added words can take away from the value of a supplication.

Therefore, as part of the etiquette of dua, we must not add or subtract anything from them, and should read them exactly as they are written. We should not repeat phrases unless the dua repeats them, nor should we repeat something more or less than it is written. We should also not add or remove sections, nor mix and match different duas.

We should have complete submission to the Imam (as) and not change his words.

"Oh you who believe, do not put yourselves before Allah and His Messenger, and fear Allah. Indeed Allah is hearing and knowing." (Quran 49:1)

For certain supplications, such as Dua Mashlool, it has been mentioned that they should not be read without wudhu. It would therefore be a good idea to make sure you have wudhu before reading any lengthy dua or ziyarah. In fact, it is recommended for a believer to always be in a state of wudhu (Mizan al Hikma Part 403, e.g. Hadith 6527).

Allah (swt) says in Surah Nisa, verse 43 "Do not approach the prayer while you are intoxicated..." and Imam Baqir (as) says "Do not stand to pray with laziness, drowsiness, or reluctance, for indeed that is from the traits of hypocrisy...". (Tafseer al Ayashi)

A person should focus while they are reciting a dua or ziyarah, they should pay attention to the meaning of the words. A person should speak what is in the dua or

Dua Ghareeq

ziyarah as if they were saying it, rather than just reading it. It is the difference between reading a book and delivering a written speech.

Imagine you are speaking directly to Allah (swt), or that you are speaking to the member of the Ahlul Bayt you are addressing. Allah (swt) promises that He responds when He is called upon (Quran 2:186), while returning Salam is obligatory in Islam. So when you call on Allah (swt) or send Salam to the Ahlul Bayt, they respond. When you pay attention to them, they pay attention to you.

Imam Mahdi (afs) states: "So increase in dua for hastening the reappearance, for in that is your relief" (Kamaaluddin, Sayyid Rizvi translation, page 467).

Finally, Abu Dharr narrates from the Prophet (saaw), "The dua remains veiled until one sends blessings on me and my family." (Wasail al Shia Vol. 7, Section 2, Chapter 36, Hadith 8835).

Always begin and end every dua with salawat on the Prophet (saaw) and his family.

Dua Hujjah

Recite regularly to express and increase your love for Imam Mahdi (afs). Making dua for your Imam (afs) gives you countless blessings as detailed in the book Mikyal al Makaram.

Oh Allah be;	اللّٰهُمَّ كُنْ
for Your guardian (over the believers), the Hujjah (proof), son of Hassan	لِوَلِيِّكَ الْحُجَّةِ ابْنِ الْحَسَنِ
Your blessings be upon him and his fathers;	صَلَوَاتُكَ عَلَيْهِ وَعَلَى آبَائِهِ
In this hour and in every hour	فِي هٰذِهِ السَّاعَةِ وَفِي كُلِّ سَاعَةٍ
A Guardian and a Protector	وَلِيّاً وَحَافِظاً
A Leader and a Supporter	وَقَائِداً وَنَاصِراً
A Guide and an Eye	وَدَلِيلاً وَعَيْناً
Until You establish him in Your earth, obeyed willingly	حَتَّىٰ تُسْكِنَهُ أَرْضَكَ طَوْعاً
And grant him enjoyment in it for a long time	وَتُمَتِّعَهُ فِيهَا طَوِيلاً
By Your mercy oh most merciful of the merciful	بِرَحْمَتِكَ يَا أَرْحَمَ الرَّاحِمِينَ

Dua Faraj

This Dua was taught to us by Imam Mahdi (afs). It brings immediate relief to the one who recites it. (Al-Baladul Ameen p 607)

In the name of Allah, the most Compassionate, the most Merciful	بِسْمِ اللهِ الرَّحْمٰنِ الرَّحِيْمِ
My God! The trial has become great and the concealment evident	إِلٰهِي عَظُمَ الْبَلَاءُ وَبَرِحَ الْخَفَاءُ
And the cover has been lifted and hope cut off	وَانْكَشَفَ الْغِطَاءُ وَانْقَطَعَ الرَّجَاءُ
And the earth has become narrow and the sky restrained	وَضَاقَتِ الْأَرْضُ وَمُنِعَتِ السَّمَاءُ
And You are the One help is sought from and to You complaints are made	وَأَنْتَ الْمُسْتَعَانُ وَإِلَيْكَ الْمُشْتَكَى
And upon You is the reliance in difficulty and ease	وَعَلَيْكَ الْمُعَوَّلُ فِي الشِّدَّةِ وَالرَّخَاءِ
Oh Allah, send blessings upon Muhammad and the family of Muhammad	اَللّٰهُمَّ صَلِّ عَلَىٰ مُحَمَّدٍ وَآلِ مُحَمَّدٍ
The possessors of command whose obedience you have made obligatory on us	أُولِي الْأَمْرِ الَّذِيْنَ فَرَضْتَ عَلَيْنَا طَاعَتَهُمْ
And made us recognize their status through this	وَعَرَّفْتَنَا بِذٰلِكَ مَنْزِلَتَهُمْ
So relieve from us, by their right, a relief, immediate, close, like the blink of an eye or closer	فَفَرِّجْ عَنَّا بِحَقِّهِمْ فَرَجاً عَاجِلاً قَرِيْباً كَلَمْحِ الْبَصَرِ أَوْ هُوَ أَقْرَبُ
Oh Muhammad, oh Ali, oh Ali, oh Muhammad	يَامُحَمَّدُ يَاعَلِيُّ يَاعَلِيُّ يَامُحَمَّدُ
Suffice me, for you two suffice	اِكْفِيَانِي فَإِنَّكُمَا كَافِيَانِ
Support me for you two support	وَانْصُرَانِي فَإِنَّكُمَا نَاصِرَانِ
Oh our master, oh master of the time	يَامَوْلَانَا يَاصَاحِبَ الزَّمَانِ

Continuous Calling

Help! Help! Help!	ٱلْغَوْثَ ٱلْغَوْثَ ٱلْغَوْثَ
Rescue me! Rescue me! Rescue me!	أَدْرِكْنِيْ أَدْرِكْنِيْ أَدْرِكْنِيْ
This hour! This hour! This hour!	ٱلسَّاعَةَ ٱلسَّاعَةَ ٱلسَّاعَةَ

Slap your right thigh as you repeat:

With haste! With haste! With haste!	ٱلْعَجَلَ ٱلْعَجَلَ ٱلْعَجَلَ
Oh Most Merciful of the merciful, by the right of Muhammad and his pure Household	يَا أَرْحَمَ ٱلرَّاحِمِيْنَ بِحَقِّ مُحَمَّدٍ وَآلِهِ ٱلطَّاهِرِيْنَ

Dua Ahd

Imam Sadiq (as) says that the one who recites this dua 40 mornings in a row will be among the companions of the Imam (afs). (Bihar al-Anwar vol 83, p 284)

Oh Allah, Lord of the Great Light	اَللَّهُمَّ رَبَّ ٱلنُّورِ ٱلْعَظِيمِ
Lord of the Elevated Throne	وَرَبَّ ٱلْكُرْسِيِّ ٱلرَّفِيعِ
Lord of the swirling sea	وَرَبَّ ٱلْبَحْرِ ٱلْمَسْجُورِ
Who brought down the Torah, and Injeel, and Zabur	وَمُنْزِلَ ٱلتَّوْرَاةِ وَٱلإِنْجِيلِ وَٱلزَّبُورِ
Lord of the shade and the Heat	وَرَبَّ ٱلظِّلِّ وَٱلْحَرُورِ
Who brought down the great Quran	وَمُنْزِلَ ٱلْقُرْآنِ ٱلْعَظِيمِ
Lord of the close angels	وَرَبَّ ٱلْمَلاَئِكَةِ ٱلْمُقَرَّبِينَ
And the Prophets and Messengers	وَٱلأَنْبِيَاءِ وَٱلْمُرْسَلِينَ
Oh Allah, I ask You by Your noble Name	اَللَّهُمَّ إِنِّي أَسْأَلُكَ بِٱسْمِكَ ٱلْكَرِيمِ
By the light of Your illuminated Face	وَبِنُورِ وَجْهِكَ ٱلْمُنِيرِ
By Your ancient kingdom	وَمُلْكِكَ ٱلْقَدِيمِ
Oh Living, oh Sustainer	يَا حَيُّ يَا قَيُّومُ
I ask You by Your Name which lit up the heavens and the earths	أَسْأَلُكَ بِٱسْمِكَ ٱلَّذِي أَشْرَقَتْ بِهِ ٱلسَّمَاوَاتُ وَٱلأَرَضُونَ
And by Your name which rectifies the former ones and the latter ones	وَبِٱسْمِكَ ٱلَّذِي يَصْلَحُ بِهِ ٱلأَوَّلُونَ وَٱلآخِرُونَ
Oh Living before all life	يَا حَيّاً قَبْلَ كُلِّ حَيٍّ
Oh Living after all life	وَيَا حَيّاً بَعْدَ كُلِّ حَيٍّ
Oh Living when there is no life	وَيَا حَيّاً حِينَ لاَ حَيَّ

Oh Reviver of the dead and causer of the living to die	يَا مُحْيِيَ الْمَوْتَى وَمُمِيتَ الْأَحْيَاءِ
Oh Ever-living, there is no god but You	يَا حَيُّ لَا إِلَهَ إِلَّا أَنْتَ
Oh Allah, convey to our Master, the guiding Imam al-Mahdi, the Qaim (Riser) by Your command	اَللَّهُمَّ بَلِّغْ مَوْلَانَا الْإِمَامَ الْهَادِىَ الْمَهْدِىَّ الْقَائِمَ بِأَمْرِكَ
Blessings of Allah on him and his pure fathers	صَلَوَاتُ اللَّهِ عَلَيْهِ وَعَلَى آبَائِهِ الطَّاهِرِينَ
On behalf of all the believing men and believing women	عَنْ جَمِيعِ الْمُؤْمِنِينَ وَالْمُؤْمِنَاتِ
In the easts and wests of the Earth	فِي مَشَارِقِ الْأَرْضِ وَمَغَارِبِهَا
Its plains and its mountains	سَهْلِهَا وَجَبَلِهَا
Its land and its sea	وَبَرِّهَا وَبَحْرِهَا
And on behalf of me and my parents	وَعَنِّي وَعَنْ وَالِدَيَّ
From the blessings that weigh as much as the throne of Allah	مِنَ الصَّلَوَاتِ زِنَةَ عَرْشِ اللَّهِ
And the ink of His words	وَمِدَادَ كَلِمَاتِهِ
And what His knowledge enumerated and encompassed with His book	وَمَا أَحْصَاهُ عِلْمُهُ وَأَحَاطَ بِهِ كِتَابُهُ
Oh Allah I renew this for him in the mornings of this day	اَللَّهُمَّ إِنِّي أُجَدِّدُ لَهُ فِي صَبِيحَةِ يَوْمِي هَذَا
And the days I will live	وَمَا عِشْتُ مِنْ أَيَّامِي
A covenant, a contract, and a allegiance on my neck	عَهْداً وَعَقْداً وَبَيْعَةً لَهُ فِي عُنُقِي
I never turn away or deviate from it	لَا أَحُولُ عَنْهَا وَلَا أَزُولُ أَبَداً
Oh Allah make me from his supporters	اَللَّهُمَّ اجْعَلْنِي مِنْ أَنْصَارِهِ

And helpers and defenders of him	وَأَعْوَانِهِ وَٱلذَّابِّينَ عَنْهُ
And those who hasten to him in fulfilling his needs	وَٱلْمُسَارِعِينَ إِلَيْهِ فِي قَضَاءِ حَوَائِجِهِ
And those who comply with his commands	وَٱلْمُمْتَثِلِينَ لِأَوَامِرِهِ
And the defenders of him	وَٱلْمُحَامِينَ عَنْهُ
And the foremost to his wishes	وَٱلسَّابِقِينَ إِلَىٰ إِرَادَتِهِ
And those martyred between his hands	وَٱلْمُسْتَشْهَدِينَ بَيْنَ يَدَيْهِ
Oh Allah, if death comes between me and him, which you have inevitably decreed for your servants	اَللَّهُمَّ إِنْ حَالَ بَيْنِي وَبَيْنَهُ ٱلْمَوْتُ ٱلَّذِي جَعَلْتَهُ عَلَىٰ عِبَادِكَ حَتْماً مَقْضِيّاً
Then remove me from my grave wrapped in my shroud	فَأَخْرِجْنِي مِنْ قَبْرِي مُؤْتَزِراً كَفَنِي
Brandishing my sword	شَاهِراً سَيْفِي
Bearing my spear	مُجَرِّداً قَنَاتِي
Responding to the call of the caller whether local or faraway	مُلَبِّياً دَعْوَةَ ٱلدَّاعِي فِي ٱلْحَاضِرِ وَٱلْبَادِي
Oh Allah show me the righteous appearance	اَللَّهُمَّ أَرِنِي ٱلطَّلْعَةَ ٱلرَّشِيدَةَ
And the praiseworthy illuminated forehead	وَٱلْغُرَّةَ ٱلْحَمِيدَةَ
Bless my sight with vision of him	وَٱكْحُلْ نَاظِرِي بِنَظْرَةٍ مِنِّي إِلَيْهِ
And hasten his relief	وَعَجِّلْ فَرَجَهُ
And ease his emergence	وَسَهِّلْ مَخْرَجَهُ
And spread his method	وَأَوْسِعْ مَنْهَجَهُ
And make me follow his path	وَٱسْلُكْ بِي مَحَجَّتَهُ
And implement his commands	وَأَنْفِذْ أَمْرَهُ

And strengthen his back	وَٱشْدُدْ أَزْرَهُ
And construct through him, oh Allah, your lands	وَٱعْمُرِ ٱللَّهُمَّ بِهِ بِلَادَكَ
And revive through him your worship	وَأَحْيِ بِهِ عِبَادَكَ
For you said, and your sayings are truth	فَإِنَّكَ قُلْتَ وَقَوْلُكَ ٱلْحَقُّ:
"Corruption has appeared in the land and sea	﴿ظَهَرَ ٱلْفَسَادُ فِي ٱلْبَرِّ وَٱلْبَحْرِ
Because of what the hands of men have caused" (Quran 30:41)	بِمَا كَسَبَتْ أَيْدِي ٱلنَّاسِ﴾
So reveal to us, oh Allah, Your guardian (over the believers)	فَأَظْهِرِ ٱللَّهُمَّ لَنَا وَلِيَّكَ
And the son of the daughter of Your Prophet	وَٱبْنَ بِنْتِ نَبِيِّكَ
The namesake of your Messenger	ٱلْمُسَمَّى بِٱسْمِ رَسُولِكَ
May Allah's blessings be upon him and his family	صَلَّى ٱللَّهُ عَلَيْهِ وَآلِهِ
Until nothing of falsehood prevails except that he tears it apart	حَتَّى لَا يَظْفَرَ بِشَيْءٍ مِنَ ٱلْبَاطِلِ إِلَّا مَزَّقَهُ
And he confirms the truth and establishes it	وَيُحِقَّ ٱلْحَقَّ وَيُحَقِّقَهُ
And make him, oh Allah, a refuge for your oppressed servants	وَٱجْعَلْهُ ٱللَّهُمَّ مَفْزَعاً لِمَظْلُومِ عِبَادِكَ
And a supporter for those without a supporter other than You	وَنَاصِراً لِمَنْ لَا يَجِدُ لَهُ نَاصِراً غَيْرَكَ
And a renewal for what has been abandoned from the rulings of Your book	وَمُجَدِّداً لِمَا عُطِّلَ مِنْ أَحْكَامِ كِتَابِكَ

Dua Ahd

And an establisher for what has come of the landmarks of your religion and the Sunnah (way) of Your Prophet	وَمُشَيِّداً لِمَا وَرَدَ مِنْ أَعْلَامِ دِينِكَ وَسُنَنِ نَبِيِّكَ
Allah's blessings on him and his family	صَلَّى ٱللَّهُ عَلَيْهِ وَآلِهِ
And make him, oh Allah, from those you have protected from the aggression of the aggressors	وَٱجْعَلْهُ ٱللَّهُمَّ مِمَّنْ حَصَّنْتَهُ مِنْ بَأْسِ ٱلْمُعْتَدِينَ
Oh Allah, delight Your Prophet Muhammad,	اَللَّهُمَّ وَسُرَّ نَبِيَّكَ مُحَمَّداً
Allah's blessings on him and his family	صَلَّى ٱللَّهُ عَلَيْهِ وَآلِهِ
With his sighting, and those that follow his call	بِرُؤْيَتِهِ وَمَنْ تَبِعَهُ عَلَى دَعْوَتِهِ
And have mercy on our meekness after him	وَٱرْحَمِ ٱسْتِكَانَتَنَا بَعْدَهُ
Oh Allah, relieve this crisis upon this community through his appearance	اَللَّهُمَّ ٱكْشِفْ هٰذِهِ ٱلْغُمَّةَ عَنْ هٰذِهِ ٱلْأُمَّةِ بِحُضُورِهِ
And hasten for us his appearance	وَعَجِّلْ لَنَا ظُهُورَهُ
"Indeed, they see it as far and We see it as near" (Quran 70:6-7)	﴿إِنَّهُمْ يَرَوْنَهُ بَعِيداً وَنَرَاهُ قَرِيباً﴾
By Your mercy oh most merciful of the merciful	بِرَحْمَتِكَ يَا أَرْحَمَ ٱلرَّاحِمِينَ

You may then slap your right thigh with your hand three times and, at each time, say the following:

Haste! Haste! Oh master, the possessor of time	الْعَجَلَ الْعَجَلَ يَامَوْلَايَ يَا صَاحِبَ ٱلزَّمَانِ

Dua Nudbah

Dua Nudbah is a supplication of lamentation and longing for Imam Mahdi (afs). It expresses grief over the injustices faced by the Prophet's family (saaw) and yearns for the reappearance of the Imam to establish justice. This dua is traditionally recited on Fridays and the four Shia Eids: Eid al-Fitr (1 Shawwal), Eid al-Adha (10 Dhul-Hijjah), Eid al-Ghadir (18 Dhul-Hijjah), and Eid al-Mubahalah (24 Dhul-Hijjah). (Iqbal Al A'mal, vol 2, page 233)

All praise belongs to Allah, Lord of all the worlds	ٱلْحَمْدُ لِلَّهِ رَبِّ ٱلْعَالَمِينَ
And may Allah send blessings upon our chief, Muhammad, His Prophet	وَصَلَّى ٱللَّهُ عَلَى سَيِّدِنَا مُحَمَّدٍ نَبِيِّهِ
And upon his Household and grant abundant peace	وَآلِهِ وَسَلَّمَ تَسْلِيماً
Oh Allah, all praise is for You	ٱللَّهُمَّ لَكَ ٱلْحَمْدُ
For what has occurred due to Your decree	عَلَى مَا جَرَىٰ بِهِ قَضَاؤُكَ
In Your chosen guardians whom You wisely selected for Yourself and Your religion	فِي أَوْلِيَائِكَ ٱلَّذِينَ ٱسْتَخْلَصْتَهُمْ لِنَفْسِكَ وَدِينِكَ
When You chose for them the abundant rewards with You	إِذِ ٱخْتَرْتَ لَهُمْ جَزِيلَ مَا عِنْدَكَ
From the eternal bliss	مِنَ ٱلنَّعِيمِ ٱلْمُقِيمِ
Which has no end and no drain	ٱلَّذِي لَا زَوَالَ لَهُ وَلَا ٱضْمِحْلَالَ
After You stipulated asceticism on them	بَعْدَ أَنْ شَرَطْتَ عَلَيْهِمُ ٱلزُّهْدَ
In the ranks of this lowly world	فِي دَرَجَاتِ هٰذِهِ ٱلدُّنْيَا ٱلدَّنِيَّةِ
And its ornaments and decorations	وَزُخْرُفِهَا وَزِبْرِجِهَا
So they accepted this stipulation	فَشَرَطُوا لَكَ ذٰلِكَ
And You knew that they would fulfill this	وَعَلِمْتَ مِنْهُمُ ٱلْوَفَاءَ بِهِ

Dua Nudbah

So You accepted them and brought them near	فَقَبِلْتَهُمْ وَقَرَّبْتَهُمْ
And advanced for them the elevated remembrance	وَقَدَّمْتَ لَهُمُ ٱلذِّكْرَ ٱلْعَلِيَّ
And the manifest praise	وَٱلثَّنَاءَ ٱلْجَلِيَّ
And sent down Your angels upon them	وَاهْبَطْتَ عَلَيْهِمْ مَلاَئِكَتَكَ
And honoured them with Your revelation	وَكَرَّمْتَهُمْ بِوَحْيِكَ
And assisted them with Your knowledge	وَرَفَدْتَهُمْ بِعِلْمِكَ
And made them the pathway to You	وَجَعَلْتَهُمُ ٱلذَّرِيعَةَ إِلَيْكَ
And the means to Your satisfactions	وَٱلْوَسِيلَةَ إِلَىٰ رِضْوَانِكَ
So some You settled in Your garden	فَبَعْضٌ أَسْكَنْتَهُ جَنَّتَكَ
Until You brought him out from it	إِلَىٰ أَنْ أَخْرَجْتَهُ مِنْهَا
And some You carried in Your ark	وَبَعْضٌ حَمَلْتَهُ فِي فُلْكِكَ
And saved him and those who believed with him	وَنَجَّيْتَهُ وَمَنْ آمَنَ مَعَهُ
From destruction, by Your mercy	مِنَ ٱلْهَلَكَةِ بِرَحْمَتِكَ
And some You took as an close friend	وَبَعْضٌ ٱتَّخَذْتَهُ لِنَفْسِكَ خَلِيلاً
And he asked You for a truthful tongue among the later generations, so You answered him	وَسَأَلَكَ لِسَانَ صِدْقٍ فِي ٱلْآخِرِينَ فَأَجَبْتَهُ
And you made that Ali (the truthful tongue)	وَجَعَلْتَ ذَٰلِكَ عَلِيّاً
And some You spoke to from a tree, directly	وَبَعْضٌ كَلَّمْتَهُ مِنْ شَجَرَةٍ تَكْلِيماً
And made for him from his brother a support and minister	وَجَعَلْتَ لَهُ مِنْ أَخِيهِ رِدْءاً وَوَزِيراً

And some You caused to be born without a father	وَبَعْضٌ أَوْلَدْتَهُ مِنْ غَيْرِ أَبٍ
And gave him clear proofs	وَآتَيْتَهُ الْبَيِّنَاتِ
And supported him with the Holy Spirit	وَأَيَّدْتَهُ بِرُوحِ الْقُدُسِ
And for each You legislated law	وَكُلٌّ شَرَعْتَ لَهُ شَرِيعَةً
And set out a path	وَنَهَجْتَ لَهُ مِنْهَاجاً
And chose successors	وَتَخَيَّرْتَ لَهُ أَوْصِيَاءَ
Preserver after preserver	مُسْتَحْفِظاً بَعْدَ مُسْتَحْفِظٍ
From one period to another	مِنْ مُدَّةٍ إِلَى مُدَّةٍ
Establishment for Your religion	إِقَامَةً لِدِينِكَ
And a proof over Your servants	وَحُجَّةً عَلَى عِبَادِكَ
And so that truth would not depart from its place	وَلِئَلاَّ يَزُولَ الْحَقُّ عَنْ مَقَرِّهِ
And falsehood would not overwhelm its people	وَيَغْلِبَ الْبَاطِلُ عَلَى أَهْلِهِ
And so no one would say:	وَلاَ يَقُولَ أَحَدٌ
"If only You had sent us a warning messenger	﴿لَوْ لاَ أَرْسَلْتَ إِلَيْنَا رَسُولاً مُنْذِراً
And established for us a guiding standard	وَأَقَمْتَ لَنَا عَلَماً هَادِياً
So we could follow Your signs before being humiliated and disgraced" – Quran 20:134	فَنَتَّبِعَ آيَاتِكَ مِنْ قَبْلِ أَنْ نَذِلَّ وَنَخْزَى﴾
Until You ended the matter with Your beloved and chosen one Muhammad	إِلَى أَنِ انْتَهَيْتَ بِالْأَمْرِ إِلَى حَبِيبِكَ وَنَجِيبِكَ مُحَمَّدٍ

Dua Nudbah

May Allah's blessings be upon him and his family	صَلَّى ٱللَّهُ عَلَيْهِ وَآلِهِ
So he was as You chose him	فَكَانَ كَمَا ٱنْتَجَبْتَهُ
The chief of those You created	سَيِّدَ مَنْ خَلَقْتَهُ
And the optimal of those You chose	وَصَفْوَةَ مَنِ ٱصْطَفَيْتَهُ
And the most virtuous of those You selected	وَأَفْضَلَ مَنِ ٱجْتَبَيْتَهُ
And the most noble of those You relied upon	وَأَكْرَمَ مَنِ ٱعْتَمَدْتَهُ
You advanced him over Your prophets	قَدَّمْتَهُ عَلَىٰ أَنْبِيَائِكَ
And sent him to the two weighty things (Jinn and Mankind) from Your servants	وَبَعَثْتَهُ إِلَى ٱلثَّقَلَيْنِ مِنْ عِبَادِكَ
And made accessible for him Your easts and Your wests	وَأَوْطَأْتَهُ مَشَارِقَكَ وَمَغَارِبَكَ
And subjected the Buraq to him	وَسَخَّرْتَ لَهُ ٱلْبُرَاقَ
And ascended his spirit to Your heaven	وَعَرَجْتَ بِرُوحِهِ إِلَىٰ سَمَائِكَ
And You entrusted him with knowledge of what was	وَأَوْدَعْتَهُ عِلْمَ مَا كَانَ
And what will be until the end of Your creation	وَمَا يَكُونُ إِلَىٰ ٱنْقِضَاءِ خَلْقِكَ
Then You supported him with intense fear	ثُمَّ نَصَرْتَهُ بِٱلرُّعْبِ
And surrounded him with Gabriel and Michael	وَحَفَفْتَهُ بِجَبْرَئِيلَ وَمِيكَائِيلَ
And the marked ones from Your angels	وَٱلْمُسَوِّمِينَ مِنْ مَلَائِكَتِكَ
And You promised him that You would make his religion prevail over all religion	وَوَعَدْتَهُ أَنْ تُظْهِرَ دِينَهُ عَلَى ٱلدِّينِ كُلِّهِ

Continuous Calling

Even if the polytheists dislike it	وَلَوْ كَرِهَ ٱلْمُشْرِكُونَ
And that was after You settled him in a truthful position among his people	وَذَٰلِكَ بَعْدَ أَنْ بَوَّأْتَهُ مُبَوَّأً صِدْقٍ مِنْ أَهْلِهِ
And You made for him and for them the first House	وَجَعَلْتَ لَهُ وَلَهُمْ أَوَّلَ بَيْتٍ
And established for people, that which is in Bakkah	وُضِعَ لِلنَّاسِ لَلَّذِى بِبَكَّةَ
Blessed and a guidance for the worlds	مُبَارَكًا وَهُدًى لِلْعَالَمِينَ
In it are clear signs	فِيهِ آيَاتٌ بَيِّنَاتٌ
The station of Ibrahim	مَقَامُ إِبْرَاهِيمَ
And whoever enters it is safe	وَمَنْ دَخَلَهُ كَانَ آمِنًا
You also said, "Allah only desires to keep away the uncleanliness from you,	وَقُلْتَ ﴿إِنَّمَا يُرِيدُ ٱللَّهُ لِيُذْهِبَ عَنْكُمُ ٱلرِّجْسَ
Oh Ahlul Bayt	أَهْلَ ٱلْبَيْتِ
And purify you a thorough purification." – Quran 33:33	وَيُطَهِّرَكُمْ تَطْهِيرًا﴾
Then You made the reward of Muhammad	ثُمَّ جَعَلْتَ أَجْرَ مُحَمَّدٍ
Your blessings upon him and his family	صَلَوَاتُكَ عَلَيْهِ وَآلِهِ
Affectionate love for them in Your Book	مَوَدَّتَهُمْ فِى كِتَابِكَ
So You said "Say: I do not ask you for any reward for it	فَقُلْتَ ﴿قُلْ لَا أَسْأَلُكُمْ عَلَيْهِ أَجْرًا
Except love for my near relatives" – Quran 42:23	إِلَّا ٱلْمَوَدَّةَ فِى ٱلْقُرْبَىٰ﴾

Dua Nudbah

And You said, "Whatever reward I have asked of you, that is only for yourselves" – Quran 34:47	وَقُلْتَ ﴿مَا سَأَلْتُكُمْ مِنْ أَجْرٍ فَهُوَ لَكُمْ﴾
And You said "I do not ask you for any reward for it	وَقُلْتَ ﴿مَا أَسْأَلُكُمْ عَلَيْهِ مِنْ أَجْرٍ
Except for whoever wishes to take to his Lord a way" – Quran 25:57	إِلاَّ مَنْ شَاءَ أَنْ يَتَّخِذَ إِلَى رَبِّهِ سَبِيلاً﴾
So they were the way to You	فَكَانُوا هُمُ ٱلسَّبِيلَ إِلَيْكَ
And the path to Your satisfaction	وَٱلْمَسْلَكَ إِلَى رِضْوَانِكَ
So when his days came to an end	فَلَمَّا ٱنْقَضَتْ أَيَّامُهُ
He appointed his guardian Ali son of Abu Talib	أَقَامَ وَلِيَّهُ عَلِيَّ بْنَ أَبِي طَالِبٍ
Your blessings upon them both and their families, as a guide	صَلَوَاتُكَ عَلَيْهِمَا وَآلِهِمَا هَادِياً
As he was the warner	إِذْ كَانَ هُوَ ٱلْمُنْذِرَ
"And for every people there is a guide" – Quran 13:7	﴿وَلِكُلِّ قَوْمٍ هَادٍ﴾
So he said, while the crowd was before him:	فَقَالَ وَٱلْمَلَا أَمَامَهُ:
"Whoever I am his master	"مَنْ كُنْتُ مَوْلاَهُ
Then Ali is his master	فَعَلِيٌّ مَوْلاَهُ
Oh Allah, befriend who befriends him	ٱللَّهُمَّ وَالِ مَنْ وَالاَهُ
And oppose who opposes him	وَعَادِ مَنْ عَادَاهُ
And help who helps him	وَٱنْصُرْ مَنْ نَصَرَهُ
And abandon who abandons him"	وَٱخْذُلْ مَنْ خَذَلَهُ"
And he said: "Whoever I am his prophet, Ali is his commander"	وَقَالَ: "مَنْ كُنْتُ أَنَا نَبِيَّهُ فَعَلِيٌّ أَمِيرُهُ"

And he said: "I and Ali are from one tree	وَقَالَ: "أَنَا وَعَلِيٌّ مِنْ شَجَرَةٍ وَاحِدَةٍ
And the rest of people are from various trees"	وَسَائِرُ ٱلنَّاسِ مِنْ شَجَرٍ شَتَّى"
And he placed him in the position of Aaron to Moses	وَأَحَلَّهُ مَحَلَّ هَارُونَ مِنْ مُوسَى
So he said to him:, "Your position to me is as same as Aaron's position to Moses	فَقَالَ لَهُ: "أَنْتَ مِنِّي بِمَنْزِلَةِ هَارُونَ مِنْ مُوسَى
Except that there is no prophet after me"	إِلَّا أَنَّهُ لَا نَبِيَّ بَعْدِي"
And he married him to his daughter, the chief of the women of the worlds	وَزَوَّجَهُ ٱبْنَتَهُ سَيِّدَةَ نِسَاءِ ٱلْعَالَمِينَ
And made lawful for him from his mosque what was lawful for him	وَأَحَلَّ لَهُ مِنْ مَسْجِدِهِ مَا حَلَّ لَهُ
And closed the doors except his door	وَسَدَّ ٱلْأَبْوَابَ إِلَّا بَابَهُ
Then he entrusted him with his knowledge and wisdom	ثُمَّ أَوْدَعَهُ عِلْمَهُ وَحِكْمَتَهُ
So he said: "I am the city of knowledge	فَقَالَ: "أَنَا مَدِينَةُ ٱلْعِلْمِ
And Ali is its gate	وَعَلِيٌّ بَابُهَا
So whoever wants the city and the wisdom	فَمَنْ أَرَادَ ٱلْمَدِينَةَ وَٱلْحِكْمَةَ
Let him come to it through its gate"	فَلْيَأْتِهَا مِنْ بَابِهَا"
Then he said: "You are my brother and my successor and my inheritor	ثُمَّ قَالَ: "أَنْتَ أَخِي وَوَصِيِّي وَوَارِثِي
Your flesh is from my flesh	لَحْمُكَ مِنْ لَحْمِي
And your blood is from my blood	وَدَمُكَ مِنْ دَمِي
And your peace is my peace	وَسِلْمُكَ سِلْمِي

Dua Nudbah

And your war is my war	وَحَرْبُكَ حَرْبِي
And faith is mixed with your flesh and blood	وَالْإِيمَانُ مُخَالِطٌ لَحْمَكَ وَدَمَكَ
As it mixed with my flesh and blood	كَمَا خَالَطَ لَحْمِي وَدَمِي
And tomorrow you are my representative at the pool	وَأَنْتَ غَداً عَلَى الْحَوْضِ خَلِيفَتِي
And you settle my debts	وَأَنْتَ تَقْضِي دَيْنِي
And fulfill my promises	وَتُنْجِزُ عِدَاتِي
And your followers will be on pulpits of light	وَشِيعَتُكَ عَلَى مَنَابِرَ مِنْ نُورٍ
Their faces brightened around me in Paradise	مُبْيَضَّةً وُجُوهُهُمْ حَوْلِي فِي الْجَنَّةِ
And they are my neighbours	وَهُمْ جِيرَانِي
And if not for you, oh Ali	وَلَوْلَا أَنْتَ يَا عَلِيُّ
The believers would not be known after me"	لَمْ يُعْرَفِ الْمُؤْمِنُونَ بَعْدِي"
And he was after him guidance from misguidance	وَكَانَ بَعْدَهُ هُدًى مِنَ الضَّلَالِ
And light from blindness	وَنُوراً مِنَ الْعَمَى
And Allah's sturdy rope	وَحَبْلَ اللَّهِ الْمَتِينَ
And His straight path.	وَصِرَاطَهُ الْمُسْتَقِيمَ
None preceded him in kinship of womb	لَا يُسْبَقُ بِقَرَابَةٍ فِي رَحِمٍ
Nor in precedence in religion	وَلَا بِسَابِقَةٍ فِي دِينٍ
And none could reach a merit from his merits	وَلَا يُلْحَقُ فِي مَنْقَبَةٍ مِنْ مَنَاقِبِهِ
He emulates the patterns of the Messenger	يَحْذُو حَذْوَ الرَّسُولِ

May Allah's blessings be upon them both and their families	صَلَّى ٱللَّهُ عَلَيْهِمَا وَآلِهِمَا
And he fought for the sake of true interpretation	وَيُقَاتِلُ عَلَى ٱلتَّأْوِيلِ
And no blame of any blamer took him away from Allah	وَلاَ تَأْخُذُهُ فِي ٱللَّهِ لَوْمَةُ لَائِمٍ
He exterminated the chiefs of the Arabs	قَدْ وَتَرَ فِيهِ صَنَادِيدَ ٱلْعَرَبِ
And he killed their heroes	وَقَتَلَ أَبْطَالَهُمْ
And fought their wolves	وَنَاوَشَ ذُؤْبَانَهُمْ
So he deposited in their hearts hatreds	فَأَوْدَعَ قُلُوبَهُمْ أَحْقَاداً
From Badr and Khaybar and Hunayn and others	بَدْرِيَّةً وَخَيْبَرِيَّةً وَحُنَيْنِيَّةً وَغَيْرَهُنَّ
So they persisted upon his enmity	فَأَضَبَّتْ عَلَى عَدَاوَتِهِ
And intensified to opposing him	وَأَكَبَّتْ عَلَى مُنَابَذَتِهِ
Until he killed the oath breakers, the unjust, and the deviators	حَتَّى قَتَلَ ٱلنَّاكِثِينَ وَٱلْقَاسِطِينَ وَٱلْمَارِقِينَ
And when he fulfilled his vow	وَلَمَّا قَضَى نَحْبَهُ
And he was killed by the most wretched of the later ones following the most wretched of the former ones	وَقَتَلَهُ أَشْقَى ٱلْآخِرِينَ يَتْبَعُ أَشْقَى ٱلْأَوَّلِينَ
The command of Allah's Messenger was not followed	لَمْ يُمْتَثَلْ أَمْرُ رَسُولِ ٱللَّهِ
May Allah's blessings be upon him and his family	صَلَّى ٱللَّهُ عَلَيْهِ وَآلِهِ
Regarding the guides after the guides	فِي ٱلْهَادِينَ بَعْدَ ٱلْهَادِينَ
And the nation persisted upon their hatred of him	وَٱلْأُمَّةُ مُصِرَّةٌ عَلَى مَقْتِهِ

Dua Nudbah

United upon cutting ties with his kinship	مُجْتَمِعَةٌ عَلَى قَطِيعَةِ رَحِمِهِ
And excluding his children	وَإِقْصَاءِ وُلْدِهِ
Except for a few who fulfilled the observance of truth regarding them	إِلاَّ ٱلْقَلِيلَ مِمَّنْ وَفَىٰ لِرِعَايَةِ ٱلْحَقِّ فِيهِمْ
So those who were killed were killed	فَقُتِلَ مَنْ قُتِلَ
And those who were captured were captured	وَسُبِيَ مَنْ سُبِيَ
And those who were exiled were exiled	وَأُقْصِيَ مَنْ أُقْصِيَ
And the decree flowed for them	وَجَرَىٰ ٱلْقَضَاءُ لَهُمْ
With what is hoped for it of good reward	بِمَا يُرْجَىٰ لَهُ حُسْنُ ٱلْمَثُوبَةِ
As the earth belongs to Allah	إِذْ كَانَتِ ٱلأَرْضُ لِلَّهِ
He causes whom He wills of His servants to inherit it	يُورِثُهَا مَنْ يَشَاءُ مِنْ عِبَادِهِ
And the end result is for the God-fearing	وَٱلْعَاقِبَةُ لِلْمُتَّقِينَ
And glory be to our Lord	وَسُبْحَانَ رَبِّنَا
Indeed the promise of our Lord is to be fulfilled	إِنْ كَانَ وَعْدُ رَبِّنَا لَمَفْعُولاً
And Allah will never break His promise	وَلَنْ يُخْلِفَ ٱللَّهُ وَعْدَهُ
And He is the Mighty, the Wise	وَهُوَ ٱلْعَزِيزُ ٱلْحَكِيمُ
So for the pure from the household of Muhammad and Ali	فَعَلَىٰ ٱلأَطَايِبِ مِنْ أَهْلِ بَيْتِ مُحَمَّدٍ وَعَلِيٍّ
May Allah's blessings be upon them both and their families	صَلَّى ٱللَّهُ عَلَيْهِمَا وَآلِهِمَا
Let the weepers weep	فَلْيَبْكِ ٱلْبَاكُونَ

And for them let the lamenters lament	وَإِيَّاهُمْ فَلْيَنْدُبِ ٱلنَّادِبُونَ
And for their like let the tears flow	وَلِمِثْلِهِمْ فَلْتَذْرِفِ ٱلدُّمُوعُ
And let the criers cry out	وَلْيَصْرُخِ ٱلصَّارِخُونَ
And let the wailers wail	وَيَضِجَّ ٱلضَّاجُّونَ
And let the clamourers raise their clamour	وَيَعِجَّ ٱلْعَاجُّونَ
Where is Hassan? Where is Hussein?	أَيْنَ ٱلْحَسَنُ أَيْنَ ٱلْحُسَيْنُ
Where are the sons of Hussein?	أَيْنَ أَبْنَاءُ ٱلْحُسَيْنِ
A righteous one after a righteous one	صَالِحٌ بَعْدَ صَالِحٍ
And a truthful one after a truthful one	وَصَادِقٌ بَعْدَ صَادِقٍ
Where is the path after the path?	أَيْنَ ٱلسَّبِيلُ بَعْدَ ٱلسَّبِيلِ
Where is the chosen one after the chosen one?	أَيْنَ ٱلْخِيَرَةُ بَعْدَ ٱلْخِيَرَةِ
Where are the rising suns?	أَيْنَ ٱلشُّمُوسُ ٱلطَّالِعَةُ
Where are the shining moons?	أَيْنَ ٱلْأَقْمَارُ ٱلْمُنِيرَةُ
Where are the radiant stars?	أَيْنَ ٱلْأَنْجُمُ ٱلزَّاهِرَةُ
Where are the banners of the religion?	أَيْنَ أَعْلَامُ ٱلدِّينِ
And the foundations of knowledge?	وَقَوَاعِدُ ٱلْعِلْمِ
Where is the remainder of Allah?	أَيْنَ بَقِيَّةُ ٱللَّهِ
Which is never devoid of the guiding progeny	ٱلَّتِي لَا تَخْلُو مِنَ ٱلْعِتْرَةِ ٱلْهَادِيَةِ
Where is the one prepared to sever the root of the oppressors?	أَيْنَ ٱلْمُعَدُّ لِقَطْعِ دَابِرِ ٱلظَّلَمَةِ
Where is the awaited one for rectifying the crookedness and distortion?	أَيْنَ ٱلْمُنْتَظَرُ لِإِقَامَةِ ٱلْأَمْتِ وَٱلْعِوَجِ

Dua Nudbah

Where is the hoped one for removing oppression and aggression?	أَيْنَ ٱلْمُرْتَجَىٰ لِإِزَالَةِ ٱلْجَوْرِ وَٱلْعُدْوَانِ
Where is the reserved one for renewing the duties and traditions?	أَيْنَ ٱلْمُدَّخَرُ لِتَجْدِيدِ ٱلْفَرَائِضِ وَٱلسُّنَنِ
Where is the chosen one for restoring the creed and the law?	أَيْنَ ٱلْمُتَخَيَّرُ لِإِعَادَةِ ٱلْمِلَّةِ وَٱلشَّرِيعَةِ
Where is the hoped one for reviving the book and its limits?	أَيْنَ ٱلْمُؤَمَّلُ لِإِحْيَاءِ ٱلْكِتَابِ وَحُدُودِهِ
Where is the reviver of the landmarks of religion and its people?	أَيْنَ مُحْيِي مَعَالِمِ ٱلدِّينِ وَأَهْلِهِ
Where is the breaker of the thorn of the aggressors?	أَيْنَ قَاصِمُ شَوْكَةِ ٱلْمُعْتَدِينَ
Where is the demolisher of the structures of polytheism and hypocrisy?	أَيْنَ هَادِمُ أَبْنِيَةِ ٱلشِّرْكِ وَٱلنِّفَاقِ
Where is the annihilator of the people of immorality, disobedience, and tyranny?	أَيْنَ مُبِيدُ أَهْلِ ٱلْفُسُوقِ وَٱلْعِصْيَانِ وَٱلطُّغْيَانِ
Where is the harvester of the branches of error and dissension?	أَيْنَ حَاصِدُ فُرُوعِ ٱلْغَيِّ وَٱلشِّقَاقِ
Where is the eraser of the traces of evasiveness and desires?	أَيْنَ طَامِسُ آثَارِ ٱلزَّيْغِ وَٱلْأَهْوَاءِ
Where is the severer of the snares of lies and fabrication?	أَيْنَ قَاطِعُ حَبَائِلِ ٱلْكِذْبِ وَٱلِافْتِرَاءِ
Where is the destroyer of the insolent and rebellious?	أَيْنَ مُبِيدُ ٱلْعُتَاةِ وَٱلْمَرَدَةِ
Where is the uprooter of the people of stubbornness, misguidance, and atheism?	أَيْنَ مُسْتَأْصِلُ أَهْلِ ٱلْعِنَادِ وَٱلتَّضْلِيلِ وَٱلْإِلْحَادِ
Where is the one who honours the friends and humiliates the enemies?	أَيْنَ مُعِزُّ ٱلْأَوْلِيَاءِ وَمُذِلُّ ٱلْأَعْدَاءِ

Continuous Calling

Where is the gatherer of the word upon piety?	أَيْنَ جَامِعُ ٱلْكَلِمَةِ عَلَى ٱلتَّقْوَى
Where is the door of Allah through which He is approached?	أَيْنَ بَابُ ٱللَّهِ ٱلَّذِي مِنْهُ يُؤْتَى
Where is the face of Allah towards which the friends turn?	أَيْنَ وَجْهُ ٱللَّهِ ٱلَّذِي إِلَيْهِ يَتَوَجَّهُ ٱلْأَوْلِيَاءُ
Where is the means of connection between the earth and the heavens?	أَيْنَ ٱلسَّبَبُ ٱلْمُتَّصِلُ بَيْنَ ٱلْأَرْضِ وَٱلسَّمَاءِ
Where is the master of the day of victory?	أَيْنَ صَاحِبُ يَوْمِ ٱلْفَتْحِ
And the raiser of the flag of guidance?	وَنَاشِرُ رَايَةِ ٱلْهُدَى
Where is the uniter of the scattered parts of righteousness and contentment?	أَيْنَ مُؤَلِّفُ شَمْلِ ٱلصَّلَاحِ وَٱلرِّضَا
Where is the one demanding the vengeance of the Prophets and their sons?	أَيْنَ ٱلطَّالِبُ بِذُحُولِ ٱلْأَنْبِيَاءِ وَأَبْنَاءِ ٱلْأَنْبِيَاءِ
Where is the one demanding the blood of the one killed in Karbala?	أَيْنَ ٱلطَّالِبُ بِدَمِ ٱلْمَقْتُولِ بِكَرْبَلَاءَ
Where is the supported over whoever transgressed against him and fabricated?	أَيْنَ ٱلْمَنْصُورُ عَلَى مَنِ ٱعْتَدَى عَلَيْهِ وَٱفْتَرَى
Where is the constrained one who is answered when he supplicates?	أَيْنَ ٱلْمُضْطَرُّ ٱلَّذِي يُجَابُ إِذَا دَعَا
Where is the chest of creation, possessor of righteousness and piety?	أَيْنَ صَدْرُ ٱلْخَلَائِقِ ذُو ٱلْبِرِّ وَٱلتَّقْوَى
Where is the son of the chosen Prophet?	أَيْنَ ٱبْنُ ٱلنَّبِيِّ ٱلْمُصْطَفَى
And the son of Ali, the Approved one?	وَٱبْنُ عَلِيٍّ ٱلْمُرْتَضَى

Dua Nudbah

And the son of Khadijah, the illustrious?	وَٱبْنُ خَدِيجَةَ ٱلْغَرَّاءِ
And the son of Fatima, the great?	وَٱبْنُ فَاطِمَةَ ٱلْكُبْرَىٰ
May my father and mother be sacrificed for you	بِأَبِي أَنْتَ وَأُمِّي
And may my soul be protection and defence for you	وَنَفْسِي لَكَ ٱلْوِقَاءُ وَٱلْحِمَىٰ
Oh son of the close chiefs	يَا بْنَ ٱلسَّادَةِ ٱلْمُقَرَّبِينَ
Oh son of the noble honoured ones	يَا بْنَ ٱلنُّجَبَاءِ ٱلْأَكْرَمِينَ
Oh son of the guided guides	يَا بْنَ ٱلْهُدَاةِ ٱلْمَهْدِيِّينَ
Oh son of the refined chosen ones	يَا بْنَ ٱلْخِيَرَةِ ٱلْمُهَذَّبِينَ
Oh son of the noble distinguished ones	يَا بْنَ ٱلْغَطَارِفَةِ ٱلْأَنْجَبِينَ
Oh son of the purified good ones	يَا بْنَ ٱلْأَطَايِبِ ٱلْمُطَهَّرِينَ
Oh son of the selected generous ones	يَا بْنَ ٱلْخَضَارِمَةِ ٱلْمُنْتَجَبِينَ
Oh son of the brilliant honoured ones	يَا بْنَ ٱلْقَمَاقِمَةِ ٱلْأَكْرَمِينَ
Oh son of the illuminating full moons	يَا بْنَ ٱلْبُدُورِ ٱلْمُنِيرَةِ
Oh son of the shining lamps	يَا بْنَ ٱلسُّرُجِ ٱلْمُضِيئَةِ
Oh son of the piercing meteors	يَا بْنَ ٱلشُّهُبِ ٱلثَّاقِبَةِ
Oh son of the radiant stars	يَا بْنَ ٱلْأَنْجُمِ ٱلزَّاهِرَةِ
Oh son of the clear paths	يَا بْنَ ٱلسُّبُلِ ٱلْوَاضِحَةِ
Oh son of the prominent banners	يَا بْنَ ٱلْأَعْلَامِ ٱللَّائِحَةِ
Oh son of the complete sciences	يَا بْنَ ٱلْعُلُومِ ٱلْكَامِلَةِ
Oh son of the famous traditions	يَا بْنَ ٱلسُّنَنِ ٱلْمَشْهُورَةِ
Oh son of the inherited landmarks	يَا بْنَ ٱلْمَعَالِمِ ٱلْمَأْثُورَةِ

Oh son of the present miracles	يَا بْنَ ٱلْمُعْجِزَاتِ ٱلْمَوْجُودَةِ
Oh son of the witnessed proofs	يَا بْنَ ٱلدَّلَائِلِ ٱلْمَشْهُودَةِ
Oh son of the straight path	يَا بْنَ ٱلصِّرَاطِ ٱلْمُسْتَقِيمِ
Oh son of the great news	يَا بْنَ ٱلنَّبَإِ ٱلْعَظِيمِ
Oh son of the one who is in the Mother of the Book with Allah, Ali the Wise	يَا بْنَ مَنْ هُوَ فِي أُمِّ ٱلْكِتَابِ لَدَى ٱللّٰهِ عَلِيٌّ حَكِيمٌ
Oh son of the signs and clear proofs	يَا بْنَ ٱلْآيَاتِ وَٱلْبَيِّنَاتِ
Oh son of the manifest indications	يَا بْنَ ٱلدَّلَائِلِ ٱلظَّاهِرَاتِ
Oh son of the clear, dazzling evidences	يَا بْنَ ٱلْبَرَاهِينِ ٱلْوَاضِحَاتِ ٱلْبَاهِرَاتِ
Oh son of the conclusive arguments	يَا بْنَ ٱلْحُجَجِ ٱلْبَالِغَاتِ
Oh son of the plentiful blessings	يَا بْنَ ٱلنِّعَمِ ٱلسَّابِغَاتِ
Oh son of Ta-Ha and the decisive verses	يَا بْنَ طٰهٰ وَٱلْمُحْكَمَاتِ
Oh son of Ya-Sin and the scatterers	يَا بْنَ يٰسٓ وَٱلذَّارِيَاتِ
Oh son of the Mount and the charging steeds	يَا بْنَ ٱلطُّورِ وَٱلْعَادِيَاتِ
Oh son of the one who drew nearer and nearer	يَا بْنَ مَنْ دَنَا فَتَدَلَّىٰ
Until he was two bow-lengths away or nearer	فَكَانَ قَابَ قَوْسَيْنِ أَوْ أَدْنَىٰ
In nearness and closeness to the most High	دُنُوّاً وَٱقْتِرَاباً مِنَ ٱلْعَلِيِّ ٱلْأَعْلَىٰ
If only I knew where you have settled	لَيْتَ شِعْرِي أَيْنَ ٱسْتَقَرَّتْ بِكَ ٱلنَّوَىٰ
Rather, which land or soil is carrying you	بَلْ أَيُّ أَرْضٍ تُقِلُّكَ أَوْ ثَرَىٰ
Is it at Radwa or elsewhere or at Tuwa	أَبِرَضْوَىٰ أَوْ غَيْرِهَا أَمْ ذِي طُوَىٰ

Dua Nudbah

It is hard upon me that I see creation but you are not seen	عَزِيزٌ عَلَيَّ أَنْ أَرَى ٱلْخَلْقَ وَلاَ تُرَى
And I hear neither a whisper nor private conversation from you	وَلاَ أَسْمَعُ لَكَ حَسِيساً وَلاَ نَجْوَى
It is hard upon me that trials surround you without me	عَزِيزٌ عَلَيَّ أَنْ تُحِيطَ بِكَ دُونِيَ ٱلْبَلْوَى
And neither my cry nor complaint reaches you	وَلاَ يَنَالُكَ مِنِّي ضَجِيجٌ وَلاَ شَكْوَى
May my soul be sacrificed for you, oh hidden one who is not absent from us	بِنَفْسِي أَنْتَ مِنْ مُغَيَّبٍ لَمْ يَخْلُ مِنَّا
May my soul be sacrificed for you, oh distant one who is not distant from us	بِنَفْسِي أَنْتَ مِنْ نَازِحٍ مَا نَزَحَ عَنَّا
May my soul be sacrificed for you, oh wish of a yearning one who wishes	بِنَفْسِي أَنْتَ أُمْنِيَّةُ شَائِقٍ يَتَمَنَّى
From believing men and women who remember and yearn	مِنْ مُؤْمِنٍ وَمُؤْمِنَةٍ ذَكَرَا فَحَنَّا
May my soul be sacrificed for you, oh possessor of unrivalled might	بِنَفْسِي أَنْتَ مِنْ عَقِيدِ عِزٍّ لاَ يُسَامَى
May my soul be sacrificed for you, oh root of unmatched glory	بِنَفْسِي أَنْتَ مِنْ أَثِيلِ مَجْدٍ لاَ يُجَارَى
May my soul be sacrificed for you, oh one of incomparable inherited blessings	بِنَفْسِي أَنْتَ مِنْ تِلاَدِ نِعَمٍ لاَ تُضَاهَى
May my soul be sacrificed for you, oh one of unequalled noble rank	بِنَفْسِي أَنْتَ مِنْ نَصِيفِ شَرَفٍ لاَ يُسَاوَى
Until when shall I be bewildered about you, oh my master? Until when?	إِلَى مَتَى أَحَارُ فِيكَ يَا مَوْلاَيَ وَإِلَى مَتَى
And which address and which private conversation can I describe you?	وَأَيَّ خِطَابٍ أَصِفُ فِيكَ وَأَيَّ نَجْوَى
It is hard for me to be answered without you and that I speak privately	عَزِيزٌ عَلَيَّ أَنْ أُجَابَ دُونَكَ وَأُنَاغَى

Continuous Calling

It is hard for me to weep for you while creation forsakes you	عَزِيزٌ عَلَىَّ أَنْ أَبْكِيَكَ وَيَخْذُلَكَ ٱلْوَرَى
It is hard for me that what happened to you happened without them	عَزِيزٌ عَلَىَّ أَنْ يَجْرِىَ عَلَيْكَ دُونَهُمْ مَا جَرَى
Is there any helper with whom I might prolong wailing and weeping?	هَلْ مِنْ مُعِينٍ فَأُطِيلَ مَعَهُ ٱلْعَوِيلَ وَٱلْبُكَاءَ
Is there any griever whose grief I might aid when alone?	هَلْ مِنْ جَزُوعٍ فَأُسَاعِدَ جَزَعَهُ إِذَا خَلَا
Has any eye become dust-filled that my eye might aid it in its dust?	هَلْ قَذِيَتْ عَيْنٌ فَسَاعَدَتْهَا عَيْنِي عَلَى ٱلْقَذَى
Is there a way to you, oh son of Ahmad, that you might be met?	هَلْ إِلَيْكَ يَا بْنَ أَحْمَدَ سَبِيلٌ فَتُلْقَى
Will our day be connected to you by a promise so we might be fortunate?	هَلْ يَتَّصِلُ يَوْمُنَا مِنْكَ بِعِدَةٍ فَنَحْظَى
When will we arrive at your refreshing springs and be satisfied?	مَتَى نَرِدُ مَنَاهِلَكَ ٱلرَّوِيَّةَ فَنَرْوَى
When will we drink deeply from your sweet water?	مَتَى نَنْتَقِعُ مِنْ عَذْبِ مَائِكَ
For the thirst has been long	فَقَدْ طَالَ ٱلصَّدَى
When will we come to you morning and evening so our eyes might be cooled?	مَتَى نُغَادِيكَ وَنُرَاوِحُكَ فَنُقِرَّ عَيْناً
When will you see us and we see you, while you have unfurled the banner of victory?	مَتَى تَرَانَا وَنَرَاكَ وَقَدْ نَشَرْتَ لِوَاءَ ٱلنَّصْرِ
I wonder, do you see us surrounding you while you lead the assembly?	تُرَى أَتَرَانَا نَحُفُّ بِكَ وَأَنْتَ تَؤُمُّ ٱلْمَلَأَ

Dua Nudbah

And you will have filled the earth with justice	وَقَدْ مَلَأْتَ ٱلْأَرْضَ عَدْلاً
And made your enemies taste humiliation and punishment	وَأَذَقْتَ أَعْدَاءَكَ هَوَاناً وَعِقَاباً
And destroyed the insolent and the deniers of truth	وَأَبَرْتَ ٱلْعُتَاةَ وَجَحَدَةَ ٱلْحَقِّ
And cut off the root of the arrogant ones	وَقَطَعْتَ دَابِرَ ٱلْمُتَكَبِّرِينَ
And uprooted the foundations of the oppressors	وَٱجْتَثَثْتَ أُصُولَ ٱلظَّالِمِينَ
And we say: Praise be to Allah, Lord of the worlds	وَنَحْنُ نَقُولُ ٱلْحَمْدُ لِلَّهِ رَبِّ ٱلْعَالَمِينَ
Oh Allah, You are the remover of afflictions and trials	اَللَّهُمَّ أَنْتَ كَشَّافُ ٱلْكُرَبِ وَٱلْبَلْوَىٰ
And to You I seek justice, for with You is justice	وَإِلَيْكَ أَسْتَعْدِي فَعِنْدَكَ ٱلْعَدْوَىٰ
And You are the Lord of the Hereafter and the world	وَأَنْتَ رَبُّ ٱلْآخِرَةِ وَٱلدُّنْيَا
So help, oh Helper of those seeking help, Your afflicted slave	فَأَغِثْ يَا غِيَاثَ ٱلْمُسْتَغِيثِينَ عُبَيْدَكَ ٱلْمُبْتَلَىٰ
And show him his chief, oh firmly Strong One	وَأَرِهِ سَيِّدَهُ يَا شَدِيدَ ٱلْقُوَىٰ
And remove from him through him the grief and anguish	وَأَزِلْ عَنْهُ بِهِ ٱلْأَسَىٰ وَٱلْجَوَىٰ
And cool his burning thirst, oh One who is established on the throne	وَبَرِّدْ غَلِيلَهُ يَا مَنْ عَلَى ٱلْعَرْشِ ٱسْتَوَىٰ
And to whom is the return and the end	وَمَنْ إِلَيْهِ ٱلرُّجْعَىٰ وَٱلْمُنْتَهَىٰ
Oh Allah, and we are Your servants yearning for Your guardian (over the believers)	اَللَّهُمَّ وَنَحْنُ عَبِيدُكَ ٱلتَّائِقُونَ إِلَىٰ وَلِيِّكَ

Continuous Calling

The one who reminds of You and Your prophet	ٱلْمُذَكِّرِ بِكَ وَبِنَبِيِّكَ
You created him for us as a protection and refuge	خَلَقْتَهُ لَنَا عِصْمَةً وَمَلَاذاً
And established him for us as a support and shelter	وَأَقَمْتَهُ لَنَا قِوَاماً وَمَعَاذاً
And made him for the believers among us an Imam	وَجَعَلْتَهُ لِلْمُؤْمِنِينَ مِنَّا إِمَاماً
So convey to him, from us, greetings and peace	فَبَلِّغْهُ مِنَّا تَحِيَّةً وَسَلَاماً
And increase us thereby, oh Lord, in honour	وَزِدْنَا بِذَلِكَ يَا رَبِّ إِكْرَاماً
And make his dwelling place for us a settlement and station	وَٱجْعَلْ مُسْتَقَرَّهُ لَنَا مُسْتَقَرّاً وَمُقَاماً
And complete Your favour by placing him before us as our Imam	وَأَتْمِمْ نِعْمَتَكَ بِتَقْدِيـمِكَ إِيَّاهُ أَمَامَنَا
Until You lead us to Your gardens	حَتَّى تُورِدَنَا جِنَانَكَ
And the companionship of the martyrs from Your sincere ones	وَمُرَافَقَةَ ٱلشُّهَدَاءِ مِنْ خُلَصَائِكَ
Oh Allah, send blessings upon Muhammad and the family of Muhammad	ٱللَّهُمَّ صَلِّ عَلَى مُحَمَّدٍ وَآلِ مُحَمَّدٍ
And send blessings upon Muhammad his grandfather and Your messenger	وَصَلِّ عَلَى مُحَمَّدٍ جَدِّهِ وَرَسُولِكَ
The greater chief	ٱلسَّيِّدِ ٱلْأَكْبَرِ
And upon his father the lesser chief	وَعَلَى أَبِيهِ ٱلسَّيِّدِ ٱلْأَصْغَرِ
And his grandmother the greater truthful one	وَجَدَّتِهِ ٱلصِّدِّيقَةِ ٱلْكُبْرَى
Fatima daughter of Muhammad	فَاطِمَةَ بِنْتِ مُحَمَّدٍ

Dua Nudbah

May Allah's blessings be upon him and his family	صَلَّى ٱللَّهُ عَلَيْهِ وَآلِهِ
And upon those You chose from his righteous forefathers	وَعَلَىٰ مَنِ ٱصْطَفَيْتَ مِنْ آبَائِهِ ٱلْبَرَرَةِ
And upon him the most excellent and most perfect	وَعَلَيْهِ أَفْضَلَ وَأَكْمَلَ
And most complete and most lasting	وَأَتَمَّ وَأَدْوَمَ
And most abundant and most plentiful	وَأَكْثَرَ وَأَوْفَرَ
That You have blessed upon any of Your chosen ones	مَا صَلَّيْتَ عَلَىٰ أَحَدٍ مِنْ أَصْفِيَائِكَ
And your well-chosen among Your creation	وَخِيَرَتِكَ مِنْ خَلْقِكَ
And send blessings upon him blessings without limit to their number	وَصَلِّ عَلَيْهِ صَلَاةً لَا غَايَةَ لِعَدَدِهَا
And no end to their extent	وَلَا نِهَايَةَ لِمَدَدِهَا
And no exhaustion to their duration	وَلَا نَفَادَ لِأَمَدِهَا
Oh Allah, establish through him the truth	ٱللَّهُمَّ وَأَقِمْ بِهِ ٱلْحَقَّ
And refute through him falsehood	وَأَدْحِضْ بِهِ ٱلْبَاطِلَ
And grant triumph through him to Your allies	وَأَدِلْ بِهِ أَوْلِيَاءَكَ
And humiliate through him Your enemies	وَأَذْلِلْ بِهِ أَعْدَاءَكَ
And connect between us and him, oh Allah	وَصِلِ ٱللَّهُمَّ بَيْنَنَا وَبَيْنَهُ
A connection that leads us to accompany his predecessors	وُصْلَةً تُؤَدِّي إِلَىٰ مُرَافَقَةِ سَلَفِهِ
And make us among those who grasp their protection	وَٱجْعَلْنَا مِمَّنْ يَأْخُذُ بِحُجْزَتِهِمْ

And dwell in their shade	وَيَمْكُثُ فِي ظِلِّهِمْ
And help us in fulfilling his rights	وَأَعِنَّا عَلَى تَأْدِيَةِ حُقُوقِهِ إِلَيْهِ
And striving in his obedience	وَالْاِجْتِهَادِ فِي طَاعَتِهِ
And avoiding disobeying him	وَاجْتِنَابِ مَعْصِيَتِهِ
And bestow upon us with his satisfaction	وَامْنُنْ عَلَيْنَا بِرِضَاهُ
And grant us his kindness and his mercy	وَهَبْ لَنَا رَأْفَتَهُ وَرَحْمَتَهُ
And his prayer and his goodness	وَدُعَاءَهُ وَخَيْرَهُ
Through which we attain abundance from Your mercy	مَا نَنَالُ بِهِ سَعَةً مِنْ رَحْمَتِكَ
And success with You	وَفَوْزاً عِنْدَكَ
And make our prayers through him accepted	وَاجْعَلْ صَلَاتَنَا بِهِ مَقْبُولَةً
And our sins through him forgiven	وَذُنُوبَنَا بِهِ مَغْفُورَةً
And our supplications through him answered	وَدُعَاءَنَا بِهِ مُسْتَجَاباً
And make our provisions through him expanded	وَاجْعَلْ أَرْزَاقَنَا بِهِ مَبْسُوطَةً
And our worries through him relieved	وَهُمُومَنَا بِهِ مَكْفِيَّةً
And our needs through him fulfilled	وَحَوَائِجَنَا بِهِ مَقْضِيَّةً
And turn to us with Your Noble Face	وَأَقْبِلْ إِلَيْنَا بِوَجْهِكَ الْكَرِيمِ
And accept our drawing near to You	وَاقْبَلْ تَقَرُّبَنَا إِلَيْكَ
And look upon us with a merciful look	وَانْظُرْ إِلَيْنَا نَظْرَةً رَحِيمَةً
Through which we complete the honour with You	نَسْتَكْمِلُ بِهَا الْكَرَامَةَ عِنْدَكَ

Dua Nudbah

Then do not turn it away from us by Your generosity	ثُمَّ لاَ تَصْرِفْهَا عَنَّا بِجُودِكَ
And quench us from the pool of his grandfather	وَأَسْقِنَا مِنْ حَوْضِ جَدِّهِ
May Allah's blessings be upon him and his family	صَلَّى ٱللَّهُ عَلَيْهِ وَآلِهِ
From his cup and by his hand	بِكَأْسِهِ وَبِيَدِهِ
A quenching, satisfying drink	رَيّاً رَوِيّاً
Pleasant, wholesome	هَنِيئاً سَائِغاً
With no thirst after it	لاَ ظَمَأَ بَعْدَهُ
Oh Most Merciful of the merciful	يَا أَرْحَمَ ٱلرَّاحِمِينَ

It is recommended to pray 2 rakat ziyarat after completing this dua and ask for your needs. (Mafatih al Jinan)

Dua Tawassul

Shaykh Majlisi says that he found this dua written on a manuscript with one of our scholars, the narrator says for whatever request he recited it, it was granted right away (Bihar Anwar vol 99, p247). Many Shias choose to recite this once a week on Tuesday nights.

Prophet Muhammad (saaw)

Oh Allah, I ask and turn to You	اَللَّهُمَّ إِنِّي أَسْأَلُكَ وَأَتَوَجَّهُ إِلَيْكَ
Through your prophet, the Prophet of Mercy	بِنَبِيِّكَ نَبِيِّ ٱلرَّحْمَةِ
Muhammad, may Allah's blessings be on him and his family	مُحَمَّدٍ صَلَّى ٱللَّهُ عَلَيْهِ وَآلِهِ
Oh father of Qasim	يَا أَبَا ٱلْقَاسِمِ
Oh messenger of Allah	يَا رَسُولَ ٱللَّهِ
Oh Imam of mercy	يَا إِمَامَ ٱلرَّحْمَةِ
Oh our chief and our master	يَا سَيِّدَنَا وَمَوْلاَنَا
We turned to you, and we sought your intercession	إِنَّا تَوَجَّهْنَا وَٱسْتَشْفَعْنَا
And we implored Allah through you	وَتَوَسَّلْنَا بِكَ إِلَى ٱللَّهِ
And we placed between your hands our needs	وَقَدَّمْنَاكَ بَيْنَ يَدَىْ حَاجَاتِنَا
Oh respected one with Allah	يَا وَجِيهاً عِنْدَ ٱللَّهِ
Intercede for us with Allah	إِشْفَعْ لَنَا عِنْدَ ٱللَّهِ

Imam Ali (as)

Oh father of Hassan	يَا أَبَا ٱلْحَسَنِ
Oh commander of the faithful	يَا أَمِيرَ ٱلْمُؤْمِنِينَ
Oh Ali the son of Abu Talib	يَا عَلِيُّ بْنَ أَبِي طَالِبٍ

Dua Tawassul

Oh Allah's proof against His creation	يَا حُجَّةَ ٱللَّهِ عَلَىٰ خَلْقِهِ
Oh our chief and our master	يَا سَيِّدَنَا وَمَوْلَانَا
We turned to you, and we sought your intercession	إِنَّا تَوَجَّهْنَا وَٱسْتَشْفَعْنَا
And we implored Allah through you	وَتَوَسَّلْنَا بِكَ إِلَى ٱللَّهِ
And we placed between your hands our needs	وَقَدَّمْنَاكَ بَيْنَ يَدَيْ حَاجَاتِنَا
Oh respected one with Allah	يَا وَجِيهاً عِنْدَ ٱللَّهِ
Intercede for us with Allah	إِشْفَعْ لَنَا عِنْدَ ٱللَّهِ

Sayyeda Fatima (as)

Oh Fatima, the Radiant	يَا فَاطِمَةُ ٱلزَّهْرَاءُ
Oh the daughter of Muhammad	يَا بِنْتَ مُحَمَّدٍ
Oh delight of the Messenger's eyes	يَا قُرَّةَ عَيْنِ ٱلرَّسُولِ
Oh our chieftess and our master	يَا سَيِّدَتَنَا وَمَوْلَاتَنَا
We turned to you, and we sought your intercession	إِنَّا تَوَجَّهْنَا وَٱسْتَشْفَعْنَا
And we implored Allah through you	وَتَوَسَّلْنَا بِكِ إِلَى ٱللَّهِ
And we placed between your hands our needs	وَقَدَّمْنَاكِ بَيْنَ يَدَيْ حَاجَاتِنَا
Oh respected one with Allah	يَا وَجِيهَةً عِنْدَ ٱللَّهِ
Intercede for us with Allah	إِشْفَعِي لَنَا عِنْدَ ٱللَّهِ

Imam Hassan (as)

Oh father of Muhammad	يَا أَبَا مُحَمَّدٍ
Oh Hassan the son of Ali	يَا حَسَنُ بْنَ عَلِيٍّ
Oh well-chosen one	أَيُّهَا ٱلْمُجْتَبَىٰ

Oh the son of the Messenger of Allah	يَا بْنَ رَسُولِ ٱللَّهِ
Oh Allah's proof against His creation	يَا حُجَّةَ ٱللَّهِ عَلَىٰ خَلْقِهِ
Oh our chief and our master	يَا سَيِّدَنَا وَمَوْلَانَا
We turned to you, and we sought your intercession	إِنَّا تَوَجَّهْنَا وَٱسْتَشْفَعْنَا
And we implored Allah through you	وَتَوَسَّلْنَا بِكَ إِلَىٰ ٱللَّهِ
And we placed between your hands our needs	وَقَدَّمْنَاكَ بَيْنَ يَدَيْ حَاجَاتِنَا
Oh respected one with Allah	يَا وَجِيهاً عِنْدَ ٱللَّهِ
Intercede for us with Allah	إِشْفَعْ لَنَا عِنْدَ ٱللَّهِ

Imam Hussein(as)

Oh father of Abdullah	يَا أَبَا عَبْدِ ٱللَّهِ
Oh Hussein the son of Ali	يَا حُسَيْنُ بْنَ عَلِيٍّ
Oh martyr	أَيُّهَا ٱلشَّهِيدُ
Oh the son of the Messenger of Allah	يَا بْنَ رَسُولِ ٱللَّهِ
Oh Allah's proof against His creation	يَا حُجَّةَ ٱللَّهِ عَلَىٰ خَلْقِهِ
Oh our chief and our master	يَا سَيِّدَنَا وَمَوْلَانَا
We turned to you, and we sought your intercession	إِنَّا تَوَجَّهْنَا وَٱسْتَشْفَعْنَا
And we implored Allah through you	وَتَوَسَّلْنَا بِكَ إِلَىٰ ٱللَّهِ
And we placed between your hands our needs	وَقَدَّمْنَاكَ بَيْنَ يَدَيْ حَاجَاتِنَا
Oh respected one with Allah	يَا وَجِيهاً عِنْدَ ٱللَّهِ
Intercede for us with Allah	إِشْفَعْ لَنَا عِنْدَ ٱللَّهِ

Imam Zainal Abideen (as)

Oh father of Hassan	يَا أَبَا ٱلْحَسَنِ
Oh Ali the son of Hussein	يَا عَلِيُّ بْنَ ٱلْحُسَيْنِ
Oh the adornment of worshippers	يَا زَيْنَ ٱلْعَابِدِينَ
Oh the son of the Messenger of Allah	يَا بْنَ رَسُولِ ٱللَّهِ
Oh Allah's proof against His creation	يَا حُجَّةَ ٱللَّهِ عَلَىٰ خَلْقِهِ
Oh our chief and our master	يَا سَيِّدَنَا وَمَوْلاَنَا
We turned to you, and we sought your intercession	إِنَّا تَوَجَّهْنَا وَٱسْتَشْفَعْنَا
And we implored Allah through you	وَتَوَسَّلْنَا بِكَ إِلَىٰ ٱللَّهِ
And we placed between your hands our needs	وَقَدَّمْنَاكَ بَيْنَ يَدَيْ حَاجَاتِنَا
Oh respected one with Allah	يَا وَجِيهاً عِنْدَ ٱللَّهِ
Intercede for us with Allah	إِشْفَعْ لَنَا عِنْدَ ٱللَّهِ

Imam Baqir (as)

Oh father of Ja'far	يَا أَبَا جَعْفَرٍ
Oh Muhammad the son of Ali	يَا مُحَمَّدُ بْنَ عَلِيٍّ
Oh the opener (of knowledge)	أَيُّهَا ٱلْبَاقِرُ
Oh the son of the Messenger of Allah	يَا بْنَ رَسُولِ ٱللَّهِ
Oh Allah's proof against His creation	يَا حُجَّةَ ٱللَّهِ عَلَىٰ خَلْقِهِ
Oh our chief and our master	يَا سَيِّدَنَا وَمَوْلاَنَا
We turned to you, and we sought your intercession	إِنَّا تَوَجَّهْنَا وَٱسْتَشْفَعْنَا
And we implored Allah through you	وَتَوَسَّلْنَا بِكَ إِلَىٰ ٱللَّهِ

And we placed between your hands our needs	وَقَدَّمْنَاكَ بَيْنَ يَدَىْ حَاجَاتِنَا
Oh respected one with Allah	يَا وَجِيهاً عِنْدَ ٱللَّهِ
Intercede for us with Allah	إِشْفَعْ لَنَا عِنْدَ ٱللَّهِ

Imam Sadiq (as)

Oh father of Abdallah	يَا أَبَا عَبْدِ ٱللَّهِ
Oh Ja'far the son of Muhammad	يَا جَعْفَرَ بْنَ مُحَمَّدٍ
Oh the truthful one	أَيُّهَا ٱلصَّادِقُ
Oh the son of the Messenger of Allah	يَا بْنَ رَسُولِ ٱللَّهِ
Oh Allah's proof against His creation	يَا حُجَّةَ ٱللَّهِ عَلَى خَلْقِهِ
Oh our chief and our master	يَا سَيِّدَنَا وَمَوْلَانَا
We turned to you, and we sought your intercession	إِنَّا تَوَجَّهْنَا وَٱسْتَشْفَعْنَا
And we implored Allah through you	وَتَوَسَّلْنَا بِكَ إِلَى ٱللَّهِ
And we placed between your hands our needs	وَقَدَّمْنَاكَ بَيْنَ يَدَىْ حَاجَاتِنَا
Oh respected one with Allah	يَا وَجِيهاً عِنْدَ ٱللَّهِ
Intercede for us with Allah	إِشْفَعْ لَنَا عِنْدَ ٱللَّهِ

Imam Kadhem (as)

Oh father of Hassan	يَا أَبَا ٱلْحَسَنِ
Oh Musa the son of Ja'far	يَا مُوسَى بْنَ جَعْفَرٍ
Oh the suppressor (of rage)	أَيُّهَا ٱلْكَاظِمُ
Oh the son of the Messenger of Allah	يَا بْنَ رَسُولِ ٱللَّهِ
Oh Allah's proof against His creation	يَا حُجَّةَ ٱللَّهِ عَلَى خَلْقِهِ

Dua Tawassul

Oh our chief and our master	يَا سَيِّدَنَا وَمَوْلَانَا
We turned to you, and we sought your intercession	إِنَّا تَوَجَّهْنَا وَاسْتَشْفَعْنَا
And we implored Allah through you	وَتَوَسَّلْنَا بِكَ إِلَى اللَّهِ
And we placed between your hands our needs	وَقَدَّمْنَاكَ بَيْنَ يَدَيْ حَاجَاتِنَا
Oh respected one with Allah	يَا وَجِيهاً عِنْدَ اللَّهِ
Intercede for us with Allah	إِشْفَعْ لَنَا عِنْدَ اللَّهِ

Imam Redha (as)

Oh father of Hassan	يَا أَبَا الْحَسَنِ
Oh Ali the son of Musa	يَا عَلِيُّ بْنَ مُوسَى
Oh the contented one	أَيُّهَا الرِّضَا
Oh the son of the Messenger of Allah	يَا بْنَ رَسُولِ اللَّهِ
Oh Allah's proof against His creation	يَا حُجَّةَ اللَّهِ عَلَى خَلْقِهِ
Oh our chief and our master	يَا سَيِّدَنَا وَمَوْلَانَا
We turned to you, and we sought your intercession	إِنَّا تَوَجَّهْنَا وَاسْتَشْفَعْنَا
And we implored Allah through you	وَتَوَسَّلْنَا بِكَ إِلَى اللَّهِ
And we placed between your hands our needs	وَقَدَّمْنَاكَ بَيْنَ يَدَيْ حَاجَاتِنَا
Oh respected one with Allah	يَا وَجِيهاً عِنْدَ اللَّهِ
Intercede for us with Allah	إِشْفَعْ لَنَا عِنْدَ اللَّهِ

Imam Jawad (as)

Oh father of Ja'far	يَا أَبَا جَعْفَرٍ
Oh Muhammad the son of Ali	يَا مُحَمَّدُ بْنَ عَلِيٍّ

Continuous Calling

Oh the pious, the generous	أَيُّهَا ٱلتَّقِيُّ ٱلْجَوَادُ
Oh the son of the Messenger of Allah	يَا بْنَ رَسُولِ ٱللَّهِ
Oh Allah's proof against His creation	يَا حُجَّةَ ٱللَّهِ عَلَىٰ خَلْقِهِ
Oh our chief and our master	يَا سَيِّدَنَا وَمَوْلَانَا
We turned to you, and we sought your intercession	إِنَّا تَوَجَّهْنَا وَٱسْتَشْفَعْنَا
And we implored Allah through you	وَتَوَسَّلْنَا بِكَ إِلَىٰ ٱللَّهِ
And we placed between your hands our needs	وَقَدَّمْنَاكَ بَيْنَ يَدَيْ حَاجَاتِنَا
Oh respected one with Allah	يَا وَجِيهاً عِنْدَ ٱللَّهِ
Intercede for us with Allah	إِشْفَعْ لَنَا عِنْدَ ٱللَّهِ

Imam Hadi (as)

Oh father of Hassan	يَا أَبَا ٱلْحَسَنِ
Oh Ali the son of Muhammad	يَا عَلِيُّ بْنَ مُحَمَّدٍ
Oh the guide, the immaculate	أَيُّهَا ٱلْهَادِى ٱلتَّقِيُّ
Oh the son of the Messenger of Allah	يَا بْنَ رَسُولِ ٱللَّهِ
Oh Allah's proof against His creation	يَا حُجَّةَ ٱللَّهِ عَلَىٰ خَلْقِهِ
Oh our chief and our master	يَا سَيِّدَنَا وَمَوْلَانَا
We turned to you, and we sought your intercession	إِنَّا تَوَجَّهْنَا وَٱسْتَشْفَعْنَا
And we implored Allah through you	وَتَوَسَّلْنَا بِكَ إِلَىٰ ٱللَّهِ
And we placed between your hands our needs	وَقَدَّمْنَاكَ بَيْنَ يَدَيْ حَاجَاتِنَا
Oh respected one with Allah	يَا وَجِيهاً عِنْدَ ٱللَّهِ
Intercede for us with Allah	إِشْفَعْ لَنَا عِنْدَ ٱللَّهِ

Dua Tawassul

Imam Askari (as)

Oh father of Muhammad	يَا أَبَا مُحَمَّدٍ
Oh Hassan the son of Ali	يَا حَسَنُ بْنَ عَلِيٍّ
Oh the immaculate resident of Askar	أَيُّهَا ٱلزَّكِيُّ ٱلْعَسْكَرِيُّ
Oh the son of the Messenger of Allah	يَا بْنَ رَسُولِ ٱللَّهِ
Oh Allah's proof against His creation	يَا حُجَّةَ ٱللَّهِ عَلَىٰ خَلْقِهِ
Oh our chief and our master	يَا سَيِّدَنَا وَمَوْلَانَا
We turned to you, and we sought your intercession	إِنَّا تَوَجَّهْنَا وَٱسْتَشْفَعْنَا
And we implored Allah through you	وَتَوَسَّلْنَا بِكَ إِلَى ٱللَّهِ
And we placed between your hands our needs	وَقَدَّمْنَاكَ بَيْنَ يَدَيْ حَاجَاتِنَا
Oh respected one with Allah	يَا وَجِيهاً عِنْدَ ٱللَّهِ
Intercede for us with Allah	إِشْفَعْ لَنَا عِنْدَ ٱللَّهِ

Imam Mahdi (afs)

Stand up and place your right hand on your head

Oh successor of Hassan	يَا وَصِيَّ ٱلْحَسَنِ
And the inheritor, the proof	وَٱلْخَلَفُ ٱلْحُجَّةُ
Oh the one who rises, the awaited, the guided	أَيُّهَا ٱلْقَائِمُ ٱلْمُنْتَظَرُ ٱلْمَهْدِيُّ
Oh the son of the Messenger of Allah	يَا بْنَ رَسُولِ ٱللَّهِ
Oh Allah's proof against His creation	يَا حُجَّةَ ٱللَّهِ عَلَىٰ خَلْقِهِ
Oh our chief and our master	يَا سَيِّدَنَا وَمَوْلَانَا
We turned to you, and we sought your intercession	إِنَّا تَوَجَّهْنَا وَٱسْتَشْفَعْنَا
And we implored Allah through you	وَتَوَسَّلْنَا بِكَ إِلَى ٱللَّهِ

Continuous Calling

And we placed between your hands our needs	وَقَدَّمْنَاكَ بَيْنَ يَدَىْ حَاجَاتِنَا
Oh respected one with Allah	يَا وَجِيهاً عِنْدَ ٱللَّهِ
Intercede for us with Allah	إِشْفَعْ لَنَا عِنْدَ ٱللَّهِ

Pause here and pray to Allah (swt) for the reappearance of the Imam (afs) as well as for his health, comfort, and peace.

Then ask for Allah (swt) to assist the oppressed Muslims throughout the world and to answer the prayers of the distressed from your community.

Finally, ask Allah (swt) for all of the things you desire of this world and the next. Pray for assistance in your worship and in gaining recognition of Allah (swt). Then continue:

Oh my chiefs and my masters	يَا سَادَتِي وَمَوَالِيَّ
I turned to you	إِنِّي تَوَجَّهْتُ بِكُمْ
My Imams and my supporters	أَئِمَّتِي وَعُدَّتِي
For the day of my poverty and my need	لِيَوْمِ فَقْرِي وَحَاجَتِي
Towards Allah	إِلَى ٱللَّهِ
I implored Allah through you	وَتَوَسَّلْتُ بِكُمْ إِلَى ٱللَّهِ
I sought intercession through you to Allah	وَٱسْتَشْفَعْتُ بِكُمْ إِلَى ٱللَّهِ
So intercede for me with Allah	فَٱشْفَعُوا لِي عِنْدَ ٱللَّهِ
And save me from my sins before Allah	وَٱسْتَنْقِذُونِي مِنْ ذُنُوبِي عِنْدَ ٱللَّهِ
For you are my means to Allah	فَإِنَّكُمْ وَسِيلَتِي إِلَى ٱللَّهِ
And through love of you, and nearness to you, I hope for salvation before Allah	وَبِحُبِّكُمْ وَبِقُرْبِكُمْ أَرْجُو نَجَاةً مِنَ ٱللَّهِ
So be my hope before Allah	فَكُونُوا عِنْدَ ٱللَّهِ رَجَائِي
Oh my chiefs, oh friends of Allah	يَا سَادَتِي يَاأَوْلِيَاءَ ٱللَّهِ

Dua Tawassul

May Allah's blessing be upon them all	صَلَّى ٱللَّهُ عَلَيْهِمْ أَجْمَعِينَ
And may Allah curse the enemies of Allah, who wronged them	وَلَعَنَ ٱللَّهُ أَعْدَاءَ ٱللَّهِ ظَالِمِيهِمْ
From the earlier and later generations	مِنَ ٱلْأَوَّلِينَ وَٱلْآخِرِينَ
Amen, Lord of the worlds.	آمِينَ رَبَّ ٱلْعَالَمِينَ

Continuous Calling

Dua Kumayl

This dua was taught to Kumayl ibn Ziad by Imam Ali (as). Imam Ali (as) identifies it as the dua of Khidr (as). He recommends we recite it on Thursday nights and says that by it, all our affairs will be sorted and we would not move away from forgiveness. (Iqbal al-a'mal, p. 220)

In the name of Allah, the most Compassionate, the most Merciful	بِسْمِ اللَّهِ الرَّحْمَنِ الرَّحِيمِ
Oh Allah, I ask You by your Mercy which encompasses all things	اللَّهُمَّ إِنِّي أَسْأَلُكَ بِرَحْمَتِكَ الَّتِي وَسِعَتْ كُلَّ شَيْءٍ
And by Your Power with which you subdued all things	وَبِقُوَّتِكَ الَّتِي قَهَرْتَ بِهَا كُلَّ شَيْءٍ
And all things humbled before it	وَخَضَعَ لَهَا كُلُّ شَيْءٍ
And all things submitted to it	وَذَلَّ لَهَا كُلُّ شَيْءٍ
And by Your invincibility by which you overwhelmed all things	وَبِجَبَرُوتِكَ الَّتِي غَلَبْتَ بِهَا كُلَّ شَيْءٍ
And by Your honour, which nothing can stand up to	وَبِعِزَّتِكَ الَّتِي لَا يَقُومُ لَهَا شَيْءٌ
And by Your greatness, which has filled all things	وَبِعَظَمَتِكَ الَّتِي مَلَأَتْ كُلَّ شَيْءٍ
And by Your authority, which rises above all things	وَبِسُلْطَانِكَ الَّذِي عَلَا كُلَّ شَيْءٍ
And by Your face, eternal, after the extinction of all things	وَبِوَجْهِكَ الْبَاقِي بَعْدَ فَنَاءِ كُلِّ شَيْءٍ
And by Your names, which filled the foundations of all things	وَبِأَسْمَائِكَ الَّتِي مَلَأَتْ أَرْكَانَ كُلِّ شَيْءٍ
And by Your knowledge, which surrounded all things	وَبِعِلْمِكَ الَّذِي أَحَاطَ بِكُلِّ شَيْءٍ
And by the light of Your face, which illuminated all things	وَبِنُورِ وَجْهِكَ الَّذِي أَضَاءَ لَهُ كُلُّ شَيْءٍ

Dua Kumayl

Oh Light! Oh Holy One!	يَا نُورُ يَا قُدُّوسُ
Oh First of the first	يَا أَوَّلَ الْأَوَّلِينَ
And oh Last of the last	وَيَا آخِرَ الْآخِرِينَ
Oh Allah, forgive my sins which tear apart the safeguards	اللَّهُمَّ اغْفِرْ لِي الذُّنُوبَ الَّتِي تَهْتِكُ الْعِصَمَ
Oh Allah, forgive my sins which bring down adversities	اللَّهُمَّ اغْفِرْ لِي الذُّنُوبَ الَّتِي تُنْزِلُ النِّقَمَ
Oh Allah, forgive my sins which alter blessings	اللَّهُمَّ اغْفِرْ لِي الذُّنُوبَ الَّتِي تُغَيِّرُ النِّعَمَ
Oh Allah, forgive my sins which cage supplications	اللَّهُمَّ اغْفِرْ لِي الذُّنُوبَ الَّتِي تَحْبِسُ الدُّعَاءَ
Oh Allah, forgive my sins which cut off hopes	اللَّهُمَّ اغْفِرْ لِي الذُّنُوبَ الَّتِي تَقْطَعُ الرَّجَاءَ
Oh Allah, forgive my sins which bring down tribulations	اللَّهُمَّ اغْفِرْ لِي الذُّنُوبَ الَّتِي تُنْزِلُ الْبَلَاءَ
Oh Allah, forgive every sin I have sinned, and every mistake I have made	اللَّهُمَّ اغْفِرْ لِي كُلَّ ذَنْبٍ أَذْنَبْتُهُ وَكُلَّ خَطِيئَةٍ أَخْطَأْتُهَا
Oh Allah, I seek nearness to You by Your remembrance	اللَّهُمَّ إِنِّي أَتَقَرَّبُ إِلَيْكَ بِذِكْرِكَ
And I seek intercession from You with Yourself	وَأَسْتَشْفِعُ بِكَ إِلَى نَفْسِكَ
And I ask You by Your generosity to bring me closer to Your nearness	وَأَسْأَلُكَ بِجُودِكَ أَنْ تُدْنِيَنِي مِنْ قُرْبِكَ
And to provide me gratitude of You	وَأَنْ تُوزِعَنِي شُكْرَكَ

Continuous Calling

And to inspire me with Your remembrance	وَأَنْ تُلْهِمَنِي ذِكْرَكَ
Oh Allah, I ask You a request, submissive, abased, and humble	اللَّهُمَّ إِنِّي أَسْأَلُكَ سُؤَالَ خَاضِعٍ مُتَذَلِّلٍ خَاشِعٍ
That You pardon me and have mercy on me and make me, with Your decree, pleased	أَنْ تُسَامِحَنِي وَتَرْحَمَنِي وَتَجْعَلَنِي بِقَسَمِكَ رَاضِياً قَانِعاً
And satisfied and in all situations humble	وَفِي جَمِيعِ الْأَحْوَالِ مُتَوَاضِعاً
Oh Allah, I ask You the question of one who's poverty is extreme	اللَّهُمَّ وَأَسْأَلُكَ سُؤَالَ مَنِ اشْتَدَّتْ فَاقَتُهُ
And who submitted to You, in difficulty, his needs	وَأَنْزَلَ بِكَ عِنْدَ الشَّدَائِدِ حَاجَتَهُ
And his desire for what You have is great	وَعَظُمَ فِيمَا عِنْدَكَ رَغْبَتُهُ
Oh Allah, Your authority is great and Your station is loft	اللَّهُمَّ عَظُمَ سُلْطَانُكَ وَعَلَا مَكَانُكَ
And Your plan is hidden and Your command is apparent	وَخَفِيَ مَكْرُكَ وَظَهَرَ أَمْرُكَ
Your dominance overpowered and Your power flows	وَغَلَبَ قَهْرُكَ وَجَرَتْ قُدْرَتُكَ
There is no escape from Your governance	وَلَا يُمْكِنُ الْفِرَارُ مِنْ حُكُومَتِكَ
Oh Allah, I do not find a forgiver for my sins	اللَّهُمَّ لَا أَجِدُ لِذُنُوبِي غَافِراً
Or for my ugliness a concealer	وَلَا لِقَبَائِحِي سَاتِراً
Or a transformer of my ugly deeds to good other than You	وَلَا لِشَيْءٍ مِنْ عَمَلِي الْقَبِيحِ بِالْحَسَنِ مُبَدِّلاً غَيْرَكَ

Dua Kumayl

There is no god but You	لَا إِلَهَ إِلَّا أَنْتَ
Glorified and praised You are	سُبْحَانَكَ وَبِحَمْدِكَ
I have wronged myself	ظَلَمْتُ نَفْسِي
And I became bold in my ignorance	وَتَجَرَّأْتُ بِجَهْلِي
And I relied upon Your previous remembrance and favour upon me	وَسَكَنْتُ إِلَى قَدِيمِ ذِكْرِكَ لِي وَمَنِّكَ عَلَيَّ
Oh Allah, my Master	اللَّهُمَّ مَوْلَايَ
How many ugly things You concealed	كَمْ مِنْ قَبِيحٍ سَتَرْتَهُ
And how many disastrous trials You lifted	وَكَمْ مِنْ فَادِحٍ مِنَ الْبَلَاءِ أَقَلْتَهُ
And how many slips You prevented	وَكَمْ مِنْ عِثَارٍ وَقَيْتَهُ
And how many detested things You repelled	وَكَمْ مِنْ مَكْرُوهٍ دَفَعْتَهُ
And how much beautiful praise, which I am not worthy of, You spread	وَكَمْ مِنْ ثَنَاءٍ جَمِيلٍ لَسْتُ أَهْلًا لَهُ نَشَرْتَهُ
Oh Allah, my trial is great	اللَّهُمَّ عَظُمَ بَلَائِي
And my evil state has exceeded	وَأَفْرَطَ بِي سُوءُ حَالِي
And my deeds have fallen short	وَقَصُرَتْ بِي أَعْمَالِي
And my chains have restrained me	وَقَعَدَتْ بِي أَغْلَالِي
And my long hopes have imprisoned my benefit	وَحَبَسَنِي عَنْ نَفْعِي بُعْدُ آمَالِي
And the world deceived me with its deception and my crimes and my procrastination	وَخَدَعَتْنِي الدُّنْيَا بِغُرُورِهَا وَنَفْسِي بِجِنَايَتِهَا وَمِطَالِي

Oh my Chief, so I ask You by Your honour to not let my evil actions and deeds veil my supplication	يَا سَيِّدِى فَأَسْأَلُكَ بِعِزَّتِكَ أَنْ لَا يَحْجُبَ عَنْكَ دُعَائِى سُوءُ عَمَلِى وَفِعَالِى
And to not expose me through the hidden things you saw from my secrets	وَلَا تَفْضَحَنِى بِخَفِىِّ مَا اطَّلَعْتَ عَلَيْهِ مِنْ سِرِّى
And do not hasten me with punishment for what I did in private	وَلَا تُعَاجِلْنِى بِالْعُقُوبَةِ عَلَى مَا عَمِلْتُهُ فِى خَلَوَاتِى
From my evil actions and misdeeds	مِنْ سُوءِ فِعْلِى وَإِسَاءَتِى
And my constant negligence and ignorance	وَدَوَامِ تَفْرِيطِى وَجَهَالَتِى
And my plentiful desires and neglect	وَكَثْرَةِ شَهَوَاتِى وَغَفْلَتِى
And by Your honour, oh Allah, in all situations be kind to me	وَكُنِ اللَّهُمَّ بِعِزَّتِكَ لِى فِى كُلِّ الْأَحْوَالِ رَؤُوفاً
And in all matters be gracious	وَعَلَىَّ فِى جَمِيعِ الْأُمُورِ عَطُوفاً
My God and my Lord, who other than You do I ask to remove my suffering and to consider my affairs	إِلَهِى وَرَبِّى مَنْ لِى غَيْرُكَ أَسْأَلُهُ كَشْفَ ضُرِّى وَالنَّظَرَ فِى أَمْرِى
My God and my Master, You decreed a judgment on me in which I followed my own desires	إِلَهِى وَمَوْلَاىَ أَجْرَيْتَ عَلَىَّ حُكْماً اتَّبَعْتُ فِيهِ هَوَى نَفْسِى
And I was not cautious of my enemy's adornment	وَلَمْ أَحْتَرِسْ فِيهِ مِنْ تَزْيِينِ عَدُوِّى
So he deceived me with what I desire and my decree pleased him	فَغَرَّنِى بِمَا أَهْوَى وَأَسْعَدَهُ عَلَى ذَلِكَ الْقَضَاءُ

Dua Kumayl

So, with what happened to me, I transgressed some of Your limits	فَتَجَاوَزْتُ بِمَا جَرَى عَلَىَّ مِنْ ذَلِكَ بَعْضَ حُدُودِكَ
And I opposed some of Your commands	وَخَالَفْتُ بَعْضَ أَوَامِرِكَ
So You have an argument against me in all of this	فَلَكَ الْحُجَّةُ عَلَىَّ فِي جَمِيعِ ذَلِكَ
And I have no argument in what happened to me by Your decree	وَلَا حُجَّةَ لِي فِيمَا جَرَى عَلَىَّ فِيهِ قَضَاؤُكَ
Your judgement and trial bound me	وَأَلْزَمَنِي حُكْمُكَ وَبَلَاؤُكَ
I have come to you, my God, after my shortcoming and immoderation toward myself	وَقَدْ أَتَيْتُكَ يَا إِلَهِي بَعْدَ تَقْصِيرِي وَإِسْرَافِي عَلَى نَفْسِي
Apologetic, regretful,	مُعْتَذِراً نَادِماً
Broken, pleading,	مُنْكَسِراً مُسْتَقِيلاً
Seeking forgiveness, repentant,	مُسْتَغْفِراً مُنِيباً
Acknowledging, submitting, confessing	مُقِرّاً مُذْعِناً مُعْتَرِفاً
I do not find escape from what has become of me	لَا أَجِدُ مَفَرّاً مِمَّا كَانَ مِنِّي
And no refuge to turn towards in my affairs	وَلَا مَفْزَعاً أَتَوَجَّهُ إِلَيْهِ فِى أَمْرِى
Other than your acceptance of my excuse and Your entering me into the vastness of your mercy	غَيْرَ قَبُولِكَ عُذْرِى وَإِدْخَالِكَ إِيَاىَ فِى سَعَةٍ مِن رَّحْمَتِكَ
Oh Allah, accept my excuse	اللَّهُمَّ فَاقْبَلْ عُذْرِى
And have mercy on the severity of my suffering	وَارْحَمْ شِدَّةَ ضُرِّى
And release me from the severity of my bonds	وَفُكَّنِى مِن شَدِّ وَثَاقِى

Continuous Calling

Oh Lord, have mercy on my weak body, and delicate skin, and thin bones	يَا رَبِّ ارْحَمْ ضَعْفَ بَدَنِي وَرِقَّةَ جِلْدِي وَدِقَّةَ عَظْمِي
Oh the One who originated my creation, my mention, my upbringing, my goodness, and my nourishment	يَا مَنْ بَدَأَ خَلْقِي وَذِكْرِي وَتَرْبِيَتِي وَبِرِّي وَتَغْذِيَتِي
Grant me, as my Originator, Your generosity and your previous goodness	هَبْنِي لِابْتِدَاءِ كَرَمِكَ وَسَالِفِ بِرِّكَ بِي
Oh my God, my Chief, my Lord	يَا إِلَهِي وَسَيِّدِي وَرَبِّي
Would You punish me with Your fire after my monotheism?	أَتُرَاكَ مُعَذِّبِي بِنَارِكَ بَعْدَ تَوْحِيدِكَ
And after recognition of You filled my heart?	وَبَعْدَ مَا انْطَوَى عَلَيْهِ قَلْبِي مِنْ مَعْرِفَتِكَ
And my tongue constantly remembered you?	وَلَهِجَ بِهِ لِسَانِي مِنْ ذِكْرِكَ
And my mind believed from Your love?	وَاعْتَقَدَهُ ضَمِيرِي مِنْ حُبِّكَ
And after the sincerity of my confession and submissive supplication to Your Lordship?	وَبَعْدَ صِدْقِ اعْتِرَافِي وَدُعَائِي خَاضِعاً لِرُبُوبِيَّتِكَ
Far be it! You are too generous to waste the one You nurtured	هَيْهَاتَ أَنْتَ أَكْرَمُ مِنْ أَنْ تُضَيِّعَ مَنْ رَبَّيْتَهُ
Or to push away the one You brought close	أَوْ تُبْعِدَ مَنْ أَدْنَيْتَهُ
Or to exile the one You sheltered	أَوْ تُشَرِّدَ مَنْ آوَيْتَهُ
Or to surrender to tribulation the one You suffieed and had mercy on	أَوْ تُسَلِّمَ إِلَى الْبَلَاءِ مَنْ كَفَيْتَهُ وَرَحِمْتَهُ
I wish I knew, oh my Chief, and my God, and my Master	وَلَيْتَ شِعْرِي يَا سَيِّدِي وَإِلَهِي وَمَوْلَايَ

Do you allow flames upon the faces which bowed to Your greatness in prostration?	أَتُسَلِّطُ النَّارَ عَلَى وُجُوهٍ خَرَّتْ لِعَظَمَتِكَ سَاجِدَةً
And on the tongues that spoke truthfully about Your Oneness and were grateful to You in praise?	وَعَلَى أَلْسُنٍ نَطَقَتْ بِتَوْحِيدِكَ صَادِقَةً وَبِشُكْرِكَ مَادِحَةً
And on the hearts that recognised and realised Your divinity?	وَعَلَى قُلُوبٍ اعْتَرَفَتْ بِإِلَهِيَّتِكَ مُحَقِّقَةً
And on the minds that contained knowledge of You until they became humble?	وَعَلَى ضَمَائِرَ حَوَتْ مِنَ الْعِلْمِ بِكَ حَتَّى صَارَتْ خَاشِعَةً
And on the limbs which strived towards the places of Your worship obediently and sought Your forgiveness submissively?	وَعَلَى جَوَارِحَ سَعَتْ إِلَى أَوْطَانِ تَعَبُّدِكَ طَائِعَةً وَأَشَارَتْ بِاسْتِغْفَارِكَ مُذْعِنَةً
No such assumption is made about you! Nor has any news of this reached us from Your grace	مَا هَكَذَا الظَّنُّ بِكَ وَلَا أُخْبِرْنَا بِفَضْلِكَ عَنْكَ
Oh Generous! Oh my Lord	يَا كَرِيمُ يَا رَبِّ
You know my weakness before even a little of this world's trials and punishments	وَأَنْتَ تَعْلَمُ ضَعْفِي عَنْ قَلِيلٍ مِنْ بَلَاءِ الدُّنْيَا وَعُقُوبَاتِهَا
And what happens in it that its people dislike	وَمَا يَجْرِي فِيهَا مِنَ الْمَكَارِهِ عَلَى أَهْلِهَا
Even though the disliked trials are little in length, easy to withstand, and short in duration	عَلَى أَنَّ ذَلِكَ بَلَاءٌ وَمَكْرُوهٌ قَلِيلٌ مَكْثُهُ يَسِيرٌ بَقَاؤُهُ قَصِيرٌ مُدَّتُهُ
So how can I endure the trials of the Hereafter and the grave occurrences in it?	فَكَيْفَ احْتِمَالِي لِبَلَاءِ الْآخِرَةِ وَجَلِيلِ وُقُوعِ الْمَكَارِهِ فِيهَا

And it is an extended trial, an enduring duration, and is not lightened for its people	وَهُوَ بَلَاءٌ تَطُولُ مُدَّتُهُ وَيَدُومُ مَقَامُهُ وَلَا يُخَفَّفُ عَنْ أَهْلِهِ
Because it only occurs from Your anger, Your vengeance, and Your displeasure	لِأَنَّهُ لَا يَكُونُ إِلَّا عَنْ غَضَبِكَ وَانْتِقَامِكَ وَسَخَطِكَ
And neither the heaven or the earth can withstand it	وَهَذَا مَا لَا تَقُومُ لَهُ السَّمَاوَاتُ وَالْأَرْضُ
My Chief, what about me?	يَا سَيِّدِى فَكَيْفَ بِى
For I am your servant weak, low, contemptible, needy, and submissive	وَأَنَا عَبْدُكَ الضَّعِيفُ الذَّلِيلُ الْحَقِيرُ الْمِسْكِينُ الْمُسْتَكِينُ
Oh my God, my Lord, my Chief, and my Master	يَا إِلَهِى وَرَبِّى وَسَيِّدِى وَمَوْلَاى
About which matters should I complain to You?	لِأَيِّ الْأُمُورِ إِلَيْكَ أَشْكُو
And for what should I groan and cry?	وَلِمَا مِنْهَا أَضِجُّ وَأَبْكِى
For the pain of the punishment and its severity?	لِأَلِيمِ الْعَذَابِ وَشِدَّتِهِ
Or for the length of the trial and its duration?	أَمْ لِطُولِ الْبَلَاءِ وَمُدَّتِهِ
So if You took me to the punishment with Your enemies	فَلَئِنْ صَيَّرْتَنِى لِلْعُقُوبَاتِ مَعَ أَعْدَائِكَ
And You gathered me with the people of Your trials	وَجَمَعْتَ بَيْنِى وَبَيْنَ أَهْلِ بَلَائِكَ
And You separated me from Your beloved ones and friends	وَفَرَّقْتَ بَيْنِى وَبَيْنَ أَحِبَّائِكَ وَأَوْلِيَائِكَ
Then suppose, my God, my Chief, my Master, and my Lord, I was patient over Your punishment	فَهَبْنِى يَا إِلَهِى وَسَيِّدِى وَمَوْلَاى وَرَبِّى صَبَرْتُ عَلَى عَذَابِكَ

Dua Kumayl

How will I be patient over separation from You?	فَكَيْفَ أَصْبِرُ عَلَى فِرَاقِكَ
And suppose I was patient over the heat of the fire	وَهَبْنِي صَبَرْتُ عَلَى حَرِّ نَارِكَ
How will I be patient not gazing at Your nobility?	فَكَيْفَ أَصْبِرُ عَنِ النَّظَرِ إِلَى كَرَامَتِكَ
Or how can I reside in the Fire while I hope for Your forgiveness?	أَمْ كَيْفَ أَسْكُنُ فِي النَّارِ وَرَجَائِي عَفْوُكَ
So by Your Might, my Chief and my Master, I swear sincerely if You left me speaking	فَبِعِزَّتِكَ يَا سَيِّدِي وَمَوْلَايَ أُقْسِمُ صَادِقاً لَئِنْ تَرَكْتَنِي نَاطِقاً
I will groan to You among its people the groaning of the hopeful	لَأَضِجَّنَّ إِلَيْكَ بَيْنَ أَهْلِهَا ضَجِيجَ الآمِلِينَ
And I will shout to You the shouting of the shouters for help	وَلَأَصْرُخَنَّ إِلَيْكَ صُرَاخَ المُسْتَصْرِخِينَ
And I will cry to You the cries of the bereaved	وَلَأَبْكِيَنَّ عَلَيْكَ بُكَاءَ الفَاقِدِينَ
And I will call to You where are You oh Guardian of the believers	وَلَأُنَادِيَنَّكَ أَيْنَ كُنْتَ يَا وَلِيَّ المُؤْمِنِينَ
Oh Goal of the hopes of those with recognition	يَا غَايَةَ آمَالِ العَارِفِينَ
Oh Helper of those seeking help	يَا غِيَاثَ المُسْتَغِيثِينَ
Oh the love of the hearts of the truthful	يَا حَبِيبَ قُلُوبِ الصَّادِقِينَ
Oh God of the worlds	وَيَا إِلَهَ العَالَمِينَ

Continuous Calling

Would You, oh my God, with Your praise, hear in it the voice of a Muslim servant	أَفَتُرَاكَ سُبْحَانَكَ يَا إِلَهِي وَبِحَمْدِكَ تَسْمَعُ فِيهَا صَوْتَ عَبْدٍ مُسْلِمٍ
Imprisoned in it due to his opposition	سُجِنَ فِيهَا بِمُخَالَفَتِهِ
Tasting the taste of its punishment due to his disobedience	وَذَاقَ طَعْمَ عَذَابِهَا بِمَعْصِيَتِهِ
And detained between its layers due to his crime and his wrongdoing	وَحُبِسَ بَيْنَ أَطْبَاقِهَا بِجُرْمِهِ وَجَرِيرَتِهِ
And he shouts out to You, hoping for Your mercy	وَهُوَ يَضِجُّ إِلَيْكَ ضَجِيجَ مُؤَمِّلٍ لِرَحْمَتِكَ
And he calls You with the tongue of the people of monotheism	وَيُنَادِيكَ بِلِسَانِ أَهْلِ تَوْحِيدِكَ
And he invokes you by Your Lordship	وَيَتَوَسَّلُ إِلَيْكَ بِرُبُوبِيَّتِكَ
Oh my Master, then how can he remain in the punishment and he hopes for Your previous leniency?	يَا مَوْلَايَ فَكَيْفَ يَبْقَى فِي الْعَذَابِ وَهُوَ يَرْجُو مَا سَلَفَ مِنْ حِلْمِكَ
Or how can the Fire hurt him and he aspires for Your favour and Your mercy?	أَمْ كَيْفَ تُؤْلِمُهُ النَّارُ وَهُوَ يَأْمَلُ فَضْلَكَ وَرَحْمَتَكَ
Or how can its flames burn him and You hear his voice and see his place?	أَمْ كَيْفَ يُحْرِقُهُ لَهِيبُهَا وَأَنْتَ تَسْمَعُ صَوْتَهُ وَتَرَى مَكَانَهُ
Or how can its roaring engulf him and You know his weakness?	أَمْ كَيْفَ يَشْتَمِلُ عَلَيْهِ زَفِيرُهَا وَأَنْتَ تَعْلَمُ ضَعْفَهُ
Or how can he be disturbed between its layers and You know his truthfulness?	أَمْ كَيْفَ يَتَقَلْقَلُ بَيْنَ أَطْبَاقِهَا وَأَنْتَ تَعْلَمُ صِدْقَهُ
Or how can its guards rebuke him and he calls You "Oh Lord"?	أَمْ كَيْفَ تَزْجُرُهُ زَبَانِيَتُهَا وَهُوَ يُنَادِيكَ يَا رَبَّهُ

Or how can he hope for Your favour in freeing him from it and You leave him in it?	أَمْ كَيْفَ يَرْجُو فَضْلَكَ فِي عِتْقِهِ مِنْهَا فَتَتْرُكُهُ فِيهَا
This is far from what is expected of You	هَيْهَاتَ مَا ذَلِكَ الظَّنُّ بِكَ
And isn't recognised from Your grace	وَلَا الْمَعْرُوفُ مِن فَضْلِكَ
And does not resemble how You treated the monotheists from Your kindness and goodness	وَلَا مُشْبِهٌ لِمَا عَامَلْتَ بِهِ الْمُوَحِّدِينَ مِنْ بِرِّكَ وَإِحْسَانِكَ
So I am certain that if not for Your previous judgement to punish the deniers	فَبِالْيَقِينِ أَقْطَعُ لَوْلَا مَا حَكَمْتَ بِهِ مِن تَعْذِيبِ جَاحِدِيكَ
And You decreed the eternality of Your stubborn deniers	وَقَضَيْتَ بِهِ مِنْ إِخْلَادِ مُعَانِدِيكَ
You would have made the Fire completely cool and peaceful	لَجَعَلْتَ النَّارَ كُلَّهَا بَرْداً وَسَلَاماً
And it would not be anyone's dwelling nor station	وَمَا كَانَ لأَحَدٍ فِيهَا مَقَرّاً وَلَا مُقَاماً
But you, holy are Your names, swore that you would fill it with the disbelievers	لَكِنَّكَ تَقَدَّسَتْ أَسْمَاؤُكَ أَقْسَمْتَ أَنْ تَمْلَأَهَا مِنَ الْكَافِرِينَ
From the jinn and mankind collectively	مِنَ الْجِنَّةِ وَالنَّاسِ أَجْمَعِينَ
And you would make it eternal for the stubborn ones	وَأَنْ تُخَلِّدَ فِيهَا الْمُعَانِدِينَ
And You, exalted is Your praise, said in the beginning, extending the favours graciously	وَأَنْتَ جَلَّ ثَنَاؤُكَ قُلْتَ مُبْتَدِئاً وَتَطَوَّلْتَ بِالإِنْعَامِ مُتَكَرِّماً
"Then is he who became a believer like he who became a transgressor? They are not equal" (Quran 32:18)	﴿أَفَمَن كَانَ مُؤْمِناً كَمَن كَانَ فَاسِقاً لَّا يَسْتَوُونَ﴾

My God, my Chief, so I ask You by the determination you determined	إِلَهِي وَسَيِّدِي فَأَسْأَلُكَ بِالْقُدْرَةِ الَّتِي قَدَّرْتَهَا
And by the decree which You made definite and unchanging and You overcame the one decreed upon	وَبِالْقَضِيَّةِ الَّتِي حَتَمْتَهَا وَحَكَمْتَهَا وَغَلَبْتَ مَنْ عَلَيْهِ أَجْرَيْتَهَا
That you relieve me in this night and in this hour	أَنْ تَهَبَ لِي فِي هذِهِ اللَّيْلَةِ وَفِي هذِهِ السَّاعَةِ
Every crime I committed	كُلَّ جُرْمٍ أَجْرَمْتُهُ
And every sin I sinned	وَكُلَّ ذَنْبٍ أَذْنَبْتُهُ
And every ugly deed I concealed	وَكُلَّ قَبِيحٍ أَسْرَرْتُهُ
And every ignorant act I did	وَكُلَّ جَهْلٍ عَمِلْتُهُ
Whether I hid it or announced it	كَتَمْتُهُ أَوْ أَعْلَنْتُهُ
Concealed it or exposed it	أَخْفَيْتُهُ أَوْ أَظْهَرْتُهُ
And every evil deed You commanded the noble recorders to record	وَكُلَّ سَيِّئَةٍ أَمَرْتَ بِإِثْبَاتِهَا الْكِرَامَ الْكَاتِبِينَ
Those You entrusted to guard over what comes from me	الَّذِينَ وَكَّلْتَهُمْ بِحِفْظِ مَا يَكُونُ مِنِّي
And you made them witnesses over me with my limbs	وَجَعَلْتَهُمْ شُهُوداً عَلَيَّ مَعَ جَوَارِحِي
And You oversaw me from behind them	وَكُنْتَ أَنْتَ الرَّقِيبَ عَلَيَّ مِنْ وَرَائِهِمْ
And the Witness for what was hidden from them	وَالشَّاهِدَ لِمَا خَفِيَ عَنْهُمْ
And by Your mercy, You concealed it	وَبِرَحْمَتِكَ أَخْفَيْتَهُ
And by Your favour, You covered it	وَبِفَضْلِكَ سَتَرْتَهُ

And that You provide my share from every good You send down	وَأَنْ تُوَفِّرَ حَظِّى مِنْ كُلِّ خَيْرٍ تُنْزِلُهُ
Or charity You bestow	أَوْ إِحْسَانٍ تُفْضِلُهُ
Or kindness You spread	أَوْ بِرٍّ تَنْشُرُهُ
Or sustenance You extend	أَوْ رِزْقٍ تَبْسُطُهُ
Or sin You forgive	أَوْ ذَنْبٍ تَغْفِرُهُ
Or mistake You cover	أَوْ خَطَأٍ تَسْتُرُهُ
Oh my Lord, oh my Lord, oh my Lord	يَا رَبِّ يَا رَبِّ يَا رَبِّ
Oh my God, my Chief, my Master, the Owner of my servitude	يَا إِلَهِى وَسَيِّدِى وَمَوْلَاىَ وَمَالِكَ رِقِّ
Oh the one in whose hands is my forelock	يَا مَنْ بِيَدِهِ نَاصِيَتِى
Oh knowledgeable in my harm and poverty	يَا عَلِيماً بِضُرِّى وَمَسْكَنَتِى
Oh aware in my destitution and want	يَا خَبِيراً بِفَقْرِى وَفَاقَتِى
Oh my Lord, oh my Lord, oh my Lord	يَا رَبِّ يَا رَبِّ يَا رَبِّ
I ask You by Your right and Your holiness	أَسْأَلُكَ بِحَقِّكَ وَقُدْسِكَ
And Your greatest attributes and names	وَأَعْظَمِ صِفَاتِكَ وَأَسْمَائِكَ
That You make my time in the night and day filled with Your remembrance	أَنْ تَجْعَلَ أَوْقَاتِى فِى اللَّيْلِ وَالنَّهَارِ بِذِكْرِكَ مَعْمُورَةً
And with Your continuous service	وَبِخِدْمَتِكَ مَوْصُولَةً
And my deeds accepted with You	وَأَعْمَالِى عِنْدَكَ مَقْبُولَةً
Until all my deeds and recitations become one continuous routine	حَتَّى تَكُونَ أَعْمَالِى وَأَوْرَادِى كُلُّهَا وِرْداً وَاحِداً

Continuous Calling

And my state in Your service is endless	وَحَالِي فِي خِدْمَتِكَ سَرْمَداً
Oh my Chief, oh the One I rely on	يَا سَيِّدِي يَا مَنْ عَلَيْهِ مُعَوَّلِي
Oh the One I complain to about my state	يَا مَنْ إِلَيْهِ شَكَوْتُ أَحْوَالِي
Oh my Lord, oh my Lord, oh my Lord	يَا رَبِّ يَا رَبِّ يَا رَبِّ
Strengthen my limbs in Your service	قَوِّ عَلَى خِدْمَتِكَ جَوَارِحِي
And strengthen my conscience in determination	وَاشْدُدْ عَلَى الْعَزِيمَةِ جَوَانِحِي
And grant me diligence in Your fear	وَهَبْ لِي الْجِدَّ فِي خَشْيَتِكَ
And continuous connection to Your service	وَالدَّوَامَ فِي الِاتِّصَالِ بِخِدْمَتِكَ
Until I roam towards You in the fields of the foremost	حَتَّى أَسْرَحَ إِلَيْكَ فِي مَيَادِينِ السَّابِقِينَ
And I hasten towards You among the pioneers	وَأُسْرِعَ إِلَيْكَ فِي الْمُبَادِرِينَ
And I yearn for Your closeness amongst those who yearn	وَأَشْتَاقَ إِلَى قُرْبِكَ فِي الْمُشْتَاقِينَ
And I draw near to You with the nearness of the sincere ones	وَأَدْنُوَ مِنْكَ دُنُوَّ الْمُخْلِصِينَ
And I fear You with the fear of those with certainty	وَأَخَافَكَ مَخَافَةَ الْمُوقِنِينَ
And I gather in Your vicinity with the believers	وَأَجْتَمِعَ فِي جِوَارِكَ مَعَ الْمُؤْمِنِينَ
Oh Allah, whoever intends evil for me, repel him	اللَّهُمَّ وَمَنْ أَرَادَنِي بِسُوءٍ فَأَرِدْهُ
And whoever plots against me, outwit him	وَمَنْ كَادَنِي فَكِدْهُ
And make me from the best of Your servants with a portion, with You	وَاجْعَلْنِي مِنْ أَحْسَنِ عَبِيدِكَ نَصِيباً عِنْدَكَ

Dua Kumayl

And closest to You in station	وَأَقْرَبِهِم مَنْزِلَةً مِنْكَ
And most special in closeness with You	وَأَخَصِّهِم زُلْفَةً لَدَيْكَ
Indeed, that is not obtained except by Your grace	فَإِنَّهُ لَا يُنَالُ ذَلِكَ إِلَّا بِفَضْلِكَ
And bestow upon me Your generosity	وَجُدْ لِي بِجُودِكَ
And be kind to me with Your glory	وَاعْطِفْ عَلَيَّ بِمَجْدِكَ
And protect me with Your mercy	وَاحْفَظْنِي بِرَحْمَتِكَ
And make my tongue busy with Your remembrance	وَاجْعَلْ لِسَانِي بِذِكْرِكَ لَهِجاً
And adore my heart with love for You	وَقَلْبِي بِحُبِّكَ مُتَيَّماً
And favour me with the best of responses	وَمُنَّ عَلَيَّ بِحُسْنِ إِجَابَتِكَ
And relieve my stumbles	وَأَقِلْنِي عَثْرَتِي
And forgive my mistakes	وَاغْفِرْ زَلَّتِي
For You decreed Your servants to worship	فَإِنَّكَ قَضَيْتَ عَلَى عِبَادِكَ بِعِبَادَتِكَ
And You commanded them to supplicate to You	وَأَمَرْتَهُم بِدُعَائِكَ
And You guaranteed that You would answer them	وَضَمِنْتَ لَهُمُ الْإِجَابَةَ
So to You, my Lord, I have directed my face	فَإِلَيْكَ يَا رَبِّ نَصَبْتُ وَجْهِي
And to You, my Lord, I extended my hand	وَإِلَيْكَ يَا رَبِّ مَدَدْتُ يَدِي
So by Your glory, respond to my supplication	فَبِعِزَّتِكَ اسْتَجِبْ لِي دُعَائِي
And grant my wish	وَبَلِّغْنِي مُنَايَ

And do not cut off my hope for Your grace	وَلَا تَقْطَعْ مِن فَضْلِكَ رَجَائِي
And spare me the evil of the humans and jinn from my enemies	وَاكْفِنِي شَرَّ الْجِنِّ وَالْإِنْسِ مِنْ أَعْدَائِي
Oh the One who is quick to be satisfied	يَا سَرِيعَ الرِّضَا
Forgive the one whose only possession is supplication	إِغْفِرْ لِمَن لَا يَمْلِكُ إِلَّا الدُّعَاءَ
For You do as you will	فَإِنَّكَ فَعَّالٌ لِمَا تَشَاءُ
Oh the One Whose name is a cure	يَا مَنْ اسْمُهُ دَوَاءٌ
And Whose mention is healing	وَذِكْرُهُ شِفَاءٌ
And Whose obedience is wealth	وَطَاعَتُهُ غِنًى
Have mercy on the one whose capital is hope	إِرْحَمْ مَّن رَّأْسُ مَالِهِ الرَّجَاءُ
And whose weapon is crying	وَسِلَاحُهُ الْبُكَاءُ
Oh abundant in blessings	يَا سَابِغَ النِّعَمِ
Oh repeller of calamities	يَا دَافِعَ النِّقَمِ
Oh light of the frightened ones in the darkness	يَا نُورَ الْمُسْتَوْحِشِينَ فِي الظُّلَمِ
Oh the Knowing who was not taught	يَا عَالِمًا لَا يُعَلَّمُ
Send blessings upon Muhammad and the family of Muhammad	صَلِّ عَلَى مُحَمَّدٍ وَآلِ مُحَمَّدٍ
And do with me what is worthy of You	وَافْعَلْ بِي مَا أَنْتَ أَهْلُهُ
And may Allah bless his Messenger and the righteous Imams from his family	وَصَلَّى اللَّهُ عَلَى رَسُولِهِ وَالْأَئِمَّةِ الْمَيَامِينِ مِنْ آلِهِ
And grant them peace abundantly	وَسَلَّمَ تَسْلِيمًا كَثِيرًا

Dua Mashlool

This dua was taught by Imam Ali (as) to a man who was paralysed. He was instructed to read it after Isha Prayer. After this he went to sleep and saw the Prophet (saaw) in his dream. The Prophet (saaw) healed him and asked him to memorise the dua as it contains the great name of Allah (swt). It drives away the effects of sins and brings every time of blessing. It is highly recommended to have wudhu while reciting it. (Muhaj al Da-wat)

In the name of Allah, the most Compassionate, the most Merciful	بِسْمِ ٱللَّهِ ٱلرَّحْمٰنِ ٱلرَّحِيمِ
Oh Allah, I ask You by your Name	اَللَّهُمَّ إِنِّي أَسْأَلُكَ بِٱسْمِكَ
In the name of Allah, the most Compassionate, the most Merciful	بِسْمِ ٱللَّهِ ٱلرَّحْمٰنِ ٱلرَّحِيمِ
Oh Possessor of majesty and honour	يَا ذَا ٱلْجَلاَلِ وَٱلإِكْرَامِ
Oh Living! Oh Sustainer!	يَا حَيُّ يَا قَيُّومُ
Oh Living! There is no god but You!	يَا حَيُّ لاَ إِلٰهَ إِلاَّ أَنْتَ
Oh He Who no one knows what He is	يَا هُوَ يَا مَنْ لاَ يَعْلَمُ مَا هُوَ
Nor how He is	وَلاَ كَيْفَ هُوَ
Nor where He is	وَلاَ أَيْنَ هُوَ
Nor His circumstance, except Him	وَلاَ حَيْثُ هُوَ إِلاَّ هُوَ
Oh Possessor of kingship and sovereignty!	يَا ذَا ٱلْمُلْكِ وَٱلْمَلَكُوتِ
Oh Possessor of might and invincibility!	يَا ذَا ٱلْعِزَّةِ وَٱلْجَبَرُوتِ
Oh King! Oh Holy! Oh Peace!	يَا مَلِكُ يَا قُدُّوسُ يَا سَلاَمُ
Oh Security! Oh Overseer!	يَا مُؤْمِنُ يَا مُهَيْمِنُ

Oh Mighty! Oh Compeller! Oh Supreme!	يَا عَزِيزُ يَا جَبَّارُ يَا مُتَكَبِّرُ
Oh Creator! Oh Maker! Oh Designer!	يَا خَالِقُ يَا بَارِئُ يَا مُصَوِّرُ
Oh giver of Benefit! Oh Manager!	يَا مُفِيدُ يَا مُدَبِّرُ
Oh Severe! Oh Originator!	يَا شَدِيدُ يَا مُبْدِئُ
Oh Returner! Oh Destroyer!	يَا مُعِيدُ يَا مُبِيدُ
Oh Loving! Oh Praised! Oh Worshipped!	يَا وَدُودُ يَا مَحْمُودُ يَا مَعْبُودُ
Oh Distant! Oh Near!	يَا بَعِيدُ يَا قَرِيبُ
Oh Responder! Oh Watchful! Oh Reckoner!	يَا مُجِيبُ يَا رَقِيبُ يَا حَسِيبُ
Oh Innovator! Oh Exalted!	يَا بَدِيعُ يَا رَفِيعُ
Oh Unreachable! Oh Hearing!	يَا مَنِيعُ يَا سَمِيعُ
Oh Knowing! Oh Forbearing! Oh Generous!	يَا عَلِيمُ يَا حَلِيمُ يَا كَرِيمُ
Oh Wise! Oh Ancient!	يَا حَكِيمُ يَا قَدِيمُ
Oh most High! Oh Great One!	يَا عَلِيُّ يَا عَظِيمُ
Oh Tender! Oh Gracious!	يَا حَنَّانُ يَا مَنَّانُ
Oh Condemner! Oh Recourse!	يَا دَيَّانُ يَا مُسْتَعَانُ
Oh Majestic! Oh Beautiful!	يَا جَلِيلُ يَا جَمِيلُ
Oh Custodian! Oh Guarantor!	يَا وَكِيلُ يَا كَفِيلُ
Oh Pardoner! Oh Granter!	يَا مُقِيلُ يَا مُنِيلُ

Oh Noble! Oh Indicator!	يَا نَبِيلُ يَا دَلِيلُ
Oh Guide! Oh Originator!	يَا هَادِي يَا بَادِي
Oh First! Oh Last!	يَا أَوَّلُ يَا آخِرُ
Oh Manifest! Oh Hidden!	يَا ظَاهِرُ يَا بَاطِنُ
Oh Steadfast! Oh Eternal!	يَا قَائِمُ يَا دَائِمُ
Oh Knower! Oh Judge!	يَا عَالِمُ يَا حَاكِمُ
Oh Decreer! Oh Just!	يَا قَاضِي يَا عَادِلُ
Oh Separator! Oh Connector!	يَا فَاصِلُ يَا وَاصِلُ
Oh Pure! Oh Purifier!	يَا طَاهِرُ يَا مُطَهِّرُ
Oh Powerful! Oh Omnipotent!	يَا قَادِرُ يَا مُقْتَدِرُ
Oh Grand! Oh Supreme!	يَا كَبِيرُ يَا مُتَكَبِّرُ
Oh One! Oh Unique! Oh Self-Sufficient!	يَا وَاحِدُ يَا أَحَدُ يَا صَمَدُ
Oh He Who does not beget and was not begotten,	يَا مَنْ لَمْ يَلِدْ وَلَمْ يُولَدْ
And no one is an equal for him	وَلَمْ يَكُنْ لَهُ كُفُواً أَحَدٌ
Who has no wife	وَلَمْ يَكُنْ لَهُ صَاحِبَةٌ
And there is no Minister with Him	وَلاَ كَانَ مَعَهُ وَزِيرٌ
And He did not take with Him an adviser	وَلاَ اتَّخَذَ مَعَهُ مُشِيراً
And He did not need an assistant	وَلاَ احْتَاجَ إِلَى ظَهِيرٍ
And there was no other God with Him	وَلاَ كَانَ مَعَهُ مِنْ إِلَهٍ غَيْرُهُ
There is no god but You	لاَ إِلَهَ إِلاَّ أَنْتَ

Continuous Calling

So You are exalted above what the wrongdoers say, a great exaltation	فَتَعَالَيْتَ عَمَّا يَقُولُ ٱلظَّالِمُونَ عُلُوّاً كَبِيراً
Oh High! Oh Lofty! Oh Sublime!	يَا عَلِيُّ يَا شَامِخُ يَا بَاذِخُ
Oh Opener! Oh Abundant Giver! Oh Comforter!	يَا فَتَّاحُ يَا نَفَّاحُ يَا مُرْتَاحُ
Oh Reliever! Oh Helper! Oh Deliverer!	يَا مُفَرِّجُ يَا نَاصِرُ يَا مُنْتَصِرُ
Oh Comprehender! Oh Destroyer! Oh Avenger!	يَا مُدْرِكُ يَا مُهْلِكُ يَا مُنْتَقِمُ
Oh Resurrector! Oh Inheritor!	يَا بَاعِثُ يَا وَارِثُ
Oh Seeker! Oh Overpowerer!	يَا طَالِبُ يَا غَالِبُ
Oh He Who no escaper can escape from!	يَا مَنْ لاَ يَفُوتُهُ هَارِبٌ
Oh Acceptor of repentance! Oh Returner! Oh Bestower!	يَا تَوَّابُ يَا أَوَّابُ يَا وَهَّابُ
Oh Originator of means!	يَا مُسَبِّبَ ٱلأَسْبَابِ
Oh Opener of doors!	يَا مُفَتِّحَ ٱلأَبْوَابِ
Oh He Who answers wherever He is called upon!	يَا مَنْ حَيْثُ مَا دُعِى أَجَابَ
Oh Pure! Oh Thankful!	يَا طَهُورُ يَا شَكُورُ
Oh Pardoner! Oh Forgiver!	يَا عَفُوُّ يَا غَفُورُ
Oh Light of the light!	يَا نُورَ ٱلنُّورِ
Oh Director of affairs!	يَا مُدَبِّرَ ٱلأُمُورِ
Oh Kind! Oh Aware!	يَا لَطِيفُ يَا خَبِيرُ

Dua Mashlool

Oh Rescuer! Oh Illuminator!	يَا مُجِيرُ يَا مُنِيرُ
Oh Seeing! Oh Supporting! Oh Great one!	يَا بَصِيرُ يَا ظَهِيرُ يَا كَبِيرُ
Oh Singular! Oh Individual!	يَا وِتْرُ يَا فَرْدُ
Oh Eternal! Oh Support! Oh Self-Sufficient!	يَا أَبَدُ يَا سَنَدُ يَا صَمَدُ
Oh Sufficer! Oh Healer!	يَا كَافِي يَا شَافِي
Oh Fulfiller! Oh Reliever!	يَا وَافِي يَا مُعَافِي
Oh Charitable! Oh Beautifier!	يَا مُحْسِنُ يَا مُجْمِلُ
Oh Bestower of Favors! Oh Bountiful!	يَا مُنْعِمُ يَا مُفْضِلُ
Oh Gracious! Oh Unique!	يَا مُتَكَرِّمُ يَا مُتَفَرِّدُ
Oh He Who was exalted so He dominated!	يَا مَنْ عَلَا فَقَهَرَ
Oh He Who rules so He decreed!	يَا مَنْ مَلَكَ فَقَدَرَ
Oh He Who was hidden so He informed!	يَا مَنْ بَطَنَ فَخَبَرَ
Oh He Who was worshipped so He was thankful!	يَا مَنْ عُبِدَ فَشَكَرَ
Oh He Who was disobeyed so He forgave!	يَا مَنْ عُصِيَ فَغَفَرَ
Oh He Who is not encompassed by thoughts	يَا مَنْ لَا تَحْوِيهِ ٱلْفِكَرُ
And vision does not perceive Him	وَلَا يُدْرِكُهُ بَصَرٌ
And no trace remains hidden from Him	وَلَا يَخْفَىٰ عَلَيْهِ أَثَرٌ
Oh Provider of mankind!	يَا رَازِقَ ٱلْبَشَرِ

Oh Determiner of every decree!	يَا مُقَدِّرَ كُلِّ قَدَرٍ
Oh Lofty in place!	يَا عَالِيَ ٱلْمَكَانِ
Oh Firm in supports!	يَا شَدِيدَ ٱلْأَرْكَانِ
Oh Transformer of the times!	يَا مُبَدِّلَ ٱلزَّمَانِ
Oh Accepter of sacrifices!	يَا قَابِلَ ٱلْقُرْبَانِ
Oh Possessor of graciousness and excellence!	يَا ذَا ٱلْمَنِّ وَٱلْإِحْسَانِ
Oh Possessor of honour and authority!	يَا ذَا ٱلْعِزَّةِ وَٱلسُّلْطَانِ
Oh Compassionate! Oh Merciful!	يَا رَحِيمُ يَا رَحْمٰنُ
Oh He Who is every day in an important matter!	يَا مَنْ هُوَ كُلَّ يَوْمٍ فِي شَأْنٍ
Oh He Who is not distracted from one matter by another!	يَا مَنْ لَا يَشْغَلُهُ شَأْنٌ عَنْ شَأْنٍ
Oh Great in matter!	يَا عَظِيمَ ٱلشَّأْنِ
Oh He Who is in every place!	يَا مَنْ هُوَ بِكُلِّ مَكَانٍ
Oh Hearer of sounds!	يَا سَامِعَ ٱلْأَصْوَاتِ
Oh Responder to supplications!	يَا مُجِيبَ ٱلدَّعَوَاتِ
Oh Grantor of requests!	يَا مُنْجِحَ ٱلطَّلِبَاتِ
Oh Fulfiller of needs!	يَا قَاضِيَ ٱلْحَاجَاتِ
Oh He Who sends down blessings!	يَا مُنْزِلَ ٱلْبَرَكَاتِ
Oh He Who has mercy upon tears!	يَا رَاحِمَ ٱلْعَبَرَاتِ
Oh He Who annuls slips!	يَا مُقِيلَ ٱلْعَثَرَاتِ

Dua Mashlool

Oh Remover of troubles!	يَا كَاشِفَ ٱلْكُرُبَاتِ
Oh Guardian of good deeds!	يَا وَلِيَّ ٱلْحَسَنَاتِ
Oh Raiser of ranks!	يَا رَافِعَ ٱلدَّرَجَاتِ
Oh Giver of requests!	يَا مُؤْتِيَ ٱلسُّؤْلَاتِ
Oh Reviver of the dead!	يَا مُحْيِيَ ٱلْأَمْوَاتِ
Oh Gatherer of the scattered!	يَا جَامِعَ ٱلشَّتَاتِ
Oh He Who is aware of intentions!	يَا مُطَّلِعاً عَلَى ٱلنِّيَّاتِ
Oh Restorer of what has passed!	يَا رَادَّ مَا قَدْ فَاتَ
Oh He for Whom sounds are never Confused!	يَا مَنْ لَا تَشْتَبِهُ عَلَيْهِ ٱلْأَصْوَاتُ
Oh He Who is never annoyed by requests	يَا مَنْ لَا تُضْجِرُهُ ٱلْمَسْأَلَاتُ
And darkness does not cover him!	وَلَا تَغْشَاهُ ٱلظُّلُمَاتُ
Oh Light of the Earth and the heavens!	يَا نُورَ ٱلْأَرْضِ وَٱلسَّمَاوَاتِ
Oh Abundant in blessings	يَا سَابِغَ ٱلنِّعَمِ
Oh Repeller of calamities	يَا دَافِعَ ٱلنِّقَمِ
Oh Creator of souls!	يَا بَارِئَ ٱلنَّسَمِ
Oh Gatherer of the nations!	يَا جَامِعَ ٱلْأُمَمِ
Oh Healer of illness!	يَا شَافِيَ ٱلسَّقَمِ
Oh Creator of light and darkness!	يَا خَالِقَ ٱلنُّورِ وَٱلظُّلَمِ
Oh Possessor of generosity and nobility!	يَا ذَا ٱلْجُودِ وَٱلْكَرَمِ

Oh He on Whose throne no foot treads!	يَا مَنْ لَا يَطَأُ عَرْشَهُ قَدَمٌ
Oh Most Generous of the generous!	يَا أَجْوَدَ ٱلْأَجْوَدِينَ
Oh Most Noble of the noble!	يَا أَكْرَمَ ٱلْأَكْرَمِينَ
Oh Most Hearing of the hearers!	يَا أَسْمَعَ ٱلسَّامِعِينَ
Oh Most Seeing of the seers!	يَا أَبْصَرَ ٱلنَّاظِرِينَ
Oh Neighbour of those seeking refuge!	يَا جَارَ ٱلْمُسْتَجِيرِينَ
Oh Safety of the fearful!	يَا أَمَانَ ٱلْخَائِفِينَ
Oh Support of the refugees!	يَا ظَهْرَ ٱللَّاجِينَ
Oh Guardian of the believers!	يَا وَلِيَّ ٱلْمُؤْمِنِينَ
Oh Helper of those seeking help!	يَا غِيَاثَ ٱلْمُسْتَغِيثِينَ
Oh Goal of the seekers!	يَا غَايَةَ ٱلطَّالِبِينَ
Oh Companion of every stranger!	يَا صَاحِبَ كُلِّ غَرِيبٍ
Oh Comforter of every lonely one!	يَا مُؤْنِسَ كُلِّ وَحِيدٍ
Oh Refuge of every outcast!	يَا مَلْجَأَ كُلِّ طَرِيدٍ
Oh Shelter of every wanderer!	يَا مَأْوَى كُلِّ شَرِيدٍ
Oh Protector of every lost thing!	يَا حَافِظَ كُلِّ ضَالَّةٍ
Oh Merciful to the great elder!	يَا رَاحِمَ ٱلشَّيْخِ ٱلْكَبِيرِ
Oh Provider of the small infants!	يَا رَازِقَ ٱلطِّفْلِ ٱلصَّغِيرِ
Oh Mender of broken bones!	يَا جَابِرَ ٱلْعَظْمِ ٱلْكَسِيرِ

Dua Mashlool

Oh Releaser of every prisoner!	يَا فَاكَّ كُلِّ أَسِيرٍ
Oh Enricher of the miserable poor person!	يَا مُغْنِيَ ٱلْبَائِسِ ٱلْفَقِيرِ
Oh Safeguard of the fearful seeker of protection!	يَا عِصْمَةَ ٱلْخَائِفِ ٱلْمُسْتَجِيرِ
Oh He to Who belongs the managing and determinations!	يَا مَنْ لَهُ ٱلتَّدْبِيرُ وَٱلتَّقْدِيرُ
Oh He for Who the difficult is simple and easy!	يَا مَنِ ٱلْعَسِيرُ عَلَيْهِ سَهْلٌ يَسِيرٌ
Oh He Who does not need an explanation!	يَا مَنْ لاَ يَحْتَاجُ إِلَىٰ تَفْسِيرٍ
Oh He Who is powerful over everything!	يَا مَنْ هُوَ عَلَىٰ كُلِّ شَيْءٍ قَدِيرٌ
Oh He Who is aware of everything!	يَا مَنْ هُوَ بِكُلِّ شَيْءٍ خَبِيرٌ
Oh He Who sees everything!	يَا مَنْ هُوَ بِكُلِّ شَيْءٍ بَصِيرٌ
Oh Sender of the winds!	يَا مُرْسِلَ ٱلرِّيَاحِ
Oh Cleaver of the dawn!	يَا فَالِقَ ٱلإِصْبَاحِ
Oh Resurrector of the spirits!	يَا بَاعِثَ ٱلأَرْوَاحِ
Oh Possessor of generosity and forbearance!	يَا ذَا ٱلْجُودِ وَٱلسَّمَاحِ
Oh He in Whose Hand is every key!	يَا مَنْ بِيَدِهِ كُلُّ مِفْتَاحٍ
Oh Hearer of every sound!	يَا سَامِعَ كُلِّ صَوْتٍ
Oh Surpasser of every loss!	يَا سَابِقَ كُلِّ فَوْتٍ

Oh Giver of life to every soul after death!	يَا مُحْيِى كُلِّ نَفْسٍ بَعْدَ ٱلْمَوْتِ
Oh my Resource in my hardship!	يَا عُدَّتِى فِى شِدَّتِى
Oh my Protector in my exile!	يَا حَافِظِى فِى غُرْبَتِى
Oh my Comforter in my solitude!	يَا مُؤْنِسِى فِى وَحْدَتِى
Oh my Guardian in my blessings!	يَا وَلِيِّى فِى نِعْمَتِى
Oh my cave when the paths make me weary	يَا كَهْفِى حِينَ تُعْيِينِى ٱلْمَذَاهِبُ
And when relatives give me up	وَتُسَلِّمُنِى ٱلْأَقَارِبُ
And every companion forsakes me!	وَيَخْذُلُنِى كُلُّ صَاحِبٍ
Oh Backing of he with no backing!	يَا عِمَادَ مَنْ لَا عِمَادَ لَهُ
Oh Support of he with no support!	يَا سَنَدَ مَنْ لَا سَنَدَ لَهُ
Oh Reserve of he with no reserve!	يَا ذُخْرَ مَنْ لَا ذُخْرَ لَهُ
Oh Fortification of he with no fortification!	يَا حِرْزَ مَنْ لَا حِرْزَ لَهُ
Oh Cave of he with no cave!	يَا كَهْفَ مَنْ لَا كَهْفَ لَهُ
Oh Treasure of he with no treasure!	يَا كَنْزَ مَنْ لَا كَنْزَ لَهُ
Oh Pillar of he with no pillar!	يَا رُكْنَ مَنْ لَا رُكْنَ لَهُ
Oh Relief of he with no relief!	يَا غِيَاثَ مَنْ لَا غِيَاثَ لَهُ
Oh Neighbour of he with no neighbour!	يَا جَارَ مَنْ لَا جَارَ لَهُ
Oh my immediate Neighbour!	يَا جَارِى ٱللَّصِيقِ
Oh my sturdy Pillar!	يَا رُكْنِى ٱلْوَثِيقِ

Dua Mashlool

Oh My God in truth!	يَا إِلٰهِى بِٱلتَّحْقِيقِ
Oh Lord of the ancient house!	يَا رَبَّ ٱلْبَيْتِ ٱلْعَتِيقِ
Oh Affectionate! Oh Friend!	يَا شَفِيقُ يَا رَفِيقُ
Release me from the constricting ring	فُكَّنِى مِنْ حَلَقِ ٱلْمَضِيقِ
And turn away from me every anxiety, grief, and distress	وَٱصْرِفْ عَنِّى كُلَّ هَمٍّ وَغَمٍّ وَضِيقٍ
And suffice me from the evil of what I cannot endure	وَٱكْفِنِى شَرَّ مَا لاَ أُطِيقُ
And help me with what I can endure	وَأَعِنِّى عَلَىٰ مَا أُطِيقُ
Oh Returner of Joseph to Jacob!	يَا رَادَّ يُوسُفَ عَلَىٰ يَعْقُوبَ
Oh Remover of the affliction of Job!	يَا كَاشِفَ ضُرِّ أَيُّوبَ
Oh Forgiver of the sin of David!	يَا غَافِرَ ذَنْبِ دَاوُودَ
Oh Raiser of Jesus, the son of Mary, and his Saviour from the hands of the Jews!	يَا رَافِعَ عِيسَىٰ بْنِ مَرْيَمَ وَمُنْجِيهِ مِنْ أَيْدِى ٱلْيَهُودِ
Oh Responder to the call of Jonah in the darkness!	يَا مُجِيبَ نِدَاءِ يُونُسَ فِى ٱلظُّلُمَاتِ
Oh Chooser of Moses by the words!	يَا مُصْطَفِى مُوسَىٰ بِٱلْكَلِمَاتِ
Oh He who forgave Adam his mistake!	يَا مَنْ غَفَرَ لِآدَمَ خَطِيئَتَهُ
And raised Enoch to a high place by His mercy!	وَرَفَعَ إِدْرِيسَ مَكَاناً عَلِيّاً بِرَحْمَتِهِ

Oh He Who saved Noah from drowning!	يَا مَنْ نَجَّى نُوحاً مِنَ ٱلْغَرَقِ
Oh He Who destroyed 'Ad, the earlier!	يَا مَنْ أَهْلَكَ عَاداً ٱلْأُولَىٰ
And Thamud, and did not spare them!	وَثَمُودَ فَمَا أَبْقَىٰ
And the people of Noah before	وَقَوْمَ نُوحٍ مِنْ قَبْلُ
Indeed, they were more oppressive and rebellious!	إِنَّهُمْ كَانُوا هُمْ أَظْلَمَ وَأَطْغَىٰ
And the overturned cities, He brought down!	وَٱلْمُؤْتَفِكَةَ أَهْوَىٰ
Oh He Who destroyed the people of Lot!	يَا مَنْ دَمَّرَ عَلَىٰ قَوْمِ لُوطٍ
And annihilated the people of Shu'ayb!	وَدَمْدَمَ عَلَىٰ قَوْمِ شُعَيْبٍ
Oh He Who took Abraham as a close friend!	يَا مَنِ ٱتَّخَذَ إِبْرَاهِيمَ خَلِيلاً
Oh He Who took Moses as a speaker!	يَا مَنِ ٱتَّخَذَ مُوسَىٰ كَلِيماً
And took Muhammad, may Allah bless him and his Household, as a beloved!	وَٱتَّخَذَ مُحَمَّداً صَلَّى ٱللَّهُ عَلَيْهِ وَآلِهِ وَعَلَيْهِمْ أَجْمَعِينَ حَبِيباً
Oh Giver of wisdom to Luqman!	يَا مُؤْتِيَ لُقْمَانَ ٱلْحِكْمَةَ
And Granter of a kingdom to Soloman!	وَٱلْوَاهِبَ لِسُلَيْمَانَ مُلْكاً
That does not befit anyone after him!	لاَ يَنْبَغِي لأَحَدٍ مِنْ بَعْدِهِ
Oh He who helped Dhul-Qarnayn over the tyrant kings!	يَا مَنْ نَصَرَ ذَا ٱلْقَرْنَيْنِ عَلَى ٱلْمُلُوكِ ٱلْجَبَابِرَةِ

Oh He Who gave Khidr life!	يَا مَنْ أَعْطَى ٱلْخِضْرَ ٱلْحَيَاةَ
And returned the sun for Joshua, the son of Nun, after its setting!	وَرَدَّ لِيُوشَعَ بْنِ نُونٍ ٱلشَّمْسَ بَعْدَ غُرُوبِهَا
Oh He Who strengthened the heart of the mother of Moses!	يَا مَنْ رَبَطَ عَلَى قَلْبِ أُمِّ مُوسَىٰ
And guarded the chastity of Mary, the daughter of Imran.	وَأَحْصَنَ فَرْجَ مَرْيَمَ ٱبْنَةِ عِمْرَانَ
Oh He Who guarded John, the son of Zachariah, against sin!	يَا مَنْ حَصَّنَ يَحْيَىٰ بْنَ زَكَرِيَّا مِنَ ٱلذَّنْبِ
And calmed, from Moses, anger!	وَسَكَّنَ عَنْ مُوسَى ٱلْغَضَبَ
Oh He Who gave Zachariah the good news of John!	يَا مَنْ بَشَّرَ زَكَرِيَّا بِيَحْيَىٰ
Oh He Who redeemed Ishmael from the sacrifice with a great sacrifice!	يَا مَنْ فَدَىٰ إِسْمَاعِيلَ مِنَ ٱلذَّبْحِ بِذِبْحٍ عَظِيمٍ
Oh He Who accepted the sacrifice of Abel!	يَا مَنْ قَبِلَ قُرْبَانَ هَابِيلَ
And placed the curse upon Cain!	وَجَعَلَ ٱللَّعْنَةَ عَلَىٰ قَابِيلَ
Oh Router of the confederates for Muhammad, May Allah's blessings be upon him and his family!	يَا هَازِمَ ٱلْأَحْزَابِ لِمُحَمَّدٍ صَلَّى ٱللَّهُ عَلَيْهِ وَآلِهِ
Send blessings upon Muhammad and the family of Muhammad	صَلِّ عَلَىٰ مُحَمَّدٍ وَآلِ مُحَمَّدٍ

And on all the messengers and your closest angels	وَعَلَىٰ جَمِيعِ ٱلْمُرْسَلِينَ وَمَلَائِكَتِكَ ٱلْمُقَرَّبِينَ
And the people of obedience to You, all together	وَأَهْلِ طَاعَتِكَ أَجْمَعِينَ
And I ask you by every request requested by anyone	وَأَسْأَلُكَ بِكُلِّ مَسْأَلَةٍ سَأَلَكَ بِهَا أَحَدٌ
From who You were pleased and You decreed for them an answer	مِمَّنْ رَضِيتَ عَنْهُ فَحَتَمْتَ لَهُ عَلَى ٱلْإِجَابَةِ
Oh Allah! Oh Allah! Oh Allah!	يَا ٱللَّهُ يَا ٱللَّهُ يَا ٱللَّهُ
Oh compassionate! Oh compassionate! Oh compassionate!	يَا رَحْمٰنُ يَا رَحْمٰنُ يَا رَحْمٰنُ
Oh Merciful! Oh Merciful! Oh Merciful!	يَا رَحِيمُ يَا رَحِيمُ يَا رَحِيمُ
Oh Possessor of majesty and honour	يَا ذَا ٱلْجَلَالِ وَٱلْإِكْرَامِ
Oh Possessor of majesty and honour	يَا ذَا ٱلْجَلَالِ وَٱلْإِكْرَامِ
Oh Possessor of majesty and honour	يَا ذَا ٱلْجَلَالِ وَٱلْإِكْرَامِ
By Him! By Him! By Him! By Him! By Him! By Him! By Him!	بِهِ بِهِ بِهِ بِهِ بِهِ بِهِ بِهِ
I ask You by every name You have named Yourself with	أَسْأَلُكَ بِكُلِّ ٱسْمٍ سَمَّيْتَ بِهِ نَفْسَكَ
Or You revealed it in something from Your books	أَوْ أَنْزَلْتَهُ فِي شَيْءٍ مِنْ كُتُبِكَ
Or You kept it in the knowledge of the unseen which is with You	أَوِ ٱسْتَأْثَرْتَ بِهِ فِي عِلْمِ ٱلْغَيْبِ ٱلَّذِي عِنْدَكَ

And by the strongholds of might from Your throne	وَبِمَعَاقِدِ ٱلْعِزِّ مِنْ عَرْشِكَ
And by the ultimate mercy from Your book	وَبِمُنْتَهَى ٱلرَّحْمَةِ مِنْ كِتَابِكَ
And by: "If all the trees on the earth were pens	وَبِمَا ﴿وَلَوْ أَنَّ مَا فِي ٱلْأَرْضِ مِنْ شَجَرَةٍ أَقْلَامٌ
And the sea were replenished with seven more seas	وَٱلْبَحْرُ يَمُدُّهُ مِنْ بَعْدِهِ سَبْعَةُ أَبْحُرٍ
The words of Allah would not be spent.	مَا نَفِدَتْ كَلِمَاتُ ٱللَّهِ
Indeed Allah is Mighty, Wise" – Quran 31:27	إِنَّ ٱللَّهَ عَزِيزٌ حَكِيمٌ﴾
And I ask You by Your most excellent names	وَأَسْأَلُكَ بِأَسْمَائِكَ ٱلْحُسْنَى
which You described in Your book, where You said:	ٱلَّتِي نَعَتَّهَا فِي كِتَابِكَ فَقُلْتَ:
"To Allah belong the most excellent names, so supplicate Him by them!" – Quran 7:180	﴿وَلِلَّهِ ٱلْأَسْمَاءُ ٱلْحُسْنَى فَٱدْعُوهُ بِهَا﴾
And You said: "Call Me and I will answer you." – Quran 40:60	وَقُلْتَ: ﴿ٱدْعُونِي أَسْتَجِبْ لَكُمْ﴾
And You said: "And when My servants ask you about Me, then surely I am near	وَقُلْتَ: ﴿وَإِذَا سَأَلَكَ عِبَادِي عَنِّي فَإِنِّي قَرِيبٌ
I answer the callers call when he calls on Me." – Quran 2:186	أُجِيبُ دَعْوَةَ ٱلدَّاعِي إِذَا دَعَانِ﴾

And You said: "Say: Oh My servants have committed excesses against themselves	وَقُلْتَ: ﴿قُلْ يَا عِبَادِيَ ٱلَّذِينَ أَسْرَفُوا عَلَىٰ أَنْفُسِهِمْ
do not despair of the mercy of Allah	لَا تَقْنَطُوا مِنْ رَحْمَةِ ٱللَّهِ
Surely, Allah forgives all sins, all together	إِنَّ ٱللَّهَ يَغْفِرُ ٱلذُّنُوبَ جَمِيعاً
Surely, He is the Forgiving, the most Merciful." – Quran 39:53	إِنَّهُ هُوَ ٱلْغَفُورُ ٱلرَّحِيمُ﴾
And I ask You, oh my God	وَأَنَا أَسْأَلُكَ يَا إِلَهِي
And I call You, oh my Lord	وَأَدْعُوكَ يَا رَبِّ
And I hope in You, oh my Chief	وَأَرْجُوكَ يَا سَيِّدِي
And I long for You to respond to me, oh my Master, as You promised me	وَأَطْمَعُ فِي إِجَابَتِي يَا مَوْلَايَ كَمَا وَعَدْتَنِي
And I have called upon You as You commanded me	وَقَدْ دَعَوْتُكَ كَمَا أَمَرْتَنِي
So do with me what is worthy of You, oh Generous	فَٱفْعَلْ بِي مَا أَنْتَ أَهْلُهُ يَا كَرِيمُ
And all praise belongs to Allah, Lord of all the worlds	وَٱلْحَمْدُ لِلَّهِ رَبِّ ٱلْعَالَمِينَ
And send blessings upon Muhammad and the family of Muhammad, all together	وَصَلَّى ٱللَّهُ عَلَىٰ مُحَمَّدٍ وَآلِهِ أَجْمَعِينَ

Then ask for your needs and inshallah they will be granted.

Prophet Muhammad (saaw)

لَقَدْ جَاءَكُمْ رَسُولٌ مِنْ أَنْفُسِكُمْ عَزِيزٌ عَلَيْهِ مَا عَنِتُّمْ حَرِيصٌ عَلَيْكُمْ بِالْمُؤْمِنِينَ رَءُوفٌ رَحِيمٌ

"A Messenger has come to you from among yourselves. He is grieved by your suffering, and concerned about you, and kind and merciful to the believers."

Quran 9:128

On 17 Rabiul Awal to celebrate his birth, and on 28 Safar to commemorate his martyrdom, you can recite the following:

I bear witness that there is no god but Allah, alone, with no partners	أَشْهَدُ أَنْ لاَ إِلَهَ إِلاَّ ٱللَّهُ وَحْدَهُ لاَ شَرِيكَ لَهُ
And I bear witness that Muhammad is His servant and messenger	وَأَشْهَدُ أَنَّ مُحَمَّداً عَبْدُهُ وَرَسُولُهُ
And that he is the chief of the earlier and later generations	وَأَنَّهُ سَيِّدُ ٱلأَوَّلِينَ وَٱلآخِرِينَ
And that he is the chief of the Prophets and Messengers	وَأَنَّهُ سَيِّدُ ٱلأَنْبِيَاءِ وَٱلْمُرْسَلِينَ
Oh Allah send blessings on him and his Ahlul Bayt, the virtuous Imams	ٱللَّهُمَّ صَلِّ عَلَيْهِ وَعَلَىٰ أَهْلِ بَيْتِهِ ٱلأَئِمَّةِ ٱلطَّيِّبِينَ
Peace be upon you oh Messenger of Allah	ٱلسَّلاَمُ عَلَيْكَ يَا رَسُولَ ٱللَّهِ
Peace be upon you oh friend of Allah	ٱلسَّلاَمُ عَلَيْكَ يَا خَلِيلَ ٱللَّهِ
Peace be upon you oh Prophet of Allah	ٱلسَّلاَمُ عَلَيْكَ يَا نَبِيَّ ٱللَّهِ
Peace be upon you oh chosen by Allah	ٱلسَّلاَمُ عَلَيْكَ يَا صَفِيَّ ٱللَّهِ
Peace be upon you oh mercy of Allah	ٱلسَّلاَمُ عَلَيْكَ يَا رَحْمَةَ ٱللَّهِ
Peace be upon you oh choice of Allah	ٱلسَّلاَمُ عَلَيْكَ يَا خِيرَةَ ٱللَّهِ
Peace be upon you oh beloved of Allah	ٱلسَّلاَمُ عَلَيْكَ يَا حَبِيبَ ٱللَّهِ

Peace be upon you oh distinguished of Allah	اَلسَّلَامُ عَلَيْكَ يَا نَجِيبَ ٱللَّهِ
Peace be upon you oh seal of the Prophets	اَلسَّلَامُ عَلَيْكَ يَا خَاتَمَ ٱلنَّبِيِّينَ
Peace be upon you oh chief of the Messengers	اَلسَّلَامُ عَلَيْكَ يَا سَيِّدَ ٱلْمُرْسَلِينَ
Peace be upon you oh upholder of justice	اَلسَّلَامُ عَلَيْكَ يَا قَائِماً بِٱلْقِسْطِ
Peace be upon you oh opener of good	اَلسَّلَامُ عَلَيْكَ يَا فَاتِحَ ٱلْخَيْرِ
Peace be upon you oh essence of revelation and descent	اَلسَّلَامُ عَلَيْكَ يَا مَعْدِنَ ٱلْوَحْيِ وَٱلتَّنْزِيلِ
Peace be upon you oh communicator from Allah	اَلسَّلَامُ عَلَيْكَ يَا مُبَلِّغاً عَنِ ٱللَّهِ
Peace be upon you oh illuminating lamp	اَلسَّلَامُ عَلَيْكَ أَيُّهَا ٱلسِّرَاجُ ٱلْمُنِيرُ
Peace be upon you oh bearer of good news	اَلسَّلَامُ عَلَيْكَ يَا مُبَشِّرُ
Peace be upon you oh warner	اَلسَّلَامُ عَلَيْكَ يَا نَذِيرُ
Peace be upon you oh he who warns	اَلسَّلَامُ عَلَيْكَ يَا مُنْذِرُ
Peace be upon you oh light of Allah by which guidance is sought	اَلسَّلَامُ عَلَيْكَ يَا نُورَ ٱللَّهِ ٱلَّذِي يُسْتَضَاءُ بِهِ
Peace be upon you and on your Ahlul Bayt, the virtuous and pure	اَلسَّلَامُ عَلَيْكَ وَعَلَىٰ أَهْلِ بَيْتِكَ ٱلطَّيِّبِينَ ٱلطَّاهِرِينَ
The guides, and the guided	ٱلْهَادِينَ ٱلْمَهْدِيِّينَ
Peace be upon you and on your grandfather Abdul-Muttalib	اَلسَّلَامُ عَلَيْكَ وَعَلَىٰ جَدِّكَ عَبْدِ ٱلْمُطَّلِبِ
And upon your father, Abdullah	وَعَلَىٰ أَبِيكَ عَبْدِ ٱللَّهِ

Prophet Muhammad (saaw)

Peace be upon your mother, Amina, the daughter of Wahb	اَلسَّلَامُ عَلَى أُمِّكَ آمِنَةَ بِنْتِ وَهَبٍ
Peace be upon your uncle Hamza, the chief of martyrs	اَلسَّلَامُ عَلَى عَمِّكَ حَمْزَةَ سَيِّدِ ٱلشُّهَدَاءِ
Peace be upon your uncle Abbas, son of Abdul-Muttalib	اَلسَّلَامُ عَلَى عَمِّكَ ٱلْعَبَّاسِ بْنِ عَبْدِ ٱلْمُطَّلِبِ
Peace be upon your uncle and sponsor, Abu Talib	اَلسَّلَامُ عَلَى عَمِّكَ وَكَفِيلِكَ اَبِي طَالِبٍ
Peace be upon your cousin Jafaar the one who is flying in the eternal gardens	اَلسَّلَامُ عَلَى ٱبْنِ عَمِّكَ جَعْفَرٍ ٱلطَّيَّارِ فِي جِنَانِ ٱلْخُلْدِ
Peace be upon you oh Muhammad	اَلسَّلَامُ عَلَيْكَ يَا مُحَمَّدُ
Peace be upon you oh Ahmad	اَلسَّلَامُ عَلَيْكَ يَا اَحْمَدُ
Peace be upon you oh proof of Allah against the earlier and later generations	اَلسَّلَامُ عَلَيْكَ يَا حُجَّةَ ٱللهِ عَلَى ٱلْأَوَّلِينَ وَٱلْآخِرِينَ
And foremost in obedience of the Lord of the Worlds	وَٱلسَّابِقِ إِلَى طَاعَةِ رَبِّ ٱلْعَالَمِينَ
And the dominant over His Messengers	وَٱلْمُهَيْمِنِ عَلَى رُسُلِهِ
And the seal of His Prophets	وَٱلْخَاتِمِ لِأَنْبِيَائِهِ
And the witness upon His creation	وَٱلشَّاهِدِ عَلَى خَلْقِهِ
And the intercessor to Him	وَٱلشَّفِيعِ إِلَيْهِ
And the established with Him	وَٱلْمَكِينِ لَدَيْهِ
And the obeyed in His Kingdom	وَٱلْمُطَاعِ فِي مَلَكُوتِهِ
The praiseworthy among praises	ٱلْأَحْمَدِ مِنَ ٱلْأَوْصَافِ

The praised among all nobility	ٱلْمُحَمَّدَ لِسَائِرِ ٱلْأَشْرَافِ
The precious one of the Lord	ٱلْكَرِيمَ عِنْدَ ٱلرَّبِّ
And the one spoken to from behind the veils	وَٱلْمُكَلَّمَ مِنْ وَرَاءِ ٱلْحُجُبِ
Victorious in the race	ٱلْفَائِزَ بِٱلسِّبَاقِ
And the one who surpasses catching up to	وَٱلْفَائِتَ عَنِ ٱللِّحَاقِ
A greeting from one who recognizes your right	تَسْلِيمَ عَارِفٍ بِحَقِّكَ
Recognising his shortcoming in his duty to You	مُعْتَرِفٍ بِٱلتَّقْصِيرِ فِي قِيَامِهِ بِوَاجِبِكَ
Not denying what has come to Him from Your grace	غَيْرِ مُنْكِرٍ مَا ٱنْتَهَى إِلَيْهِ مِنْ فَضْلِكَ
Certain in your increase from your Lord	مُوقِنٍ بِٱلْمَزِيدَاتِ مِنْ رَبِّكَ
Believing in the book sent down on you	مُؤْمِنٍ بِٱلْكِتَابِ ٱلْمُنْزَلِ عَلَيْكَ
Making lawful your lawful	مُحَلِّلٍ حَلَالَكَ
Making unlawful your unlawful	مُحَرِّمٍ حَرَامَكَ
I bear witness oh Messenger of Allah with every witness	أَشْهَدُ يَا رَسُولَ ٱللَّهِ مَعَ كُلِّ شَاهِدٍ
And I bear it on every denier	وَأَتَحَمَّلُهَا عَنْ كُلِّ جَاحِدٍ
Indeed you conveyed the Message of your Lord	أَنَّكَ قَدْ بَلَّغْتَ رِسَالَاتِ رَبِّكَ
And advised to your nation	وَنَصَحْتَ لِأُمَّتِكَ
And you struggled in the way of Allah	وَجَاهَدْتَ فِي سَبِيلِ رَبِّكَ
And you proclaimed with His command	وَصَدَعْتَ بِأَمْرِهِ
And you bore the harm by His side	وَٱحْتَمَلْتَ ٱلْأَذَى فِي جَنْبِهِ

Prophet Muhammad (saaw)

And you called to His path with wisdom and good and beautiful advice	وَدَعَوْتَ إِلَى سَبِيلِهِ بِٱلْحِكْمَةِ وَٱلْمَوْعِظَةِ ٱلْحَسَنَةِ ٱلْجَمِيلَةِ
And you fulfilled the truth which was upon you	وَأَدَّيْتَ ٱلْحَقَّ ٱلَّذِى كَانَ عَلَيْكَ
And you were kind to the believers	وَأَنَّكَ قَدْ رَؤُفْتَ بِٱلْمُؤْمِنِينَ
And stern with the disbelievers	وَغَلُظْتَ عَلَى ٱلْكَافِرِينَ
And you worshipped Allah sincerely until certainty came to you	وَعَبَدْتَ ٱللَّهَ مُخْلِصاً حَتَّى اتاكَ ٱلْيَقِينُ
So Allah conveyed you to the noblest station of the honoured	فَبَلَّغَ ٱللَّهُ بِكَ اشْرَفَ مَحَلِّ ٱلْمُكَرَّمِينَ
And the highest stations of the close ones	وَأَعْلَى مَنَازِلِ ٱلْمُقَرَّبِينَ
And the highest level of the messengers to where no chaser could catch up	وَأَرْفَعَ دَرَجَاتِ ٱلْمُرْسَلِينَ حَيْثُ لاَ يَلْحَقُكَ لاَحِقٌ
And no surpasser could surpass you	وَلاَ يَفُوقُكَ فَائِقٌ
And no proceeder could proceed you	وَلاَ يَسْبِقُكَ سَابِقٌ
And no aspirer could aspire to grasp you	وَلاَ يَطْمَعُ فِى إِدْرَاكِكَ طَامِعٌ
All praise is for Allah who rescued us through you from ruin	ٱلْحَمْدُ لِلَّهِ ٱلَّذِى ٱسْتَنْقَذَنَا بِكَ مِنَ ٱلْهَلَكَةِ
And guided us through you from misguidance	وَهَدَانَا بِكَ مِنَ ٱلضَّلاَلَةِ
And enlightened us through you from darkness	وَنَوَّرَنَا بِكَ مِنَ ٱلظُّلْمَةِ

Continuous Calling

So many Allah reward you oh Messenger of Allah as an envoy, the best He has ever rewarded a Prophet of his nation	فَجَزَاكَ ٱللَّهُ يَا رَسُولَ ٱللَّهِ مِنْ مَبْعُوثٍ أَفْضَلَ مَا جَازَىٰ نَبِيّاً عَنْ أُمَّتِهِ
And a Messenger of those he was sent to	وَرَسُولاً عَمَّنْ أُرْسِلَ إِلَيْهِ
May my father and mother be sacrificed for you oh Messenger of Allah, I visit you, acknowledging your right	بِأَبِي أَنْتَ وَأُمِّي يَا رَسُولَ ٱللَّهِ زُرْتُكَ عَارِفاً بِحَقِّكَ
Confessing your grace	مُقِرّاً بِفَضْلِكَ
Seeing clearly the misguidance of those who oppose you and your Ahlul Bayt	مُسْتَبْصِراً بِضَلَالَةِ مَنْ خَالَفَكَ وَخَالَفَ أَهْلَ بَيْتِكَ
Recognising the guidance which you are on	عَارِفاً بِٱلْهُدَىٰ ٱلَّذِي أَنْتَ عَلَيْهِ
May my father, mother, myself, my family, my wealth, and my children be sacrificed for you	بِأَبِي أَنْتَ وَأُمِّي وَنَفْسِي وَأَهْلِي وَمَالِي وَوَلَدِي
I send praise upon you as Allah sends blessings upon you	أَنَا أُصَلِّي عَلَيْكَ كَمَا صَلَّىٰ ٱللَّهُ عَلَيْكَ
And blessings are sent on you by His Angels and Prophets and Messengers	وَصَلَّىٰ عَلَيْكَ مَلَائِكَتُهُ وَأَنْبِيَاؤُهُ وَرُسُلُهُ
Blessings successive and abundant and continuous	صَلَاةً مُتَتَابِعَةً وَافِرَةً مُتَوَاصِلَةً
Uninterrupted without term or end	لَا ٱنْقِطَاعَ لَهَا وَلَا أَمَدَ وَلَا أَجَلَ
May Allah send blessings upon you and your Ahlul Bayt, virtuous and pure, as you are deserving	صَلَّىٰ ٱللَّهُ عَلَيْكَ وَعَلَىٰ أَهْلِ بَيْتِكَ ٱلطَّيِّبِينَ ٱلطَّاهِرِينَ كَمَا أَنْتُمْ أَهْلُهُ

Prophet Muhammad (saaw)

Oh Allah make Your comprehensive blessings	اَللَّهُمَّ ٱجْعَلْ جَوَامِعَ صَلَوَاتِكَ
And the best of Your blessings	وَنَوَامِيَ بَرَكَاتِكَ
And the most virtuous of Your bounties	وَفَوَاضِلَ خَيْرَاتِكَ
And the most noble of Your greetings and saulations	وَشَرَائِفَ تَحِيَّاتِكَ وَتَسْلِيمَاتِكَ
And Your honours and mercies	وَكَرَامَاتِكَ وَرَحَمَاتِكَ
And the blessings of Your close angels	وَصَلَوَاتِ مَلَائِكَتِكَ ٱلْمُقَرَّبِينَ
And Your Messenger Prophets	وَأَنْبِيَائِكَ ٱلْمُرْسَلِينَ
And Your chosen Imams	وَأَئِمَّتِكَ ٱلْمُنْتَجَبِينَ
And Your righteous servants	وَعِبَادِكَ ٱلصَّالِحِينَ
And the people of the heavens and the earths	وَأَهْلِ ٱلسَّمَاوَاتِ وَٱلْأَرَضِينَ
And those who glorify You oh Lord of the worlds	وَمَنْ سَبَّحَ لَكَ يَا رَبَّ ٱلْعَالَمِينَ
From the earlier and later generations	مِنَ ٱلْأَوَّلِينَ وَٱلْآخِرِينَ
Upon Muhammad, Your servant and Messenger	عَلَى مُحَمَّدٍ عَبْدِكَ وَرَسُولِكَ
Your witness and Prophet	وَشَاهِدِكَ وَنَبِيِّكَ
Your Warner and Trustee	وَنَذِيرِكَ وَأَمِينِكَ
Your established and confidant	وَمَكِينِكَ وَنَجِيِّكَ
Your distinguished and beloved	وَنَجِيبِكَ وَحَبِيبِكَ
Your friend and chosen	وَخَلِيلِكَ وَصَفِيِّكَ
Your elite and special	وَصَفْوَتِكَ وَخَاصَّتِكَ
Your sincere and mercy	وَخَالِصَتِكَ وَرَحْمَتِكَ

Your best choice from Your creation	وَخَيْرِ خِيَرَتِكَ مِنْ خَلْقِكَ
Prophet of Mercy	نَبِيِّ الرَّحْمَةِ
Keeper of forgiveness	وَخَازِنِ ٱلْمَغْفِرَةِ
Leader of goodness and blessing	وَقَائِدِ ٱلْخَيْرِ وَٱلْبَرَكَةِ
Rescuer of servants from destruction by Your permission	وَمُنْقِذِ ٱلْعِبَادِ مِنَ ٱلْهَلَكَةِ بِإِذْنِكَ
Caller of them to Your religion	وَدَاعِيهِمْ إِلَى دِينِكَ
Establisher of Your command	الْقَيِّمِ بِأَمْرِكَ
The first of the Prophets to make the covenant	أَوَّلِ ٱلنَّبِيِّينَ مِيثَاقاً
And the last of them to be sent	وَآخِرِهِمْ مَبْعَثاً
The one immersed in the sea of Your excellence	ٱلَّذِى غَمَسْتَهُ فِي بَحْرِ ٱلْفَضِيلَةِ
And the grand status	وَٱلْمَنْزِلَةِ ٱلْجَلِيلَةِ
And the lofty station	وَٱلدَّرَجَةِ ٱلرَّفِيعَةِ
And the significant rank	وَٱلْمَرْتَبَةِ ٱلْخَطِيرَةِ
And You entrusted him in the loins of the pure	وَأَوْدَعْتَهُ ٱلْأَصْلَابَ ٱلطَّاهِرَةَ
And You transferred him from it to the wombs of the purified	وَنَقَلْتَهُ مِنْهَا إِلَى ٱلْأَرْحَامِ ٱلْمُطَهَّرَةِ
Gentleness from You to him	لُطْفاً مِنْكَ لَهُ
And Your compassion on him	وَتَحَنُّناً مِنْكَ عَلَيْهِ
When You assigned for his protection and his safeguarding	إِذْ وَكَّلْتَ لِصَوْنِهِ وَحِرَاسَتِهِ
And his preservation and his guarding	وَحِفْظِهِ وَحِيَاطَتِهِ
From Your power, a protecting eye	مِنْ قُدْرَتِكَ عَيْناً عَاصِمَةً

Prophet Muhammad (saaw)

You shielded him, through it, from filths of immorality	حَجَبْتَ بِهَا عَنْهُ مَدَانِسَ ٱلْعَهْرِ
And the faults of the promiscuous	وَمَعَايِبَ ٱلسِّفَاحِ
Until, through him, you raised the gazes of the servants	حَتَّىٰ رَفَعْتَ بِهِ نَوَاظِرَ ٱلْعِبَادِ
And revived through him the dead lands	وَأَحْيَيْتَ بِهِ مَيْتَ ٱلْبِلَادِ
That You removed the curtains of darkness by the light of his birth	بِأَنْ كَشَفْتَ عَنْ نُورِ وِلَادَتِهِ ظُلَمَ ٱلْأَسْتَارِ
And You clothed Your sanctuary with the robes of the lights	وَأَلْبَسْتَ حَرَمَكَ بِهِ حُلَلَ ٱلْأَنْوَارِ
Oh Allah, as You distinguished him with the honour of this noble rank	ٱللَّهُمَّ فَكَمَا خَصَصْتَهُ بِشَرَفِ هَٰذِهِ ٱلْمَرْتَبَةِ ٱلْكَرِيمَةِ
And the privilege of this great merit	وَذُخْرِ هَٰذِهِ ٱلْمَنْقَبَةِ ٱلْعَظِيمَةِ
Bless him as he fulfilled Your covenant	صَلِّ عَلَيْهِ كَمَا وَفَىٰ بِعَهْدِكَ
And he conveyed Your messages	وَبَلَّغَ رِسَالَاتِكَ
And he fought the people of denying monotheism	وَقَاتَلَ أَهْلَ ٱلْجُحُودِ عَلَىٰ تَوْحِيدِكَ
And cut off the womb of disbelief for the honour of Your religion	وَقَطَعَ رَحِمَ ٱلْكُفْرِ فِي إِعْزَازِ دِينِكَ
And wore the garment of trial to struggle with Your enemies	وَلَبِسَ ثَوْبَ ٱلْبَلْوَىٰ فِي مُجَاهَدَةِ أَعْدَائِكَ
And You decreed for him, for every harm that touched him	وَأَوْجَبْتَ لَهُ بِكُلِّ أَذًى مَسَّهُ
Or plot he perceived	أَوْ كَيْدٍ أَحَسَّ بِهِ
From the faction that tried to kill him,	مِنَ ٱلْفِئَةِ ٱلَّتِي حَاوَلَتْ قَتْلَهُ
A virtue that exceeds the virtues	فَضِيلَةً تَفُوقُ ٱلْفَضَائِلَ

And possessions abundant with Your gifts	وَيَمْلِكُ بِهَا ٱلْجَزِيلَ مِنْ نَوَالِكَ
And he certainly concealed his regret	وَقَدْ أَسَرَّ ٱلْحَسْرَةَ
And hid the sigh	وَأَخْفَىٰ ٱلزَّفْرَةَ
And swallowed the lump	وَتَجَرَّعَ ٱلْغُصَّةَ
And did not go beyond the outlines of Your revelation for him	وَلَمْ يَتَخَطَّ مَا مَثَّلَ لَهُ وَحْيُكَ
Oh Allah bless him and his Ahlul Bayt, with the blessings you please for them	ٱللَّهُمَّ صَلِّ عَلَيْهِ وَعَلَىٰ أَهْلِ بَيْتِهِ صَلَاةً تَرْضَاهَا لَهُمْ
And convey to them abundant greetings and peace from us	وَبَلِّغْهُمْ مِنَّا تَحِيَّةً كَثِيرَةً وَسَلَاماً
And grant us, from Your awareness in our loyalty to them, grace and kindness	وَآتِنَا مِنْ لَدُنْكَ فِي مُوَالَاتِهِمْ فَضْلاً وَإِحْسَاناً
And mercy and forgiveness	وَرَحْمَةً وَغُفْرَاناً
You possess the great bounty	إِنَّكَ ذُو ٱلْفَضْلِ ٱلْعَظِيمِ
Oh Allah, You said to Your Prophet Muhammad	ٱللَّهُمَّ إِنَّكَ قُلْتَ لِنَبِيِّكَ مُحَمَّدٍ
May Allah's blessings be upon him and his family	صَلَّىٰ ٱللَّهُ عَلَيْهِ وَآلِهِ:
"And if, when they wronged themselves	﴿وَلَوْ أَنَّهُمْ إِذْ ظَلَمُوٓاْ أَنْفُسَهُمْ
They came to you and asked forgiveness of Allah	جَآءُوكَ فَٱسْتَغْفَرُواْ ٱللَّهَ
And the Messenger asked forgiveness for them	وَٱسْتَغْفَرَ لَهُمُ ٱلرَّسُولُ
They would have found Allah accepting of repentance and merciful" – Quran 4:64	لَوَجَدُواْ ٱللَّهَ تَوَّاباً رَحِيماً﴾

Prophet Muhammad (saaw)

And I was not present during the time of Your Messenger, peace be upon him and his family	وَلَمْ أَحْضُرْ زَمَانَ رَسُولِكَ عَلَيْهِ وَآلِهِ ٱلسَّلَامُ
Oh Allah, indeed I have visited him eager, repentant from the evil of my actions	اَللَّهُمَّ وَقَدْ زُرْتُهُ رَاغِباً تَائِباً مِنْ سَيِّءِ عَمَلِي
And seeking Your forgiveness from my sins	وَمُسْتَغْفِراً لَكَ مِنْ ذُنُوبِي
And acknowledging it to You, while You are more knowledgeable about them than me	وَمُقِرّاً لَكَ بِهَا وَأَنْتَ أَعْلَمُ بِهَا مِنِّي
And turning towards You through Your Prophet, the Prophet of Mercy	وَمُتَوَجِّهاً إِلَيْكَ بِنَبِيِّكَ نَبِيِّ ٱلرَّحْمَةِ
May Your blessings be upon him and his family	صَلَوَاتُكَ عَلَيْهِ وَآلِهِ
So make me, oh Allah, by Muhammad and his Ahlul Bayt, distinguished with You	فَٱجْعَلْنِي ٱللَّهُمَّ بِمُحَمَّدٍ وَأَهْلِ بَيْتِهِ عِنْدَكَ وَجِيهاً
In this world and the hereafter, and from the close ones	فِي ٱلدُّنْيَا وَٱلْآخِرَةِ وَمِنَ ٱلْمُقَرَّبِينَ
Oh Muhammad	يَا مُحَمَّدُ
Oh Messenger of Allah	يَا رَسُولَ ٱللَّهِ
May my father and mother be sacrificed for you	بِأَبِي أَنْتَ وَأُمِّي
Oh Prophet of Allah	يَا نَبِيَّ ٱللَّهِ
Oh chief of Allah's creation	يَا سَيِّدَ خَلْقِ ٱللَّهِ
I turn through you to Allah, your Lord and my Lord	إِنِّي أَتَوَجَّهُ بِكَ إِلَى ٱللَّهِ رَبِّكَ وَرَبِّي
To forgive my sins	لِيَغْفِرَ لِي ذُنُوبِي
And to accepts my actions	وَيَتَقَبَّلَ مِنِّي عَمَلِي

And to fulfill my needs	وَيَقْضِيَ لِي حَوَائِجِي
So be for me an intercessor with my Lord and your Lord	فَكُنْ لِي شَفِيعاً عِنْدَ رَبِّكَ وَرَبِّي
Excellent is the one who is asked, the Master, my Lord	فَنِعْمَ ٱلْمَسْؤُولُ ٱلْمَوْلَى رَبِّي
And you are the excellent intercessor	وَنِعْمَ ٱلشَّفِيعُ أَنْتَ
Oh Muhammad	يَا مُحَمَّدُ
Peace be upon you and your Ahlul Bayt	ٱلسَّلَامُ عَلَيْكَ وَعَلَى أَهْلِ بَيْتِكَ
Oh Allah, make necessary for me Your forgiveness and mercy	ٱللَّهُمَّ وَأَوْجِبْ لِي مِنْكَ ٱلْمَغْفِرَةَ وَٱلرَّحْمَةَ
And the broad sustenance, good and beneficial	وَٱلرِّزْقَ ٱلْوَاسِعَ ٱلطَّيِّبَ ٱلنَّافِعَ
As you made necessary for who came to Your Prophet Muhammad;	كَمَا أَوْجَبْتَ لِمَنْ أَتَى نَبِيَّكَ مُحَمَّداً
Your blessing be upon him and his family;	صَلَوَاتُكَ عَلَيْهِ وَآلِهِ
While he was alive, acknowledging his sins	وَهُوَ حَيٌّ فَأَقَرَّ لَهُ بِذُنُوبِهِ
And the Messenger sought forgiveness for him	وَٱسْتَغْفَرَ لَهُ رَسُولُكَ
Peace be upon him and his family	عَلَيْهِ وَآلِهِ ٱلسَّلَامُ
So You forgave him by Your mercy oh the most merciful of the merciful	فَغَفَرْتَ لَهُ بِرَحْمَتِكَ يَا أَرْحَمَ ٱلرَّاحِمِينَ
Oh Allah, I hoped in You and begged You	ٱللَّهُمَّ وَقَدْ أَمَّلْتُكَ وَرَجَوْتُكَ
And stood between Your hands	وَقُمْتُ بَيْنَ يَدَيْكَ
And I desired You instead of all others	وَرَغِبْتُ إِلَيْكَ عَمَّنْ سِوَاكَ

Prophet Muhammad (saaw)

And I have hoped for Your abundant reward	وَقَدْ أَمَّلْتُ جَزِيلَ ثَوَابِكَ
And I admit and do not deny	وَإِنِّي لَمُقِرٌّ غَيْرُ مُنْكِرٍ
And I am repentant to You from what I committed	وَتَائِبٌ إِلَيْكَ مِمَّا اقْتَرَفْتُ
And seeking refuge with You in this place	وَعَائِذٌ بِكَ فِي هٰذَا ٱلْمَقَامِ
From what I sent forward from my deeds	مِمَّا قَدَّمْتُ مِنَ ٱلْأَعْمَالِ
Which You warned me in advance about and prohibited	ٱلَّتِي تَقَدَّمْتَ إِلَيَّ فِيهَا وَنَهَيْتَنِي عَنْهَا
And for which You threatened the punishment	وَأَوْعَدْتَ عَلَيْهَا ٱلْعِقَابَ
And I seek refuge in the generosity of Your face	وَأَعُوذُ بِكَرَمِ وَجْهِكَ
Lest You make me stand disgraced and humiliated	أَنْ تُقِيمَنِي مَقَامَ ٱلْخِزْيِ وَٱلذُّلِّ
On the day that covers are torn	يَوْمَ تُهْتَكُ فِيهِ ٱلْأَسْتَارُ
And secrets and scandals become apparent	وَتَبْدُو فِيهِ ٱلْأَسْرَارُ وَٱلْفَضَائِحُ
And the limbs tremble	وَتَرْعَدُ فِيهِ ٱلْفَرَائِصُ
The day of regret and remorse	يَوْمَ ٱلْحَسْرَةِ وَٱلنَّدَامَةِ
The day of falsehood	يَوْمَ ٱلْآفِكَةِ
The day that approaches	يَوْمَ ٱلْآزِفَةِ
The day of disillusionment	يَوْمَ ٱلتَّغَابُنِ
The day of separation	يَوْمَ ٱلْفَصْلِ
The day of recompense	يَوْمَ ٱلْجَزَاءِ

Continuous Calling

The day which measures 50,000 years	يَوْماً كَانَ مِقْدَارُهُ خَمْسِينَ أَلْفَ سَنَةٍ
The day of trumpeting	يَوْمَ ٱلنَّفْخَةِ
The day the shaker shakes	يَوْمَ تَرْجُفُ ٱلرَّاجِفَةُ
Events following events	تَتْبَعُهَا ٱلرَّادِفَةُ
The day of spreading	يَوْمَ ٱلنَّشْرِ
The day of presentation	يَوْمَ ٱلْعَرْضِ
The day of people standing before the Lord of the worlds	يَوْمَ يَقُومُ ٱلنَّاسُ لِرَبِّ ٱلْعَالَمِينَ
The day the fleer flees from his sibling	يَوْمَ يَفِرُّ ٱلْمَرْءُ مِنْ أَخِيهِ
And his mother and father	وَأُمِّهِ وَأَبِيهِ
And his spouse and children	وَصَاحِبَتِهِ وَبَنِيهِ
The day the earth and the edges of the sky split apart	يَوْمَ تَشَقَّقُ ٱلْأَرْضُ وَاكْنَافُ ٱلسَّمَاءِ
The day every soul comes arguing on behalf of itself	يَوْمَ تَأْتِي كُلُّ نَفْسٍ تُجَادِلُ عَنْ نَفْسِهَا
The day they are returned to Allah and He informs them about what they used to do	يَوْمَ يُرَدُّونَ إِلَى ٱللَّهِ فَيُنَبِّئُهُمْ بِمَا عَمِلُوا
The day no protector benefits any protector at all	يَوْمَ لَا يُغْنِي مَوْلًى عَنْ مَوْلًى شَيْئاً
And they cannot be supported	وَلَا هُمْ يُنْصَرُونَ
Except who Allah has mercy on	إِلَّا مَنْ رَحِمَ ٱللَّهُ
Indeed He is the Might and most Merciful	إِنَّهُ هُوَ ٱلْعَزِيزُ ٱلرَّحِيمُ
The day they are returned to the Knower of the unseen and the seen	يَوْمَ يُرَدُّونَ إِلَى عَالِمِ ٱلْغَيْبِ وَٱلشَّهَادَةِ

Prophet Muhammad (saaw)

The day they are returned to Allah, their Master, the truth	يَوْمَ يُرَدُّونَ إِلَى ٱللَّهِ مَوْلَاهُمُ ٱلْحَقِّ
The day they emerge from the graves quickly	يَوْمَ يَخْرُجُونَ مِنَ ٱلْأَجْدَاثِ سِرَاعاً
As if they are rushing towards a goal	كَأَنَّهُمْ إِلَى نُصُبٍ يُوفِضُونَ
And as if they are scattered locusts	وَكَأَنَّهُمْ جَرَادٌ مُنْتَشِرٌ
Rushing towards the caller	مُهْطِعِينَ إِلَى ٱلدَّاعِي
To Allah	إِلَى ٱللَّهِ
The day of the event	يَوْمَ ٱلْوَاقِعَةِ
The day the earth shakes violently	يَوْمَ تَرُجُّ ٱلْأَرْضُ رَجّاً
The day the sky will be like molten metal	يَوْمَ تَكُونُ ٱلسَّمَاءُ كَٱلْمُهْلِ
And the mountains like wool	وَتَكُونُ ٱلْجِبَالُ كَٱلْعِهْنِ
And no close friend will ask about his close friend	وَلَا يَسْأَلُ حَمِيمٌ حَمِيماً
The day of witnessing and being witnessed	يَوْمَ ٱلشَّاهِدِ وَٱلْمَشْهُودِ
The day the angels will be in rows	يَوْمَ تَكُونُ ٱلْمَلَائِكَةُ صَفّاً صَفّاً
Oh Allah have mercy on my situation on that day through my stance on this day	اللَّهُمَّ ٱرْحَمْ مَوْقِفِي فِي ذَلِكَ ٱلْيَوْمِ بِمَوْقِفِي فِي هَذَا ٱلْيَوْمِ
And do not disgrace me in that situation for what I brought on myself	وَلَا تُخْزِنِي فِي ذَلِكَ ٱلْمَوْقِفِ بِمَا جَنَيْتُ عَلَى نَفْسِي
And group me, oh my Lord, on that day with Your intimate friends	وَٱجْعَلْ يَا رَبِّ فِي ذَلِكَ ٱلْيَوْمِ مَعَ أَوْلِيَائِكَ مُنْطَلَقِي

Continuous Calling

And in the crowded group of Muhammad and his Ahlul Bayt peace be upon them	وَفِي زُمْرَةِ مُحَمَّدٍ وَأَهْلِ بَيْتِهِ عَلَيْهِمُ ٱلسَّلَامُ مَحْشَرِى
And make his pond my destination	وَٱجْعَلْ حَوْضَهُ مَوْرِدِى
And make the bright and noble my resurrection	وَفِي ٱلْغُرِّ ٱلْكِرَامِ مَصْدَرِى
And give me my book in my right hand	وَأَعْطِنِى كِتَابِى بِيَمِينِى
So that I suceed by my good deeds	حَتَّى أَفُوزَ بِحَسَنَاتِى
And my face becomes white from it	وَتَبْيَضَّ بِهِ وَجْهِى
And my accounting becomes easy through it	وَتُيَسَّرَ بِهِ حِسَابِى
And my scale tips through it	وَتُرَجَّحَ بِهِ مِيزَانِى
And I proceed with the winners	وَأَمْضِىَ مَعَ ٱلْفَائِزِينَ
From Your righteous servants	مِنْ عِبَادِكَ ٱلصَّالِحِينَ
To Your pleasure and Your gardens	إِلَى رِضْوَانِكَ وَجِنَانِكَ
God of the worlds	إِلٰهَ ٱلْعَالَمِينَ
Oh Allah I seek refuge with You from You exposing me on that day	اَللَّهُمَّ إِنِّى أَعُوذُ بِكَ مِنْ أَنْ تَفْضَحَنِى فِى ذٰلِكَ ٱلْيَوْمِ
Before the creation, through my wrongdoing	بَيْنَ يَدَى ٱلْخَلَائِقِ بِجَرِيرَتِى
Or that I encounter disgrace and regret by my mistakes	أَوْ أَنْ أَلْقَى ٱلْخِزْىَ وَٱلنَّدَامَةَ بِخَطِيئَتِى
Or that You reveal my sins over my good deeds	أَوْ أَنْ تُظْهِرَ فِيهِ سَيِّئَاتِى عَلَى حَسَنَاتِى
Or that You mention me by name before the creation	أَوْ أَنْ تُنَوِّهَ بَيْنَ ٱلْخَلَائِقِ بِٱسْمِى

Prophet Muhammad (saaw)

Oh Generous one, oh Generous one	يَا كَرِيمُ يَا كَرِيمُ
Forgiveness, forgiveness	ٱلْعَفْوَ ٱلْعَفْوَ
Concealment, concealment	ٱلسِّتْرَ ٱلسِّتْرَ
Oh Allah I seek refuge with You that on that day	اَللَّهُمَّ وَأَعُوذُبِكَ مِنْ أَنْ يَكُونَ فِي ذٰلِكَ ٱلْيَوْمِ
My situation is with the evil ones	فِي مَوَاقِفِ ٱلْأَشْرَارِ مَوْقِفِي
Or my position is with the wretched ones	أَوْ فِي مَقَامِ ٱلْأَشْقِيَاءِ مَقَامِي
And if You distinguished between Your creation	وَإِذَا مَيَّزْتَ بَيْنَ خَلْقِكَ
You drive each by their deeds	فَسُقْتَ كُلاًّ بِأَعْمَالِهِمْ
In groups to their abodes	زُمَراً إِلَى مَنَازِلِهِمْ
Then drive me, by Your mercy, with Your righteous servants	فَسُقْنِي بِرَحْمَتِكَ مَعَ عِبَادِكَ ٱلصَّالِحِينَ
And in the company of Your pious friends	وَفِي زُمْرَةِ أَوْلِيَائِكَ ٱلْمُتَّقِينَ
To Your gardens oh lord of the worlds	إِلَى جَنَّاتِكَ يَا رَبَّ ٱلْعَالَمِينَ

Then you may bid farewell:

Peace be upon you oh Messenger of Allah	اَلسَّلَامُ عَلَيْكَ يَا رَسُولَ ٱللهِ
Peace be upon you oh bringer of good news and warner	اَلسَّلَامُ عَلَيْكَ أَيُّهَا ٱلْبَشِيرُ ٱلنَّذِيرُ
Peace be upon you oh illuminating lamp	اَلسَّلَامُ عَلَيْكَ أَيُّهَا ٱلسِّرَاجُ ٱلْمُنِيرُ
Peace be upon you oh ambassador between Allah and His creation	اَلسَّلَامُ عَلَيْكَ أَيُّهَا ٱلسَّفِيرُ بَيْنَ ٱللهِ وَبَيْنَ خَلْقِهِ

Continuous Calling

I bear witness, oh Messenger of Allah, that you were a light in the noble loins	أَشْهَدُ يَا رَسُولَ اللَّهِ أَنَّكَ كُنْتَ نُوراً فِي الْأَصْلَابِ الشَّامِخَةِ
And in the purified wombs	وَالْأَرْحَامِ الْمُطَهَّرَةِ
Ignorance did not make you impure from its impurity	لَمْ تُنَجِّسْكَ الْجَاهِلِيَّةُ بِأَنْجَاسِهَا
Nor has it clothed you with the darkness of its garments	وَلَمْ تُلْبِسْكَ مِنْ مُدْلَهِمَّاتِ ثِيَابِهَا
And I bear witness, oh Messenger of Allah, I am a believer in you	وَأَشْهَدُ يَا رَسُولَ اللَّهِ أَنِّي مُؤْمِنٌ بِكَ
And in the Imams from your Ahlul Bayt	وَبِالْأَئِمَّةِ مِنْ أَهْلِ بَيْتِكَ
Certain about everything You came with	مُوقِنٌ بِجَمِيعِ مَا أَتَيْتَ بِهِ
Satisfied and believing	رَاضٍ مُؤْمِنٌ
And I bear witness that the Imams from your Ahlul Bayt are the beacons of guidance	وَأَشْهَدُ أَنَّ الْأَئِمَّةَ مِنْ أَهْلِ بَيْتِكَ أَعْلَامُ الْهُدَى
And the firmest handhold	وَالْعُرْوَةُ الْوُثْقَى
And the proof on the people of the world	وَالْحُجَّةُ عَلَى أَهْلِ الدُّنْيَا
Oh Allah do not make this the last covenant of visiting Your Prophet	اَللَّهُمَّ لَا تَجْعَلْهُ آخِرَ الْعَهْدِ مِنْ زِيَارَةِ نَبِيِّكَ
Peace be upon him and his family	عَلَيْهِ وَآلِهِ السَّلَامُ
And if You take my soul I bear witness in my death	وَإِنْ تَوَفَّيْتَنِي فَإِنِّي أَشْهَدُ فِي مَمَاتِي
Upon what I bore witness in my life	عَلَى مَا أَشْهَدُ عَلَيْهِ فِي حَيَاتِي
That you are Allah, there is no god but You	أَنَّكَ أَنْتَ اللَّهُ لَا إِلَهَ إِلَّا أَنْتَ
One, with no partners to You	وَحْدَكَ لَا شَرِيكَ لَكَ

Prophet Muhammad (saaw)

And Muhammad is Your servant and Messenger	وَأَنَّ مُحَمَّداً عَبْدُكَ وَرَسُولُكَ
And the Imams from his Ahlul Bayt are Your friends and supporters	وَأَنَّ ٱلْأَئِمَّةَ مِنْ أَهْلِ بَيْتِهِ أَوْلِيَاؤُكَ وَأَنْصَارُكَ
And Your proofs against Your creation	وَحُجَجُكَ عَلَى خَلْقِكَ
And Your successors among Your servants	وَخُلَفَاؤُكَ فِى عِبَادِكَ
And Your beacons in Your lands	وَأَعْلَامُكَ فِى بِلَادِكَ
And the treasurers of Your knowledge	وَخُزَّانُ عِلْمِكَ
And the preservers of Your secrets	وَحَفَظَةُ سِرِّكَ
And the interpreters of Your revelation	وَتَرَاجِمَةُ وَحْيِكَ
Oh Allah send blessings on Muhammad and the family of Muhammad	اَللَّهُمَّ صَلِّ عَلَى مُحَمَّدٍ وَآلِ مُحَمَّدٍ
And convey to the soul of Your Prophet Muhammad and his family	وَبَلِّغْ رُوحَ نَبِيِّكَ مُحَمَّدٍ وَآلِهِ
In this hour and in every hour, a greeting from me and peace	فِى سَاعَتِى هٰذِهِ وَفِى كُلِّ سَاعَةٍ تَحِيَّةً مِنِّى وَسَلَاماً
And peace be upon you oh Messenger of Allah and Allah's mercy and grace upon you	وَٱلسَّلَامُ عَلَيْكَ يَا رَسُولَ ٱللَّهِ وَرَحْمَةُ ٱللَّهِ وَبَرَكَاتُهُ
Make Allah not let this be my final greeting to you	لَا جَعَلَهُ ٱللَّهُ آخِرَ تَسْلِيمِى عَلَيْكَ

Imam Ali (as)

"You are the supporters of truth, the brothers in religion, the shields on the day of hardship, and the innermost circle of the people. By you I strike those who leave (the truth) and hope for the obedience of the forthcoming. So assist me with sincerity, without deceit. Safe from doubt. For by Allah I am the closest of the people with the people." - Imam Ali (as)

(Nahjol Balagha Sermon 118)

On 13 Rajab to celebrate his birth, on 21 Shahr Ramadan to commemorate his martyrdom, and on 18 Dhul-Hijjah to celebrate his appointment by Allah (swt) through the Prophet (saaw), you can recite this Ziyarah. It is quite lengthy but extremely detailed about his life. A shorter version is available online. This is the Ziyarah by Imam Hadi (as) on the Eid of Ghadeer when he stopped in Najaf.

Peace be upon Muhammad the Messenger of Allah;	اَلسَّلَامُ عَلَى مُحَمَّدٍ رَسُولِ اللَّهِ
Seal of the Prophets	خَاتَمِ ٱلنَّبِيِّينَ
And chief of the Messengers	وَسَيِّدِ ٱلْمُرْسَلِينَ
And the choice of the Lord of the worlds	وَصَفْوَةِ رَبِّ ٱلْعَالَمِينَ
Allah's Trustee over His Revelations	أَمِينِ ٱللَّهِ عَلَى وَحْيِهِ
And His firm commands	وَعَزَائِمِ أَمْرِهِ
And the seal of what came before	وَٱلْخَاتِمِ لِمَا سَبَقَ
And the opener for what is to come	وَٱلْفَاتِحِ لِمَا ٱسْتُقْبِلَ
And overseer over all of that;	وَٱلْمُهَيْمِنِ عَلَى ذَلِكَ كُلِّهِ
And Allah's mercy and grace	وَرَحْمَةُ ٱللَّهِ وَبَرَكَاتُهُ
And His blessings and greetings	وَصَلَوَاتُهُ وَتَحِيَّاتُهُ
Peace be upon the Prophets of Allah and His Messengers	اَلسَّلَامُ عَلَى أَنْبِيَاءِ ٱللَّهِ وَرُسُلِهِ
And His close angels	وَمَلَائِكَتِهِ ٱلْمُقَرَّبِينَ

Imam Ali (as)

And His righteous servants	وَعِبَادِهِ ٱلصَّالِحِينَ
Peace be upon you oh commander of the faithful;	اَلسَّلَامُ عَلَيْكَ يَا أَمِيرَ ٱلْمُؤْمِنِينَ
And chief of successors	وَسَيِّدَ ٱلْوَصِيِّينَ
And heir of the knowledge of the Prophets	وَوَارِثَ عِلْمِ ٱلنَّبِيِّينَ
And guardian (over the believers) of the Lord of the worlds,	وَوَلِيَّ رَبِّ ٱلْعَالَمِينَ
And my master and master of the believers;	وَمَوْلَايَ وَمَوْلَى ٱلْمُؤْمِنِينَ
And Allah's mercy and grace	وَرَحْمَةُ ٱللَّهِ وَبَرَكَاتُهُ
Peace be upon you oh my master, oh commander of the faithful,	اَلسَّلَامُ عَلَيْكَ يَا مَوْلَايَ يَا أَمِيرَ ٱلْمُؤْمِنِينَ
Oh trustee of Allah in His Earth,	يَا أَمِينَ ٱللَّهِ فِي أَرْضِهِ
And His ambassador among His creation,	وَسَفِيرَهُ فِي خَلْقِهِ
And His definite proof on His servants	وَحُجَّتَهُ ٱلْبَالِغَةَ عَلَى عِبَادِهِ
Peace be upon you oh upright religion of Allah	اَلسَّلَامُ عَلَيْكَ يَا دِينَ ٱللَّهِ ٱلْقَوِيمَ
And His straight path	وَصِرَاطَهُ ٱلْمُسْتَقِيمَ
Peace be upon you oh the great news	اَلسَّلَامُ عَلَيْكَ أَيُّهَا ٱلنَّبَأُ ٱلْعَظِيمُ
About who they differ	ٱلَّذِي هُمْ فِيهِ مُخْتَلِفُونَ
And about him, they shall be asked	وَعَنْهُ يُسْأَلُونَ
Peace be upon you oh commander of the faithful	اَلسَّلَامُ عَلَيْكَ يَا أَمِيرَ ٱلْمُؤْمِنِينَ
You believed in Allah while they were polytheists	آمَنْتَ بِٱللَّهِ وَهُمْ مُشْرِكُونَ

Continuous Calling

And you accepted the truth while they were deniers	وَصَدَّقْتَ بِٱلْحَقِّ وَهُمْ مُكَذِّبُونَ
And you struggled for Allah while they were hesitant	وَجَاهَدْتَ فِي ٱللَّهِ وَهُمْ مُحْجِمُونَ
And you worshipped Allah sincerely in His religion	وَعَبَدْتَ ٱللَّهَ مُخْلِصاً لَهُ ٱلدِّينَ
Patiently and expectantly until certainty came to you	صَابِراً مُحْتَسِباً حَتَّى أَتَاكَ ٱلْيَقِينُ
Indeed, the curse of Allah be upon the wrongdoers	أَلَا لَعْنَةُ ٱللَّهِ عَلَى ٱلظَّالِمِينَ
Peace be upon you oh chief of the Muslims	ٱلسَّلَامُ عَلَيْكَ يَا سَيِّدَ ٱلْمُسْلِمِينَ
Head of the believers	وَيَعْسُوبَ ٱلْمُؤْمِنِينَ
Imam (leader) of the pious	وَإِمَامَ ٱلْمُتَّقِينَ
And leader of the distinguished bright-faced ones;	وَقَائِدَ ٱلْغُرِّ ٱلْمُحَجَّلِينَ
And Allah's mercy and grace	وَرَحْمَةُ ٱللَّهِ وَبَرَكَاتُهُ
I bear witness that you are the brother of Allah's Messenger	أَشْهَدُ أَنَّكَ أَخُو رَسُولِ ٱللَّهِ
And his successor and heir of his knowledge	وَوَصِيُّهُ وَوَارِثُ عِلْمِهِ
And trustee on his laws	وَأَمِينُهُ عَلَى شَرْعِهِ
His successor in his nation	وَخَلِيفَتُهُ فِي أُمَّتِهِ
And the first to believe in Allah	وَأَوَّلُ مَنْ آمَنَ بِٱللَّهِ
And to accept what was revealed to His Prophet	وَصَدَّقَ بِمَا أُنْزِلَ عَلَى نَبِيِّهِ
And I bear witness that he conveyed what Allah sent down to him concerning you	وَأَشْهَدُ أَنَّهُ قَدْ بَلَّغَ عَنِ ٱللَّهِ مَا أَنْزَلَهُ فِيكَ

He proclaimed his command	فَصَدَعَ بِأَمْرِهِ
And he made obligatory on his nation obedience to you and your guardianship	وَأَوْجَبَ عَلَى أُمَّتِهِ فَرْضَ طَاعَتِكَ وَوِلَايَتِكَ
And he bound them with the pledge of allegiance to you	وَعَقَدَ عَلَيْهِمُ ٱلْبَيْعَةَ لَكَ
And he made you more deserving of the believers than themselves	وَجَعَلَكَ أَوْلَى بِٱلْمُؤْمِنِينَ مِنْ أَنْفُسِهِمْ
Just as Allah made it like that	كَمَا جَعَلَهُ ٱللَّهُ كَذَلِكَ
Then he made Allah the Exalted his witness against them	ثُمَّ أَشْهَدَ ٱللَّهَ تَعَالَى عَلَيْهِمْ
So he said "Have I not conveyed?"	فَقَالَ: "أَلَسْتُ قَدْ بَلَّغْتُ"
They answered, "By Allah, yes"	فَقَالُوا: "ٱللَّهُمَّ بَلَى"
So he said, "Oh Allah, bear witness	فَقَالَ: "ٱللَّهُمَّ ٱشْهَدْ
And You are a sufficient Witness and Judge between the servants"	وَكَفَى بِكَ شَهِيداً وَحَاكِماً بَيْنَ ٱلْعِبَادِ"
Curse of Allah on the denier of your guardianship after his acknowledgement	فَلَعَنَ ٱللَّهُ جَاحِدَ وِلَايَتِكَ بَعْدَ ٱلْإِقْرَارِ
And the breaker of their pledge to you after his covenant	وَنَاكِثَ عَهْدِكَ بَعْدَ ٱلْمِيثَاقِ
And I bear witness that you fulfilled your pledge to Allah the Exalted	وَأَشْهَدُ أَنَّكَ وَفَيْتَ بِعَهْدِ ٱللَّهِ تَعَالَى
And that Allah the Exalted fulfilled His pledge to you	وَأَنَّ ٱللَّهَ تَعَالَى مُوفٍ لَكَ بِعَهْدِهِ
"And whoever fulfills Allah's pledge over him, He will grant him a great reward" – Quran 48:10	﴿وَمَنْ أَوْفَى بِمَا عَاهَدَ عَلَيْهُ ٱللَّهَ فَسَيُؤْتِيهِ أَجْراً عَظِيماً﴾

And I bear witness that you are the commander of the faithful, the truth	وَأَشْهَدُ أَنَّكَ أَمِيرُ ٱلْمُؤْمِنِينَ ٱلْحَقُّ
Who the Revelation has spoken of your guardianship	ٱلَّذِى نَطَقَ بِوِلَايَتِكَ ٱلتَّنْزِيلُ
And the Messenger took a covenant with the people for you	وَأَخَذَ لَكَ ٱلْعَهْدَ عَلَى ٱلْأُمَّةِ بِذَٰلِكَ ٱلرَّسُولُ
And I bear witness that you, your uncle, and brother	وَأَشْهَدُ أَنَّكَ وَعَمَّكَ وَأَخَاكَ
Who traded with Allah your souls	ٱلَّذِينَ تَاجَرْتُمُ ٱللَّهَ بِنُفُوسِكُمْ
So Allah revealed about you:	فَأَنْزَلَ ٱللَّهُ فِيكُمْ:
"Surely, Allah has bought from the believers themselves and their wealth,	﴿إِنَّ ٱللَّهَ ٱشْتَرَىٰ مِنَ ٱلْمُؤْمِنِينَ أَنْفُسَهُمْ وَأَمْوَالَهُمْ
Because Paradise is for them	بِأَنَّ لَهُمُ ٱلْجَنَّةَ
They fight in Allah's way, so they kill and are killed	يُقَاتِلُونَ فِى سَبِيلِ ٱللَّهِ فَيَقْتُلُونَ وَيُقْتَلُونَ
A binding promise on Him in the Torah and the Injeel and the Qur'an	وَعْداً عَلَيْهِ حَقّاً فِى ٱلتَّوْرَاةِ وَٱلْإِنْجِيلِ وَٱلْقُرْآنِ
And who is more fulfilling of their covenant than Allah?	وَمَنْ أَوْفَىٰ بِعَهْدِهِ مِنَ ٱللَّهِ
So rejoice in your transaction which you contracted	فَٱسْتَبْشِرُوا بِبَيْعِكُمُ ٱلَّذِى بَايَعْتُمْ بِهِ
And that is the great success	وَذَٰلِكَ هُوَ ٱلْفَوْزُ ٱلْعَظِيمُ
The ones who return, who worship,	ٱلتَّائِبُونَ ٱلْعَابِدُونَ
Who praise, who travel,	ٱلْحَامِدُونَ ٱلسَّائِحُونَ

Imam Ali (as)

Who bow down (ruku'), who prostrate,	ٱلرَّاكِعُونَ ٱلسَّاجِدُونَ
Who enjoin good and forbid evil,	ٱلْآمِرُونَ بِٱلْمَعْرُوفِ وَٱلنَّاهُونَ عَنِ ٱلْمُنْكَرِ
And who guard the limits of Allah; and give good news to the believers" – Quran 9:112	وَٱلْحَافِظُونَ لِحُدُودِ ٱللَّهِ وَبَشِّرِ ٱلْمُؤْمِنِينَ﴾
I bear witness, oh commander of the faithful	أَشْهَدُ يَا أَمِيرَ ٱلْمُؤْمِنِينَ
That whoever doubts about you has not believed in the trustworthy Messenger	أَنَّ ٱلشَّاكَّ فِيكَ مَا آمَنَ بِٱلرَّسُولِ ٱلْأَمِينِ
And whoever leaves you for another is stubborn regarding the upright religion	وَأَنَّ ٱلْعَادِلَ بِكَ غَيْرَكَ عَانِدٌ عَنِ ٱلدِّينِ ٱلْقَوِيمِ
That the Lord of the worlds has chosen for us	ٱلَّذِي ٱرْتَضَاهُ لَنَا رَبُّ ٱلْعَالَمِينَ
And that He completed it on the Day of Ghadeer through your guardianship	وَأَكْمَلَهُ بِوِلَايَتِكَ يَوْمَ ٱلْغَدِيرِ
And I bear witness that you are the one intended in the saying of the Almighty, Most-merciful:	وَأَشْهَدُ أَنَّكَ ٱلْمَعْنِيُّ بِقَوْلِ ٱلْعَزِيزِ ٱلرَّحِيمِ:
"And this is My straight path, so follow it	﴿وَأَنَّ هَذَا صِرَاطِي مُسْتَقِيماً فَٱتَّبِعُوهُ
And do not follow other ways, for they will separate you from His way" – Quran 6:153	وَلَا تَتَّبِعُوا ٱلسُّبُلَ فَتَفَرَّقَ بِكُمْ عَنْ سَبِيلِهِ﴾
By Allah, he is lost, and by Allah, he leads astray whoever follows other than you	ضَلَّ وَٱللَّهِ وَأَضَلَّ مَنِ ٱتَّبَعَ سِوَاكَ
And whoever opposes you is stubborn regarding the truth	وَعَنَدَ عَنِ ٱلْحَقِّ مَنْ عَادَاكَ

Continuous Calling

Oh Allah, we listened to Your command	اَللَّهُمَّ سَمِعْنَا لِأَمْرِكَ
And obeyed and followed Your straight path	وَأَطَعْنَا وَاتَّبَعْنَا صِرَاطَكَ الْمُسْتَقِيمَ
So guide us, oh our Lord	فَاهْدِنَا رَبَّنَا
And do not deviate our hearts after You have guided us to obedience to You	وَلَا تُزِغْ قُلُوبَنَا بَعْدَ إِذْ هَدَيْتَنَا إِلَى طَاعَتِكَ
And make us of those grateful for Your favours	وَاجْعَلْنَا مِنَ الشَّاكِرِينَ لِأَنْعُمِكَ
And I bear witness that you never ceased opposing whims	وَأَشْهَدُ أَنَّكَ لَمْ تَزَلْ لِلْهَوَى مُخَالِفاً
And being allied with piety	وَلِلتُّقَى مُحَالِفاً
And you have always been capable of suppressing rage	وَعَلَى كَظْمِ الْغَيْظِ قَادِراً
And pardoning and forgiving people	وَعَنِ النَّاسِ عَافِياً غَافِراً
And when Allah is disobeyed, you are displeased	وَإِذَا عُصِيَ اللَّهُ سَاخِطاً
And when Allah is obeyed, you are pleased	وَإِذَا أُطِيعَ اللَّهُ رَاضِياً
And acting upon what he entrusted you with	وَبِمَا عَهِدَ إِلَيْكَ عَامِلاً
Keeping watch over what has been held with you	رَاعِياً لِمَا اسْتُحْفِظْتَ
Guarding what was deposited with you	حَافِظاً لِمَا اسْتُودِعْتَ
Conveying what you tasked to carry	مُبَلِّغاً مَا حُمِّلْتَ
Waiting for what you were promised	مُنْتَظِراً مَا وُعِدْتَ
And I bear witness that you did not conceal out of humiliation	وَأَشْهَدُ أَنَّكَ مَا اتَّقَيْتَ ضَارِعاً

And you did remain silent about your right, due to fear	وَلَا أَمْسَكْتَ عَنْ حَقِّكَ جَازِعاً
And you did not hold back struggling against your usurpers to give up	وَلَا أَحْجَمْتَ عَنْ مُجَاهَدَةِ غَاصِبِيكَ نَاكِلاً
And you did not show contentment contrary to what pleases Allah as a compromise	وَلَا أَظْهَرْتَ ٱلرِّضَا بِخِلَافِ مَا يُرْضِي ٱللَّهَ مُدَاهِناً
And you did not become feeble by what befell you in the path of Allah	وَلَا وَهَنْتَ لِمَا أَصَابَكَ فِي سَبِيلِ ٱللَّهِ
And you did not become weak nor did you yield from seeking your right observantly	وَلَا ضَعُفْتَ وَلَا ٱسْتَكَنْتَ عَنْ طَلَبِ حَقِّكَ مُرَاقِباً
Allah's refuge against such claims	مَعَاذَ ٱللَّهِ أَنْ تَكُونَ كَذٰلِكَ
Rather, when you were wronged, you considered your Lord	بَلْ إِذْ ظُلِمْتَ ٱحْتَسَبْتَ رَبَّكَ
And delegated your affair to Him,	وَفَوَّضْتَ إِلَيْهِ أَمْرَكَ
And you reminded them, they did not remember	وَذَكَّرْتَهُمْ فَمَا ٱذَّكَرُوا
And you preached to them, they did not take heed	وَوَعَظْتَهُمْ فَمَا ٱتَّعَظُوا
And you frightened them of Allah, they did not fear	وَخَوَّفْتَهُمُ ٱللَّهَ فَمَا تَخَوَّفُوا
And I bear witness, oh commander of the faithful, that you	وَأَشْهَدُ أَنَّكَ يَا أَمِيرَ ٱلْمُؤْمِنِينَ
Struggled for Allah, true to His struggle	جَاهَدْتَ فِي ٱللَّهِ حَقَّ جِهَادِهِ
Until Allah called you to His vicinity,	حَتَّىٰ دَعَاكَ ٱللَّهُ إِلَىٰ جِوَارِهِ
And He chose to take you to Him	وَقَبَضَكَ إِلَيْهِ بِٱخْتِيَارِهِ
And imposed against your enemies, the argument by their killing of you	وَأَلْزَمَ أَعْدَاءَكَ ٱلْحُجَّةَ بِقَتْلِهِمْ إِيَّاكَ

So that you have an argument against them	لِتَكُونَ ٱلْحُجَّةُ لَكَ عَلَيْهِمْ
Along with the conclusive arguments you have against all of His creation	مَعَ مَا لَكَ مِنَ ٱلْحُجَجِ ٱلْبَالِغَةِ عَلَى جَمِيعِ خَلْقِهِ
Peace be upon you oh commander of the faithful	ٱلسَّلَامُ عَلَيْكَ يَا أَمِيرَ ٱلْمُؤْمِنِينَ
You worshipped Allah sincerely	عَبَدْتَ ٱللَّهَ مُخْلِصاً
And you struggled in the way of Allah patiently	وَجَاهَدْتَ فِي ٱللَّهِ صَابِراً
And expended yourself, seeking Allah's reward	وَجُدْتَ بِنَفْسِكَ مُحْتَسِباً
And acted by His Book	وَعَمِلْتَ بِكِتَابِهِ
And followed His Prophet's sunnah (way)	وَٱتَّبَعْتَ سُنَّةَ نَبِيِّهِ
And established the prayers	وَأَقَمْتَ ٱلصَّلَاةَ
And gave the zakat (charity)	وَآتَيْتَ ٱلزَّكَاةَ
And enjoined what is good	وَأَمَرْتَ بِٱلْمَعْرُوفِ
And forbade what is evil as much as you could	وَنَهَيْتَ عَنِ ٱلْمُنْكَرِ مَا ٱسْتَطَعْتَ
Seeking what is with Allah	مُبْتَغِياً مَا عِنْدَ ٱللَّهِ
Desiring for what Allah has promised	رَاغِباً فِي مَا وَعَدَ ٱللَّهُ
Not caring for misfortunes	لَا تَحْفِلُ بِٱلنَّوَائِبِ
And not yielding to the hardships	وَلَا تَهِنُ عِنْدَ ٱلشَّدَائِدِ
And not holding back from a warrior	وَلَا تَحْجُمُ عَنْ مُحَارِبٍ
Inconceivable is the one who attributes anything other than this to you	أَفِكَ مَنْ نَسَبَ غَيْرَ ذَلِكَ إِلَيْكَ

And they are forging falsehood against you	وَٱفْتَرَىٰ بَاطِلاً عَلَيْكَ
And more deserving is the one who is unwavering with you	وَأَوْلَىٰ لِمَنْ عَنَدَ عَنْكَ
You certainly struggled for Allah, true to His struggle	لَقَدْ جَاهَدْتَ فِي ٱللَّهِ حَقَّ ٱلْجِهَادِ
And were patient with harm the patience of seeking reward	وَصَبَرْتَ عَلَى ٱلْأَذَىٰ صَبْرَ ٱحْتِسَابٍ
And you were the first to believe in Allah	وَأَنْتَ أَوَّلُ مَنْ آمَنَ بِٱللَّهِ
And to pray to him and struggle	وَصَلَّىٰ لَهُ وَجَاهَدَ
And show himself in the land of polytheism	وَأَبْدَىٰ صَفْحَتَهُ فِي دَارِ ٱلشِّرْكِ
While the earth was filled with misguidance	وَٱلْأَرْضُ مَشْحُونَةٌ ضَلاَلَةً
And Satan was worshipped openly	وَٱلشَّيْطَانُ يُعْبَدُ جَهْرَةً
And you said, "The many people around me do not increase my might,	وَأَنْتَ ٱلْقَائِلُ: "لاَ تَزِيدُنِي كَثْرَةُ ٱلنَّاسِ حَوْلِي عِزَّةً
Nor does their departure make me feel lonely	وَلاَ تَفَرُّقُهُمْ عَنِّي وَحْشَةً
And if humanity abandoned me, I would not be begging"	وَلَوْ أَسْلَمَنِي ٱلنَّاسُ جَمِيعاً لَمْ أَكُنْ مُتَضَرِّعاً"
You held fast to Allah and were made mighty	إِعْتَصَمْتَ بِٱللَّهِ فَعَزَزْتَ
And you preferred the hereafter over the former so you renounced this life	وَآثَرْتَ ٱلْآخِرَةَ عَلَى ٱلْأُولَىٰ فَزَهِدْتَ
And Allah supported you and guided you	وَأَيَّدَكَ ٱللَّهُ وَهَدَاكَ
And made you sincere and chose you	وَأَخْلَصَكَ وَٱجْتَبَاكَ

Continuous Calling

Your actions did not contradict	فَمَا تَنَاقَضَتْ أَفْعَالُكَ
And your words never disagreed	وَلَا ٱخْتَلَفَتْ أَقْوَالُكَ
And your situations were never fickle	وَلَا تَقَلَّبَتْ أَحْوَالُكَ
And you never claimed or forged a lie against Allah	وَلَا ٱدَّعَيْتَ وَلَا ٱفْتَرَيْتَ عَلَى ٱللَّهِ كَذِباً
And you were never inclined to the wreckage	وَلَا شَرِهْتَ إِلَى ٱلْحُطَامِ
And sin never defiled you	وَلَا دَنَّسَكَ ٱلْآثَامُ
And you never ceased to be on the clear evidence of your Lord	وَلَمْ تَزَلْ عَلَى بَيِّنَةٍ مِنْ رَبِّكَ
And certain in your matter	وَيَقِينٍ مِنْ أَمْرِكَ
Guiding to the truth and to the straight path	تَهْدِى إِلَى ٱلْحَقِّ وَإِلَى صِرَاطٍ مُسْتَقِيمٍ
I bear true witness	أَشْهَدُ شَهَادَةَ حَقٍّ
And I truly swear by Allah	وَأُقْسِمُ بِٱللَّهِ قَسَمَ صِدْقٍ
That Muhammad and his family, Allah's blessings be upon them, are the chiefs of all creation	أَنَّ مُحَمَّداً وَآلَهُ صَلَوَاتُ ٱللَّهِ عَلَيْهِمْ سَادَاتُ ٱلْخَلْقِ
And you are indeed my master and the master of the believers	وَأَنَّكَ مَوْلَايَ وَمَوْلَى ٱلْمُؤْمِنِينَ
And you are the servant of Allah and His guardian (over the believers)	وَأَنَّكَ عَبْدُ ٱللَّهِ وَوَلِيُّهُ
And the brother of the Messenger and his successor and heir	وَأَخُو ٱلرَّسُولِ وَوَصِيُّهُ وَوَارِثُهُ
And he said to you:	وَأَنَّهُ ٱلْقَائِلُ لَكَ:

Imam Ali (as)

"By Him Who sent me with the truth, whoever denies you has not believed in me,	"وَٱلَّذِي بَعَثَنِي بِٱلْحَقِّ مَا آمَنَ بِي مَنْ كَفَرَ بِكَ
And whoever rejects you has not acknowledged Allah,	وَلاَ أَقَرَّ بِٱللَّهِ مَنْ جَحَدَكَ
And whoever abandons you has gone astray,	وَقَدْ ضَلَّ مَنْ صَدَّ عَنْكَ
And he is not guided to Allah and to me who is not guided by you"	وَلَمْ يَهْتَدِ إِلَى ٱللَّهِ وَلاَ إِلَيَّ مَنْ لاَ يَهْتَدِي بِكَ
And this is the saying of my Lord, Almighty and Majestic:	وَهُوَ قَوْلُ رَبِّي عَزَّ وَجَلَّ:
"And indeed, I am most Forgiving to him who repents and believes and does good	﴿وَإِنِّي لَغَفَّارٌ لِمَنْ تَابَ وَآمَنَ وَعَمِلَ صَالِحاً
Then is guided" to your guardianship – Quran 20:82	ثُمَّ ٱهْتَدَىٰ﴾ إِلَى وِلاَيَتِكَ
My master, your grace cannot be concealed	مَوْلاَيَ فَضْلُكَ لاَ يَخْفَىٰ
And your light cannot be extinguished	وَنُورُكَ لاَ يُطْفَأُ
And indeed, who rejects you is a miserable oppressor	وَأَنَّ مَنْ جَحَدَكَ ٱلظَّلُومُ ٱلأَشْقَىٰ
My master, you are the proof against the servants	مَوْلاَيَ أَنْتَ ٱلْحُجَّةُ عَلَى ٱلْعِبَادِ
And the guide to righteousness	وَٱلْهَادِي إِلَى ٱلرَّشَادِ
And the preparation for the appointed time	وَٱلْعُدَّةُ لِلْمَعَادِ
My master Allah has raised your standing in the first	مَوْلاَيَ لَقَدْ رَفَعَ ٱللَّهُ فِي ٱلأُولَىٰ مَنْزِلَتَكَ
And raised your rank in the Hereafter	وَأَعْلَىٰ فِي ٱلآخِرَةِ دَرَجَتَكَ

And showed you what those who opposed you were blind to	وَبَصَّرَكَ مَا عَمِيَ عَلَىٰ مَنْ خَالَفَكَ
And who stood between you and Allah's gifts to you	وَحَالَ بَيْنَكَ وَبَيْنَ مَوَاهِبِ ٱللَّهِ لَكَ
So the curse of Allah upon those who violated your sanctity	فَلَعَنَ ٱللَّهُ مُسْتَحِلِّي ٱلْحُرْمَةِ مِنْكَ
And prevented you from your right	وَذَابِدِي ٱلْحَقِّ عَنْكَ
And I bear witness that they are the losers	وَأَشْهَدُ أَنَّهُمُ ٱلْأَخْسَرُونَ
Whose faces shall be scorched by Hellfire	ٱلَّذِينَ تَلْفَحُ وُجُوهَهُمُ ٱلنَّارُ
And they therein shall be grim	وَهُمْ فِيهَا كَالِحُونَ
And I bear witness that you did not advance nor hesitate	وَأَشْهَدُ أَنَّكَ مَا أَقْدَمْتَ وَلَا أَحْجَمْتَ
And did not speak nor keep silent	وَلَا نَطَقْتَ وَلَا أَمْسَكْتَ
Except by the command from Allah or the Messenger	إِلَّا بِأَمْرٍ مِنَ ٱللَّهِ وَرَسُولِهِ
You said, "By Him Who holds my soul	قُلْتَ: "وَٱلَّذِي نَفْسِي بِيَدِهِ
The messenger of Allah, may Allah's blessings be upon him and his family, looked at me	لَقَدْ نَظَرَ إِلَيَّ رَسُولُ ٱللَّهِ صَلَّى ٱللَّهُ عَلَيْهِ وَآلِهِ
As I struck with my sword on the frontline, so he said:	أَضْرِبُ بِالسَّيْفِ قُدُماً فَقَالَ:
"Oh Ali, your position to me is like Aaron to Moses	"يَا عَلِيُّ أَنْتَ مِنِّي بِمَنْزِلَةِ هَارُونَ مِنْ مُوسَىٰ
Except that there is no prophet after me	إِلَّا أَنَّهُ لَا نَبِيَّ بَعْدِي

Imam Ali (as)

And I inform you that your death and your life are with me and upon my Sunnah (way)"	وَأُعْلِمُكَ أَنَّ مَوْتَكَ وَحَيَاتَكَ مَعِي وَعَلَى سُنَّتِي"
So by Allah I did not lie nor was I lied to	فَوَاللَّهِ مَا كَذِبْتُ وَلَا كُذِّبْتُ
And I did not go astray nor have I led astray	وَلَا ضَلَلْتُ وَلَا ضُلَّ بِي
And I did not forget what my Lord entrusted to me	وَلَا نَسِيتُ مَا عَهِدَ إِلَيَّ رَبِّي
And I am on the clear evidence from my Lord that he made clear to His Prophet	وَإِنِّي لَعَلَى بَيِّنَةٍ مِنْ رَبِّي بَيَّنَهَا لِنَبِيِّهِ
And the Prophet made clear to me	وَبَيَّنَهَا ٱلنَّبِيُّ لِي
And I am on the clear path explicitly articulating it"	وَإِنِّي لَعَلَى ٱلطَّرِيقِ ٱلْوَاضِحِ أَلْفِظُهُ لَفْظًا"
I affirm by Allah that you said the truth	صَدَقْتَ وَٱللَّهِ وَقُلْتَ ٱلْحَقَّ
So the curse of Allah upon those who compare you to your adversaries	فَلَعَنَ ٱللَّهُ مَنْ سَاوَاكَ بِمَنْ نَاوَاكَ
And Allah, majestic is His name, says:	وَٱللَّهُ جَلَّ ٱسْمُهُ يَقُولُ:
"Are those who know and those who do not know equal?" – Quran 39:9	﴿هَلْ يَسْتَوِي ٱلَّذِينَ يَعْلَمُونَ وَٱلَّذِينَ لَا يَعْلَمُونَ﴾
So the curse of Allah upon those who treated you the same as those who Allah obligated to follow your guardianship	فَلَعَنَ ٱللَّهُ مَنْ عَدَلَ بِكَ مَنْ فَرَضَ ٱللَّهُ عَلَيْهِ وِلَايَتَكَ
And you are Allah's guardian (over the believers)	وَأَنْتَ وَلِيُّ ٱللَّهِ
And the brother of His Messenger	وَأَخُو رَسُولِهِ
And the defender of His religion	وَٱلذَّابُّ عَنْ دِينِهِ
And the one who the Quran spoke in his favour	وَٱلَّذِي نَطَقَ ٱلْقُرْآنُ بِتَفْضِيلِهِ

Continuous Calling

Allah, the most High, says:	قَالَ ٱللَّهُ تَعَالَى:
"And Allah preferred those who struggle (jihad) above the inactive a great reward	﴿وَفَضَّلَ ٱللَّهُ ٱلْمُجَاهِدِينَ عَلَى ٱلْقَاعِدِينَ أَجْراً عَظِيماً
Degrees from Him and forgiveness and mercy	دَرَجَاتٍ مِنْهُ وَمَغْفِرَةً وَرَحْمَةً
And Allah is Forgiving, Merciful" – Quran 4:95-96 (Paraphrased)	وَكَانَ ٱللَّهُ غَفُوراً رَحِيماً﴾
And Allah the Exalted said:	وَقَالَ ٱللَّهُ تَعَالَى:
"Have you made the providing of water for the Hajj (pilgrimage) and the maintenance of Al-Masjid Al-Haram	﴿أَجَعَلْتُمْ سِقَايَةَ ٱلْحَاجِّ وَعِمَارَةَ ٱلْمَسْجِدِ ٱلْحَرَامِ
Like the one who believes in Allah and the Last Day and struggles in the way of Allah?	كَمَنْ آمَنَ بِٱللَّهِ وَٱلْيَوْمِ ٱلْآخِرِ وَجَاهَدَ فِي سَبِيلِ ٱللَّهِ
They are not equal with Allah	لَا يَسْتَوُونَ عِنْدَ ٱللَّهِ
And Allah does not guide the wrongdoing people	وَٱللَّهُ لَا يَهْدِي ٱلْقَوْمَ ٱلظَّالِمِينَ
Those who believed and emigrated	ٱلَّذِينَ آمَنُوا وَهَاجَرُوا
And struggled in Allah's way with their wealth and themselves	وَجَاهَدُوا فِي سَبِيلِ ٱللَّهِ بِأَمْوَالِهِمْ وَأَنْفُسِهِمْ
Are greater in degrees with Allah	أَعْظَمُ دَرَجَةً عِنْدَ ٱللَّهِ
And it is they who are the successful	وَأُولَٰئِكَ هُمُ ٱلْفَائِزُونَ
Their Lord gives them good news of mercy from Him and His approval	يُبَشِّرُهُمْ رَبُّهُمْ بِرَحْمَةٍ مِنْهُ وَرِضْوَانٍ
And gardens for them, wherein is enduring blessings	وَجَنَّاتٍ لَهُمْ فِيهَا نَعِيمٌ مُقِيمٌ
Abiding therein for ever	خَالِدِينَ فِيهَا أَبَداً

Imam Ali (as)

Indeed, with Allah is a great reward" – Quran 9:19-22	إِنَّ ٱللَّهَ عِنْدَهُ أَجْرٌ عَظِيمٌ﴾
I bear witness that you are singled out for the commendation of Allah	أَشْهَدُ أَنَّكَ ٱلْمَخْصُوصُ بِمِدْحَةِ ٱللَّهِ
The sincere in obedience to Allah	ٱلْمُخْلِصُ لِطَاعَةِ ٱللَّهِ
You did not seek a substitute for guidance	لَمْ تَبْغِ بِٱلْهُدَى بَدَلاً
And you did not associate anyone in the worship of your Lord	وَلَمْ تُشْرِكْ بِعِبَادَةِ رَبِّكَ أَحَداً
And Allah the Exalted responded to His Prophet;	وَأَنَّ ٱللَّهَ تَعَالَى ٱسْتَجَابَ لِنَبِيِّهِ
May Allah's blessings be upon him and his family: concerning his dua about you	صَلَّى ٱللَّهُ عَلَيْهِ وَآلِهِ فِيكَ دَعْوَتَهُ
He then ordered him to proclaim your guardianship of his nation	ثُمَّ أَمَرَهُ بِإِظْهَارِ مَا أَوْلاَكَ لِأُمَّتِهِ
Elevating your position	إِعْلاَءً لِشَأْنِكَ
And a declaration of your proof	وَإِعْلاَناً لِبُرْهَانِكَ
And a refutation of falsehoods	وَدَحْضاً لِلْأَبَاطِيلِ
And a severance of excuses	وَقَطْعاً لِلْمَعَاذِيرِ
So when he feared the corruption (fitnah) of the disobedient	فَلَمَّا أَشْفَقَ مِنْ فِتْنَةِ ٱلْفَاسِقِينَ
And was worried about the hypocrites regarding you	وَٱتَّقَى فِيكَ ٱلْمُنَافِقِينَ
The Lord of the worlds revealed to him;	أَوْحَى إِلَيْهِ رَبُّ ٱلْعَالَمِينَ:
"Oh Messenger! Convey what has been send down to you from your Lord	﴿يَا أَيُّهَا ٱلرَّسُولُ بَلِّغْ مَا أُنْزِلَ إِلَيْكَ مِنْ رَبِّكَ
And if you do not, then you have not conveyed His message	وَإِنْ لَمْ تَفْعَلْ فَمَا بَلَّغْتَ رِسَالَتَهُ

Continuous Calling

And Allah will protect you from the people" – Quran 5:67	وَٱللَّهُ يَعْصِمُكَ مِنَ ٱلنَّاسِ ﴾
So he bore the burdens of the journey	فَوَضَعَ عَلَى نَفْسِهِ أَوْزَارَ ٱلْمَسِيرِ
And stood in the hot sand of the midday heat	وَنَهَضَ فِي رَمْضَاءِ ٱلْهَجِيرِ
And gave a sermon and made them listen	فَخَطَبَ وَأَسْمَعَ
And called out and conveyed	وَنَادَىٰ فَأَبْلَغَ
Then asked them all:	ثُمَّ سَأَلَهُمْ أَجْمَعَ
Saying "Have I conveyed?"	فَقَالَ: "هَلْ بَلَّغْتُ"
"By Allah, yes" they answered	فَقَالُوٓا: "ٱللَّهُمَّ بَلَىٰ"
So he said "Oh Allah, bear witness!"	فَقَالَ: "ٱللَّهُمَّ ٱشْهَدْ"
Then said, "Am I not more deserving of the believers than themselves?"	ثُمَّ قَالَ: "أَلَسْتُ أَوْلَىٰ بِٱلْمُؤْمِنِينَ مِنْ أَنْفُسِهِمْ"
"Yes" they answered	فَقَالُوٓا: "بَلَىٰ"
So he took your hand and said	فَأَخَذَ بِيَدِكَ وَقَالَ:
"Whoever I am his master, then this Ali is his master	"مَنْ كُنْتُ مَوْلَاهُ فَهَذَا عَلِيٌّ مَوْلَاهُ
Oh Allah, befriend with those who befriend him	ٱللَّهُمَّ وَالِ مَنْ وَالَاهُ
And be an enemy to his enemies	وَعَادِ مَنْ عَادَاهُ
And support whoever supports him	وَٱنْصُرْ مَنْ نَصَرَهُ
And abandon whoever abandons him"	وَٱخْذُلْ مَنْ خَذَلَهُ"
But none believed in what Allah sent down to His Prophet about you except a few	فَمَا آمَنَ بِمَا أَنْزَلَ ٱللَّهُ فِيكَ عَلَىٰ نَبِيِّهِ إِلَّا قَلِيلٌ

Imam Ali (as)

And it did not increase most of them except in defiance	وَلَا زَادَ أَكْثَرَهُمْ غَيْرَ تَخْيِيرٍ
And Allah the Exalted sent down to you previously, while they were detesting;	وَلَقَدْ أَنْزَلَ ٱللَّهُ تَعَالَىٰ فِيكَ مِنْ قَبْلُ وَهُمْ كَارِهُونَ:
"Oh you who believe!	﴿يَا أَيُّهَا ٱلَّذِينَ آمَنُوا
Whoever turns back among you from his religion	مَنْ يَرْتَدَّ مِنْكُمْ عَنْ دِينِهِ
Then soon Allah will bring a people who He loves and they love Him	فَسَوْفَ يَأْتِي ٱللَّهُ بِقَوْمٍ يُحِبُّهُمْ وَيُحِبُّونَهُ
Humble before the believers	أَذِلَّةٍ عَلَى ٱلْمُؤْمِنِينَ
Mighty against the disbelievers	أَعِزَّةٍ عَلَى ٱلْكَافِرِينَ
Struggling in the way of Allah	يُجَاهِدُونَ فِي سَبِيلِ ٱللَّهِ
And not fearing the blame of any critic	وَلَا يَخَافُونَ لَوْمَةَ لَائِمٍ
That is the grace of Allah, He gives it to whoever He wills	ذَٰلِكَ فَضْلُ ٱللَّهِ يُؤْتِيهِ مَنْ يَشَاءُ
And Allah is encompassing, knowing	وَٱللَّهُ وَاسِعٌ عَلِيمٌ
You Guardian is only Allah and His Messenger and those who believe	إِنَّمَا وَلِيُّكُمُ ٱللَّهُ وَرَسُولُهُ وَٱلَّذِينَ آمَنُوا
Those who establish the prayer	ٱلَّذِينَ يُقِيمُونَ ٱلصَّلَاةَ
And give charity while bowing (ruku')	وَيُؤْتُونَ ٱلزَّكَاةَ وَهُمْ رَاكِعُونَ
And whoever takes Allah and His messenger and those who believe as guardians	وَمَنْ يَتَوَلَّ ٱللَّهَ وَرَسُولَهُ وَٱلَّذِينَ آمَنُوا
Then they are the party of Allah and they are victorious" – Quran 5:54-56	فَإِنَّ حِزْبَ ٱللَّهِ هُمُ ٱلْغَالِبُونَ﴾

Continuous Calling

Our Lord! We believed in what You sent down and we have followed the Messenger	رَبَّنَا آمَنَّا بِمَا أَنْزَلْتَ وَٱتَّبَعْنَا ٱلرَّسُولَ
So write us with the witnesses	فَٱكْتُبْنَا مَعَ ٱلشَّاهِدِينَ
Our Lord, do not deviate our hearts after You guided us	رَبَّنَا لَا تُزِغْ قُلُوبَنَا بَعْدَ إِذْ هَدَيْتَنَا
And grant us from Your mercy	وَهَبْ لَنَا مِنْ لَدُنْكَ رَحْمَةً
Indeed, You are the Bestower	إِنَّكَ أَنْتَ ٱلْوَهَّابُ
Oh Allah, we know that this is the truth from You	ٱللَّهُمَّ إِنَّا نَعْلَمُ أَنَّ هَذَا هُوَ ٱلْحَقُّ مِنْ عِنْدِكَ
So curse whoever opposes him and acts arrogantly	فَٱلْعَنْ مَنْ عَارَضَهُ وَٱسْتَكْبَرَ
And denies it and disbelieves	وَكَذَّبَ بِهِ وَكَفَرَ
"And soon those who act unjustly shall know which destination they will return to" – Quran 26:227	﴿وَسَيَعْلَمُ ٱلَّذِينَ ظَلَمُوا أَيَّ مُنْقَلَبٍ يَنْقَلِبُونَ﴾
Peace be upon you oh commander of the faithful	ٱلسَّلَامُ عَلَيْكَ يَا أَمِيرَ ٱلْمُؤْمِنِينَ
And chief of the successors	وَسَيِّدَ ٱلْوَصِيِّينَ
And first of the worshippers	وَأَوَّلَ ٱلْعَابِدِينَ
And most ascetic of the ascetics	وَأَزْهَدَ ٱلزَّاهِدِينَ
And Allah's mercy and grace	وَرَحْمَةُ ٱللَّهِ وَبَرَكَاتُهُ
And His blessings and greetings	وَصَلَوَاتُهُ وَتَحِيَّاتُهُ
You served food to the needy, orphan, and captive out of love for Him	أَنْتَ مُطْعِمُ ٱلطَّعَامِ عَلَىٰ حُبِّهِ مِسْكِيناً وَيَتِيماً وَأَسِيراً

Imam Ali (as)

For the sake of Allah, not wanting reward or thanks	لِوَجْهِ ٱللَّهِ لَا تُرِيدُ مِنْهُمْ جَزَاءً وَلَا شُكُوراً
And about you Allah the Exalted sent down:	وَفِيكَ أَنْزَلَ ٱللَّهُ تَعَالَى:
"And they prefer themselves though there they are in need	﴿وَيُؤْثِرُونَ عَلَى أَنْفُسِهِمْ وَلَوْ كَانَ بِهِمْ خَصَاصَةٌ
And whoever suppresses the selfishness of his soul, then they are the successful" – Quran 59:9	وَمَنْ يُوقَ شُحَّ نَفْسِهِ فَأُولَٰئِكَ هُمُ ٱلْمُفْلِحُونَ﴾
And you are the restrainer of anger	وَأَنْتَ ٱلْكَاظِمُ لِلْغَيْظِ
And the pardoner of people	وَٱلْعَافِي عَنِ ٱلنَّاسِ
And Allah loves the good-doers	وَٱللَّهُ يُحِبُّ ٱلْمُحْسِنِينَ
And you are the patient in adversity and distress and during battle	وَأَنْتَ ٱلصَّابِرُ فِي ٱلْبَأْسَاءِ وَٱلضَّرَّاءِ وَحِينَ ٱلْبَأْسِ
And you are the one dividing equally	وَأَنْتَ ٱلْقَاسِمُ بِٱلسَّوِيَّةِ
And the just one among the subjects	وَٱلْعَادِلُ فِي ٱلرَّعِيَّةِ
And the knowledgeable about the limits set by Allah from all of origination	وَٱلْعَالِمُ بِحُدُودِ ٱللَّهِ مِنْ جَمِيعِ ٱلْبَرِيَّةِ
And Allah the Exalted has informed about what He has bestowed upon you of His grace by His saying;	وَٱللَّهُ تَعَالَى أَخْبَرَ عَمَّا أَوْلَاكَ مِنْ فَضْلِهِ بِقَوْلِهِ:
"Is he who is a believer like him who is a transgressor?	﴿أَفَمَنْ كَانَ مُؤْمِناً كَمَنْ كَانَ فَاسِقاً
They are not equal	لَا يَسْتَوُونَ
As for those who believed and did righteous deeds	أَمَّا ٱلَّذِينَ آمَنُوا وَعَمِلُوا ٱلصَّالِحَاتِ

For them their residence is in gardens, lodging for what they used to do" – Quran 32:18-19	فَلَهُمْ جَنَّاتُ ٱلْمَأْوَى نُزُلاً بِمَا كَانُوا۟ يَعْمَلُونَ﴾
And you are the one singled out with the knowledge of the revelation	وَأَنْتَ ٱلْمَخْصُوصُ بِعِلْمِ ٱلتَّنْزِيلِ
And the rulings of true interpretation	وَحُكْمِ ٱلتَّأْوِيلِ
And the text of the Messenger	وَنَصِّ ٱلرَّسُولِ
And for you are the witnessed stances	وَلَكَ ٱلْمَوَاقِفُ ٱلْمَشْهُودَةُ
And the famous stations	وَٱلْمَقَامَاتُ ٱلْمَشْهُورَةُ
And the memorable days	وَٱلْأَيَّامُ ٱلْمَذْكُورَةُ
The day of Badr and the day of Allies (Ahzab)	يَوْمُ بَدْرٍ وَيَوْمُ ٱلْأَحْزَابِ:
"When the eyes grew wild, and the hearts reached the throats	﴿إِذْ زَاغَتِ ٱلْأَبْصَارُ وَبَلَغَتِ ٱلْقُلُوبُ ٱلْحَنَاجِرَ
And they speculated about Allah, doubting	وَتَظُنُّونَ بِٱللَّهِ ٱلظُّنُونَا
There the believers were tested and shaken with a severe shaking	هُنَالِكَ ٱبْتُلِيَ ٱلْمُؤْمِنُونَ وَزُلْزِلُوا۟ زِلْزَالاً شَدِيداً
And when the hypocrites and those in whose hearts is disease said:	وَإِذْ يَقُولُ ٱلْمُنَافِقُونَ وَٱلَّذِينَ فِي قُلُوبِهِمْ مَرَضٌ:
'Allah and His Messenger did not promise us except delusion'	مَا وَعَدَنَا ٱللَّهُ وَرَسُولُهُ إِلاَّ غُرُوراً
And when a group of them said:	وَإِذْ قَالَتْ طَائِفَةٌ مِنْهُمْ:
'Oh people of Yathrib, there is no position for you, so go back'	يَا أَهْلَ يَثْرِبَ لاَ مُقَامَ لَكُمْ فَٱرْجِعُوا۟
And a party of them asked permission of the Prophet	وَيَسْتَأْذِنُ فَرِيقٌ مِنْهُمُ ٱلنَّبِيَّ

Saying, 'Surely, our houses are exposed'	يَقُولُونَ إِنَّ بُيُوتَنَا عَوْرَةٌ
And they were not exposed; they only wanted to flee" – Quran 33:11-13	وَمَا هِيَ بِعَوْرَةٍ إِنْ يُرِيدُونَ إِلَّا فِرَاراً﴾
And Allah the Exalted said:	وَقَالَ اللَّهُ تَعَالَى:
"And when the believers saw the allies, they said:	﴿وَلَمَّا رَأَى الْمُؤْمِنُونَ الْأَحْزَابَ قَالُوا
'This is what Allah and His Messenger promised us	هَذَا مَا وَعَدَنَا اللَّهُ وَرَسُولُهُ
And Allah and His Messenger spoke the truth'	وَصَدَقَ اللَّهُ وَرَسُولُهُ
And it increased them only in faith and submission" – Quran 33:22	وَمَا زَادَهُمْ إِلَّا إِيمَاناً وَتَسْلِيماً﴾
So you killed their Amr	فَقَتَلْتَ عَمْرَوهُمْ
And defeated their assembly	وَهَزَمْتَ جَمْعَهُمْ
"And Allah repelled the disbelievers in their rage	﴿وَرَدَّ اللَّهُ الَّذِينَ كَفَرُوا بِغَيْظِهِمْ
Not attaining any good	لَمْ يَنَالُوا خَيْراً
And Allah sufficed the believers in battle	وَكَفَى اللَّهُ الْمُؤْمِنِينَ الْقِتَالَ
And Allah is ever Strong and Mighty" – Quran 33:25	وَكَانَ اللَّهُ قَوِيّاً عَزِيزاً﴾
And on the day of Uhud: "When they ran uphill, not turning back for any one	وَيَوْمَ أُحُدٍ: ﴿إِذْ تُصْعِدُونَ وَلَا تَلْوُونَ عَلَى أَحَدٍ
While the Messenger was calling them from behind" – Quran 3:153 (Paraphrased)	وَالرَّسُولُ يَدْعُوهُمْ فِي أُخْرَاهُمْ﴾
And you were driving off the polytheists from the Prophet	وَأَنْتَ تَذُودُ بِهِمُ الْمُشْرِكِينَ عَنِ الَّتِي

Continuous Calling

On the right and the left	ذَاتَ ٱلْيَمِينِ وَذَاتَ ٱلشِّمَالِ
Until Allah the Exalted repelled them from you two, fearful	حَتَّى رَدَّهُمْ ٱللَّهُ تَعَالَى عَنكُمَا خَائِفِينَ
And He granted victory through you to the deserters	وَنَصَرَ بِكَ ٱلْخَاذِلِينَ
On the day of Hunayn, upon what the revelation spoke:	وَيَوْمَ حُنَيْنٍ عَلَى مَا نَطَقَ بِهِ ٱلتَّنْزِيلُ:
"When you were impressed by your great number, but it did not give you any advantage	﴿إِذْ أَعْجَبَتْكُمْ كَثْرَتُكُمْ فَلَمْ تُغْنِ عَنكُمْ شَيْئًا
And the earth narrowed in its spaciousness	وَضَاقَتْ عَلَيْكُمُ ٱلْأَرْضُ بِمَا رَحُبَتْ
Then you turned back retreating	ثُمَّ وَلَّيْتُم مُّدْبِرِينَ
Then, Allah sent down His tranquillity upon His Messenger and upon the believers" – Quran 9:25-26	ثُمَّ أَنزَلَ ٱللَّهُ سَكِينَتَهُ عَلَى رَسُولِهِ وَعَلَى ٱلْمُؤْمِنِينَ﴾
"The believers" were you and your friends	وَٱلْمُؤْمِنُونَ أَنتَ وَمَنْ يَلِيكَ
And your uncle, Abbas, was calling at the defeated:	وَعَمُّكَ ٱلْعَبَّاسُ يُنَادِى ٱلْمُنْهَزِمِينَ:
"Oh companions (mentioned) in Surah al-Baqarah!	يَا أَصْحَابَ سُورَةِ ٱلْبَقَرَةِ
Oh people of the Allegiance of the Tree!"	يَا أَهْلَ بَيْعَةِ ٱلشَّجَرَةِ
Until a people responded to him, whose needs you had secured	حَتَّى ٱسْتَجَابَ لَهُ قَوْمٌ قَدْ كَفَيْتَهُمُ ٱلْمَؤُونَةَ
And you took charge of their support	وَتَكَفَّلْتَ دُونَهُمُ ٱلْمَعُونَةَ
So they returned, despairing of any reward	فَعَادُوا آيِسِينَ مِنَ ٱلْمَثُوبَةِ

Imam Ali (as)

Hoping for Allah's promise of repentance	رَاجِينَ وَعْدَ ٱللَّهِ تَعَالَىٰ بِٱلتَّوْبَةِ
And Allah, majestic is His mention, says:	وَذَلِكَ قَوْلُ ٱللَّهِ جَلَّ ذِكْرُهُ:
"Then Allah will accept repentance after that for whoever He wills" – Quran 9:27	﴿ثُمَّ يَتُوبُ ٱللَّهُ مِنْ بَعْدِ ذَلِكَ عَلَىٰ مَنْ يَشَاءُ﴾
And you attained the rank of patience	وَأَنْتَ حَائِزٌ دَرَجَةَ ٱلصَّبْرِ
Winning immense reward	فَائِزٌ بِعَظِيمِ ٱلْأَجْرِ
And on the day of Khaybar, when Allah manifested the cowardice of the hypocrites	وَيَوْمَ خَيْبَرَ إِذْ أَظْهَرَ ٱللَّهُ خَوَرَ ٱلْمُنَافِقِينَ
And cut off the root of the disbelievers	وَقَطَعَ دَابِرَ ٱلْكَافِرِينَ
And praise be to Allah, Lord of the worlds:	وَٱلْحَمْدُ لِلَّهِ رَبِّ ٱلْعَالَمِينَ:
"And they had previously promised Allah not to turn their backs	﴿وَلَقَدْ كَانُوا عَاهَدُوا ٱللَّهَ مِنْ قَبْلُ لاَ يُوَلُّونَ ٱلْأَدْبَارَ
And the promise to Allah will be asked about" – Quran 33:15	وَكَانَ عَهْدُ ٱللَّهِ مَسْؤُولاً﴾
Oh my master, you are the conclusive proof	مَوْلاَيَ أَنْتَ ٱلْحُجَّةُ ٱلْبَالِغَةُ
And the clear proof	وَٱلْمَحَجَّةُ ٱلْوَاضِحَةُ
And the abundant blessing	وَٱلنِّعْمَةُ ٱلسَّابِغَةُ
And the illuminating evidence	وَٱلْبُرْهَانُ ٱلْمُنِيرُ
So congratulations, for what Allah has given you from His grace	فَهَنِيئاً لَكَ بِمَا آتَاكَ ٱللَّهُ مِنْ فَضْلٍ
And woe to your ignorant opposition	وَتَبّاً لِشَانِيكَ ذِى ٱلْجَهْلِ

Continuous Calling

You witnessed with the Prophet, may Allah's blessings be upon him and his family	شَهِدْتَ مَعَ ٱلنَّبِيِّ صَلَّى ٱللَّهُ عَلَيْهِ وَآلِهِ
All of his wars and campaigns	جَمِيعَ حُرُوبِهِ وَمَغَازِيهِ
Carrying the banner before him	تَحْمِلُ ٱلرَّايَةَ أَمَامَهُ
And striking with the sword in front of him	وَتَضْرِبُ بِٱلسَّيْفِ قُدَّامَهُ
Then, due to your famous determination	ثُمَّ لِحَزْمِكَ ٱلْمَشْهُورِ
And foresight into affairs	وَبَصِيرَتِكَ فِي ٱلْأُمُورِ
He appointed you in situations	أَمَرَكَ فِي ٱلْمَوَاطِنِ
And there was no commander over you	وَلَمْ يَكُنْ عَلَيْكَ أَمِيرٌ
And how many matters did your piety prevent you from executing what you had decided	وَكَمْ مِنْ أَمْرٍ صَدَّكَ عَنْ إِمْضَاءِ عَزْمِكَ فِيهِ ٱلتُّقَى
While others followed desires in the like of it	وَٱتَّبَعَ غَيْرُكَ فِي مِثْلِهِ ٱلْهَوَى
So the ignorant thought you were incapable of what they attained	فَظَنَّ ٱلْجَاهِلُونَ أَنَّكَ عَجَزْتَ عَمَّا إِلَيْهِ ٱنْتَهَى
By Allah the speculator went astray and was not guided	ضَلَّ وَٱللَّهِ ٱلظَّانُّ لِذَلِكَ وَمَا ٱهْتَدَى
And you indeed clarified what was obscure of that for whoever assumed and objected	وَلَقَدْ أَوْضَحْتَ مَا أَشْكَلَ مِنْ ذَلِكَ لِمَنْ تَوَهَّمَ وَٱمْتَرَى
By your saying, May Allah's blessings be upon you:	بِقَوْلِكَ صَلَّى ٱللَّهُ عَلَيْكَ:
"The people of foresight see the face of the loophole	"قَدْ يَرَى ٱلْحُوَّلُ ٱلْقُلَّبُ وَجْهَ ٱلْحِيلَةِ
And the barrier before it is the fear of Allah	وَدُونَهَا حَاجِزٌ مِنْ تَقْوَى ٱللَّهِ

So he leaves it as merely a sight seen by the eye	فَيَدَعُهَا رَأْىَ ٱلْعَيْنِ
While the one who is not restrained by religion seizes the opportunity"	وَيَنْتَهِزُ فُرْصَتَهَا مَنْ لاَ حَرِيجَةَ لَهُ فِي ٱلدِّينِ"
You spoke the truth, by Allah, and the falsifiers have lost	صَدَقْتَ وَٱللَّهِ وَخَسِرَ ٱلْمُبْطِلُونَ
And when the two traitors plotted against you	وَإِذْ مَاكَرَكَ ٱلنَّاكِثَانِ
They said: "We want to perform Umrah (lesser pilgrimage)"	فَقَالاَ: نُرِيدُ ٱلْعُمْرَةَ
You answered them: "By your lives, you do not want the Umrah	فَقُلْتَ لَهُمَا: لَعَمْرُكُمَا مَا تُرِيدَانِ ٱلْعُمْرَةَ
Rather, you want treachery"	لٰكِنْ تُرِيدَانِ ٱلْغَدْرَةَ
So you took allegiance from them	فَأَخَذْتَ ٱلْبَيْعَةَ عَلَيْهِمَا
And renewed the covenant	وَجَدَّدْتَ ٱلْمِيثَاقَ
But they persisted in hypocrisy	فَجَدَّا فِي ٱلنِّفَاقِ
When you warned them about their deed, they neglected and returned and did not benefit	فَلَمَّا نَبَّهْتُهُمَا عَلَىٰ فِعْلِهِمَا أَغْفَلاَ وَعَادَا وَمَا ٱنْتَفَعَا
And the end of their affair was loss	وَكَانَ عَاقِبَةُ أَمْرِهِمَا خُسْراً
Then the people of Sham followed them	ثُمَّ تَلاَهُمَا أَهْلُ ٱلشَّامِ
So you marched towards them after all excuses	فَسِرْتَ إِلَيْهِمْ بَعْدَ ٱلْإِعْذَارِ
While they did not practice the true religion	وَهُمْ لاَ يَدِينُونَ دِينَ ٱلْحَقِّ
Nor did they contemplate the Quran	وَلاَ يَتَدَبَّرُونَ ٱلْقُرْآنَ
Savages, disorganised, and astray	هَمَجٌ رُعَاعٌ ضَالُّونَ

And disbelieved in what was sent down to Muhammad about you	وَبِٱلَّذِى أُنزِلَ عَلَىٰ مُحَمَّدٍ فِيكَ كَافِرُونَ
And supporters of the people who disputed against you	وَلِأَهْلِ ٱلْخِلَافِ عَلَيْكَ نَاصِرُونَ
And Allah the Exalted has commanded following you	وَقَدْ أَمَرَ ٱللَّهُ تَعَالَىٰ بِٱتِّبَاعِكَ
And urged the believers to support you	وَنَدَبَ ٱلْمُؤْمِنِينَ إِلَىٰ نَصْرِكَ
And He said, Mighty and Majestic	وَقَالَ عَزَّ وَجَلَّ:
"Oh you who believe!	﴿يَا أَيُّهَا ٱلَّذِينَ آمَنُوا
Fear Allah and be with the truthful" – Quran 9:119	ٱتَّقُوا ٱللَّهَ وَكُونُوا مَعَ ٱلصَّادِقِينَ﴾
My master, through you the truth appeared	مَوْلَايَ بِكَ ظَهَرَ ٱلْحَقُّ
While the creation had cast it aside	وَقَدْ نَبَذَهُ ٱلْخَلْقُ
And you clarified the Sunnah (way) after eradication and confusion	وَأَوْضَحْتَ ٱلسُّنَنَ بَعْدَ ٱلدُّرُوسِ وَٱلطَّمْسِ
So for you is the precedence of struggling in confirming the revelation	فَلَكَ سَابِقَةُ ٱلْجِهَادِ عَلَىٰ تَصْدِيقِ ٱلتَّنْزِيلِ
And for you is the virtue of struggling in realizing the interpretation	وَلَكَ فَضِيلَةُ ٱلْجِهَادِ عَلَىٰ تَحْقِيقِ ٱلتَّأْوِيلِ
And your enemy is the enemy of Allah, rejecting the Messenger of Allah	وَعَدُوُّكَ عَدُوُّ ٱللَّهِ جَاحِدٌ لِرَسُولِ ٱللَّهِ
Calling to falsehood and judging unjustly	يَدْعُو بَاطِلاً وَيَحْكُمُ جَائِراً

And usurping authority, and calling his party to the Fire	وَيَتَأَمَّرُ غَاصِباً وَيَدْعُو حِزْبَهُ إِلَى ٱلنَّارِ
While Ammar struggled and called out between the two lines:	وَعَمَّارٌ يُجَاهِدُ وَيُنَادِى بَيْنَ ٱلصَّفَّيْنِ:
"The journey, the journey to Paradise!"	"ٱلرَّوَاحَ ٱلرَّوَاحَ إِلَى ٱلْجَنَّةِ"
And when he asked for a drink and was given milk, he glorified Allah and said:	وَلَمَّا ٱسْتَسْقَى فَسُقِىَ ٱللَّبَنَ كَبَّرَ وَقَالَ:
"The Messenger of Allah, may Allah's blessings be upon him and his family, said to me:	"قَالَ لِى رَسُولُ ٱللَّهِ صَلَّى ٱللَّهُ عَلَيْهِ وَآلِهِ:
'Your last drink in this world will be a sip of milk,	'آخِرُ شَرَابِكَ مِنَ ٱلدُّنْيَا ضَيَاحٌ مِنْ لَبَنٍ
And the transgressing group will kill you'"	وَتَقْتُلُكَ ٱلْفِئَةُ ٱلْبَاغِيَةُ'"
Then Abul Adiyah al-Fazari confronted him and killed him	فَٱعْتَرَضَهُ أَبُو ٱلْعَادِيَةِ ٱلْفَزَارِىُّ فَقَتَلَهُ
So upon Abul Adiyah is the curse of Allah	فَعَلَى أَبِى ٱلْعَادِيَةِ لَعْنَةُ ٱللَّهِ
And the curse of His angels and messengers altogether	وَلَعْنَةُ مَلَائِكَتِهِ وَرُسُلِهِ أَجْمَعِينَ
And upon whoever unsheathed his sword against you	وَعَلَى مَنْ سَلَّ سَيْفَهُ عَلَيْكَ
Or who you unsheathed your sword against;	وَسَلَلْتَ سَيْفَكَ عَلَيْهِ
Oh commander of the faithful;	يَا أَمِيرَ ٱلْمُؤْمِنِينَ
(Curse be upon) the polytheists and the hypocrites up to the Day of Judgement	مِنَ ٱلْمُشْرِكِينَ وَٱلْمُنَافِقِينَ إِلَى يَوْمِ ٱلدِّينِ

Continuous Calling

And upon whoever was pleased with what displeased you	وَعَلَىٰ مَنْ رَضِيَ بِمَا سَاءَكَ
And did not detest it, and closed his eye and did not denounce	وَلَمْ يَكْرَهْهُ وَأَغْمَضَ عَيْنَهُ وَلَمْ يُنْكِرْ
Or aided against you with hand or tongue	أَوْ أَعَانَ عَلَيْكَ بِيَدٍ أَوْ لِسَانٍ
Or sat back from supporting you	أَوْ قَعَدَ عَنْ نَصْرِكَ
Or deserted jihad with you	أَوْ خَذَلَ عَنِ ٱلْجِهَادِ مَعَكَ
Or belittled your virtues	أَوْ غَمَطَ فَضْلَكَ
Or rejected your right	وَجَحَدَ حَقَّكَ
Or preferred over you someone that Allah made you more worthy of him than himself	أَوْ عَدَلَ بِكَ مَنْ جَعَلَكَ ٱللَّهُ أَوْلَىٰ بِهِ مِنْ نَفْسِهِ
And the blessings of Allah upon you, and Allah's mercy and grace	وَصَلَوَاتُ ٱللَّهِ عَلَيْكَ وَرَحْمَةُ ٱللَّهِ وَبَرَكَاتُهُ
And His peace and greetings	وَسَلَامُهُ وَتَحِيَّاتُهُ
And upon the Imams from your purified family	وَعَلَىٰ ٱلْأَئِمَّةِ مِنْ آلِكَ ٱلطَّاهِرِينَ
Indeed, He is Praised and Glorious	إِنَّهُ حَمِيدٌ مَجِيدٌ
And the most amazing matter	وَٱلْأَمْرُ ٱلْأَعْجَبُ
And the most dreadful calamity after rejecting your right	وَٱلْخَطْبُ ٱلْأَفْظَعُ بَعْدَ جَحْدِكَ حَقَّكَ
Is the usurpation of Fadak from the truthful, the pure, and the radiant Lady, the chief of the women	غَصْبُ ٱلصِّدِّيقَةِ ٱلطَّاهِرَةِ ٱلزَّهْرَاءِ سَيِّدَةِ ٱلنِّسَاءِ فَدَكاً

And the rejection of your testimony and that of the two chiefs of your lineage	وَرَدُّ شَهَادَتِكَ وَشَهَادَةِ ٱلسَّيِّدَيْنِ سُلالَتِكَ
And the family of the Chosen One, May Allah's blessings be upon you all	وَعِتْرَةِ ٱلْمُصْطَفَى صَلَّى ٱللَّهُ عَلَيْكُمْ
For Allah the Exalted has elevated your rank over the nation	وَقَدْ أَعْلَى ٱللَّهُ تَعَالَى عَلَى ٱلْأُمَّةِ دَرَجَتَكُمْ
And raised your station,	وَرَفَعَ مَنْزِلَتَكُمْ
And made clear your virtue and nobility over all the worlds	وَأَبَانَ فَضْلَكُمْ وَشَرَّفَكُمْ عَلَى ٱلْعَالَمِينَ
So He kept away filth from you and purified you a thorough purification	فَأَذْهَبَ عَنْكُمُ ٱلرِّجْسَ وَطَهَّرَكُمْ تَطْهِيراً
Allah the Mighty and Majestic says:	قَالَ ٱللَّهُ عَزَّ وَجَلَّ:
"Indeed, man was created anxious	﴿إِنَّ ٱلْإِنْسَانَ خُلِقَ هَلُوعاً
When evil touches him, grieving	إِذَا مَسَّهُ ٱلشَّرُّ جَزُوعاً
And when good touches him, withholding	وَإِذَا مَسَّهُ ٱلْخَيْرُ مَنُوعاً
Except those who pray" – Quran 70:19-23	إِلَّا ٱلْمُصَلِّينَ﴾
So Allah the Exalted exempted His chosen Prophet	فَٱسْتَثْنَى ٱللَّهُ تَعَالَى نَبِيَّهُ ٱلْمُصْطَفَى
And you, oh chief of the successors, from all creation	وَأَنْتَ يَا سَيِّدَ ٱلْأَوْصِيَاءِ مِنْ جَمِيعِ ٱلْخَلْقِ
So how blind is the one who wronged you of the truth	فَمَا أَعْمَى مَنْ ظَلَمَكَ عَنِ ٱلْحَقِّ
Then they deceptively imposed only a share of the relatives to you	ثُمَّ أَقْرَضُوكَ سَهْمَ ذَوِي ٱلْقُرْبَى مَكْراً

And diverted it wrongfully from its people	وَأَحَادُوهُ عَنْ أَهْلِهِ جَوْراً
When the matter came to you, you let them continue as they were	فَلَمَّا آلَ الْأَمْرُ إِلَيْكَ أَجْرَيْتَهُمْ عَلَى مَا أَجْرَيَا
Out of desire for what is with Allah for you	رَغْبَةً عَنْهُمَا بِمَا عِنْدَ اللَّهِ لَكَ
So your trial with them resembled the trials of the Prophets, peace be upon them	فَأَشْبَهَتْ مِحْنَتُكَ بِهِمَا مِحَنَ الْأَنْبِيَاءِ عَلَيْهِمُ السَّلَامُ
During loneliness and lack of supporters	عِنْدَ الْوَحْدَةِ وَعَدَمِ الْأَنْصَارِ
And in spending nights on the bed, you resembled the one sacrificed, peace be upon him	وَأَشْبَهْتَ فِي الْبَيَاتِ عَلَى الْفِرَاشِ الذَّبِيحَ عَلَيْهِ السَّلَامُ
When you responded just as he responded	إِذْ أَجَبْتَ كَمَا أَجَابَ
And obeyed just as Ismail obeyed, patiently and seeking reward	وَأَطَعْتَ كَمَا أَطَاعَ إِسْمَاعِيلُ صَابِراً مُحْتَسِباً
When he said to him: "'Oh my son, indeed I have seen in a dream that I must sacrifice you	إِذْ قَالَ لَهُ: يَا بُنَيَّ إِنِّي أَرَى فِي الْمَنَامِ أَنِّي أَذْبَحُكَ
So look, what do you think?'	فَانْظُرْ مَاذَا تَرَى
He said: 'Oh my father, do as you are commanded	قَالَ: ﴿يَا أَبَتِ افْعَلْ مَا تُؤْمَرُ
You will find me, if Allah wills, of the patient ones'" – Quran 37:102	سَتَجِدُنِي إِنْ شَاءَ اللَّهُ مِنَ الصَّابِرِينَ﴾
And likewise, when the Prophet, may Allah's blessings be upon him and his family, made you stay the night	وَكَذَلِكَ أَنْتَ لَمَّا أَبَاتَكَ النَّبِيُّ صَلَّى اللَّهُ عَلَيْهِ وَآلِهِ

Imam Ali (as)

And commanded you to lie down in his bed	وَأَمَرَكَ أَنْ تَضْجَعَ فِي مَرْقَدِهِ
Shielding him with your own self	وَاقِيًا لَهُ بِنَفْسِكَ
You rushed to obey him	أَسْرَعْتَ إِلَى إِجَابَتِهِ مُطِيعاً
And laid yourself down ready for being killed	وَلِنَفْسِكَ عَلَى الْقَتْلِ مُوَطِّناً
So Allah the Exalted thanked your obedience	فَشَكَرَ اللَّهُ تَعَالَى طَاعَتَكَ
And made clear the beauty of your action by His words, glorified is His mention	وَأَبَانَ عَنْ جَمِيلِ فِعْلِكَ بِقَوْلِهِ جَلَّ ذِكْرُهُ:
"And among the people is he who sells himself, seeking the pleasure of Allah" – Quran 2:207	﴿وَمِنَ ٱلنَّاسِ مَنْ يَشْرِى نَفْسَهُ ٱبْتِغَاءَ مَرْضَاةِ ٱللَّهِ﴾
Then, your trial on the day of Siffin	ثُمَّ مِحْنَتُكَ يَوْمَ صِفِّينَ
And the Masahif (Qur'an copies) were raised as a ploy and trick	وَقَدْ رُفِعَتِ الْمَصَاحِفُ حِيلَةً وَمَكْراً
So doubt crept in	فَأَعْرَضَ الشَّكُّ
And the truth was turned away from	وَعُزِفَ الْحَقُّ
And speculation was followed	وَاتُّبِعَ الظَّنُّ
It resembled the trial of Harun when Musa appointed him over his people but they split from him	أَشْبَهَتْ مِحْنَةَ هَارُونَ إِذْ أَمَرَهُ مُوسَى عَلَى قَوْمِهِ فَتَفَرَّقُوا عَنْهُ
And Harun was calling out to them, saying:	وَهَارُونُ يُنَادِى بِهِمْ وَيَقُولُ:
"'Oh my people, you were only tried by it, and indeed your Lord is the Most Merciful	يَا قَوْمِ إِنَّمَا فُتِنْتُمْ بِهِ وَإِنَّ رَبَّكُمُ ٱلرَّحْمَٰنُ
So follow me and obey my order'	فَٱتَّبِعُونِى وَأَطِيعُوٓا أَمْرِى

141

Continuous Calling

They said: 'We will remain devoted to it until Musa returns to us'" – Quran 20:90-91	قَالُواْ: ﴿لَن نَّبْرَحَ عَلَيْهِ عَاكِفِينَ حَتَّىٰ يَرْجِعَ إِلَيْنَا مُوسَىٰ﴾
And likewise, when the Masahif (Qur'an copies) were raised, you said:	وَكَذَلِكَ أَنتَ لَنَّا رُفِعَتِ ٱلْمَصَاحِفُ قُلْتَ:
'Oh my people, you were only tried by it and deceived'	يَا قَوْمِ إِنَّمَا فُتِنتُمْ بِهَا وَخُدِعْتُمْ
But they disobeyed you and opposed you	فَعَصَوْكَ وَخَالَفُواْ عَلَيْكَ
And called for the appointment of the two arbitrators	وَٱسْتَدْعَوْاْ نَصْبَ ٱلْحَكَمَيْنِ
So you refused them and disavowed their action to Allah, and left it up to them	فَأَبَيْتَ عَلَيْهِمْ وَتَبَرَّأْتَ إِلَى ٱللَّهِ مِن فِعْلِهِمْ وَفَوَّضْتَهُ إِلَيْهِمْ
Then when the truth became clear	فَلَمَّا أَسْفَرَ ٱلْحَقُّ
And the evil became foolish	وَسَفِهَ ٱلْمُنْكَرُ
And they admitted their slip and injustice from the intended purpose	وَٱعْتَرَفُواْ بِٱلزَّلَلِ وَٱلْجَوْرِ عَنِ ٱلْقَصْدِ
They differed after that	ٱخْتَلَفُواْ مِنْ بَعْدِهِ
And compelled you to the foolish arbitration which you refused but they loved	وَأَلْزَمُوكَ عَلَىٰ سَفَهِ ٱلتَّحْكِيمِ ٱلَّذِي أَبَيْتَهُ وَأَحَبُّوهُ
You prohibited it, but they permitted their sin which they committed	وَحَظَرْتَهُ وَأَبَاحُواْ ذَنْبَهُمُ ٱلَّذِي ٱقْتَرَفُوهُ
And you were upon the path of foresight and guidance	وَأَنتَ عَلَىٰ نَهْجِ بَصِيرَةٍ وَهُدًى
While they were upon the ways of misguidance and blindness	وَهُمْ عَلَىٰ سُنَنِ ضَلَالَةٍ وَعَمًى
They did not cease insisting on hypocrisy	فَمَا زَالُواْ عَلَى ٱلنِّفَاقِ مُصِرِّينَ

And wavering in error	وَفِي ٱلْغَيِّ مُتَرَدِّدِينَ
Until Allah made them taste the consequences of their affair	حَتَّىٰ أَذَاقَهُمُ ٱللَّهُ وَبَالَ أَمْرِهِمْ
So He killed, by your sword, those who stubbornly opposed you, being wretched and going astray	فَأَمَاتَ بِسَيْفِكَ مَنْ عَانَدَكَ فَشَقِيَ وَهَوَىٰ
And by your proof He gave life to those who were brightened with guidance	وَأَحْيَا بِحُجَّتِكَ مَنْ سَعَدَ فَهُدِيَ
Allah's blessings be upon you, coming and going	صَلَوَاتُ ٱللَّهِ عَلَيْكَ غَادِيَةً وَرَائِحَةً
And staying and departing	وَعَاكِفَةً وَذَاهِبَةً
For no praiser can encompass your description	فَمَا يُحِيطُ ٱلْمَادِحُ وَصْفَكَ
Nor can any critic negate your virtues	وَلَا يُحْبِطُ ٱلطَّاعِنُ فَضْلَكَ
You are the best of creation in worship	أَنْتَ أَحْسَنُ ٱلْخَلْقِ عِبَادَةً
And the most sincere in asceticism	وَأَخْلَصُهُمْ زَهَادَةً
And the most enthusiastic defender of the religion	وَأَذَبُّهُمْ عَنِ ٱلدِّينِ
You established the limits of Allah with your struggle	أَقَمْتَ حُدُودَ ٱللَّهِ بِجُهْدِكَ
And crushed the armies of the defectors with your sword	وَفَلَلْتَ عَسَاكِرَ ٱلْمَارِقِينَ بِسَيْفِكَ
You extinguish the flames of wars with your fingers	تُخْمِدُ لَهَبَ ٱلْحُرُوبِ بِبَنَانِكَ
And tear apart the veils of misconceptions with your clarifications	وَتَهْتِكُ سُتُورَ ٱلشُّبَهِ بِبَيَانِكَ
And you unveil falsehood from the undeniable truth	وَتَكْشِفُ لَبْسَ ٱلْبَاطِلِ عَنْ صَرِيحِ ٱلْحَقِّ

Continuous Calling

The blame of a blamer does not take you in the cause of Allah	لَا تَأْخُذُكَ فِي ٱللَّهِ لَوْمَةُ لَائِمٍ
And the praise of Allah the Exalted suffices you	وَفِي مَدْحِ ٱللَّهِ تَعَالَى لَكَ غِنًى
From the praise of praisers and commendations of describers	عَنْ مَدْحِ ٱلْمَادِحِينَ وَتَقْرِيظِ ٱلْوَاصِفِينَ
Allah the Exalted said:	قَالَ ٱللَّهُ تَعَالَى:
"Among the believers are men true to what they promised Allah	﴿مِنَ ٱلْمُؤْمِنِينَ رِجَالٌ صَدَقُوا مَا عَاهَدُوا ٱللَّهَ عَلَيْهِ
Among them is he who has fulfilled his vow, and among them is he who waits, and they have not changed at all" – Quran 33:23	فَمِنْهُمْ مَنْ قَضَى نَحْبَهُ وَمِنْهُمْ مَنْ يَنْتَظِرُ وَمَا بَدَّلُوا تَبْدِيلًا﴾
And when you saw that you had killed the oath-breakers, and the unjust, and the rebels	وَلَمَّا رَأَيْتَ أَنْ قَتَلْتَ ٱلنَّاكِثِينَ وَٱلْقَاسِطِينَ وَٱلْمَارِقِينَ
And the Messenger of Allah, may Allah's blessings be upon him and his family, was truthful in his promise to you	وَصَدَقَكَ رَسُولُ ٱللَّهِ صَلَّى ٱللَّهُ عَلَيْهِ وَآلِهِ وَعْدَهُ
So you fulfilled his covenant, saying:	فَأَوْفَيْتَ بِعَهْدِهِ قُلْتَ:
"Is it not time that this (beard) be dyed from this (head)?	أَمَا آنَ أَنْ تُخْضَبَ هٰذِهِ مِنْ هٰذِهِ
Or when will its most wretched one be dispatched?"	أَمْ مَتَى يُبْعَثُ أَشْقَاهَا
Being confident that you are upon a clear proof from your Lord	وَاثِقًا بِأَنَّكَ عَلَى بَيِّنَةٍ مِنْ رَبِّكَ
And insightful into your affair	وَبَصِيرَةٍ مِنْ أَمْرِكَ
Advancing towards Allah	قَادِمٌ عَلَى ٱللَّهِ

Imam Ali (as)

Rejoicing in your pledge which you pledged to Him	مُسْتَبْشِرٌ بِبَيْعِكَ ٱلَّذِي بَايَعْتَهُ بِهِ
And that is the great victory	وَذٰلِكَ هُوَ ٱلْفَوْزُ ٱلْعَظِيمُ
Oh Allah, curse the killers of Your prophets and successors of Your prophets	اَللَّهُمَّ ٱلْعَنْ قَتَلَةَ أَنْبِيَائِكَ وَأَوْصِيَاءِ أَنْبِيَائِكَ
With all of Your curses	بِجَمِيعِ لَعَنَاتِكَ
And make them taste the heat of Your fire	وَأَصْلِهِمْ حَرَّ نَارِكَ
And curse whoever usurped the right of Your guardian (over the believers)	وَٱلْعَنْ مَنْ غَصَبَ وَلِيَّكَ حَقَّهُ
And denied his covenant	وَأَنْكَرَ عَهْدَهُ
And rejected him after certainty and acknowledgement of his guardianship	وَجَحَدَهُ بَعْدَ ٱلْيَقِينِ وَٱلْإِقْرَارِ بِٱلْوِلَايَةِ لَهُ
On the day you perfected the religion for him	يَوْمَ أَكْمَلْتَ لَهُ ٱلدِّينَ
Oh Allah, curse the killers of the commander of the faithful	اَللَّهُمَّ ٱلْعَنْ قَتَلَةَ أَمِيرِ ٱلْمُؤْمِنِينَ
And those who wronged him, and their followers and supporters	وَمَنْ ظَلَمَهُ وَأَشْيَاعَهُمْ وَأَنْصَارَهُمْ
Oh Allah, curse the oppressors of Husain and those who killed him	اَللَّهُمَّ ٱلْعَنْ ظَالِمِي ٱلْحُسَيْنِ وَقَاتِلِيهِ
And those who followed his enemy and their supporters	وَٱلْمُتَّبِعِينَ عَدُوَّهُ وَنَاصِرِيهِ
And those pleased with his killing and abandonment, with a lasting curse	وَٱلرَّاضِينَ بِقَتْلِهِ وَخَاذِلِيهِ لَعْناً وَبِيلاً
Oh Allah, curse the first oppressor who oppressed the family of Muhammad	اَللَّهُمَّ ٱلْعَنْ أَوَّلَ ظَالِمٍ ظَلَمَ آلَ مُحَمَّدٍ
And those who prevented them from their rights	وَمَانِعِيهِمْ حُقُوقَهُمْ

Oh Allah, specifically curse the first oppressor and usurper against the family of Muhammad	اَللَّهُمَّ خُصَّ أَوَّلَ ظَالِمٍ وَغَاصِبٍ لِآلِ مُحَمَّدٍ بِٱللَّعْنِ
And everyone who follows his practice until the Day of Resurrection	وَكُلَّ مُسْتَنٍّ بِمَا سَنَّ إِلَى يَوْمِ ٱلْقِيَامَةِ
Oh Allah, send blessings upon Muhammad, the seal of the Prophets	اَللَّهُمَّ صَلِّ عَلَىٰ مُحَمَّدٍ خَاتَمِ ٱلنَّبِيِّينَ
And upon Ali, chief of the successors, and upon his purified family	وَعَلَىٰ عَلِيٍّ سَيِّدِ ٱلْوَصِيِّينَ وَآلِهِ ٱلطَّاهِرِينَ
And make us adhere to them firmly	وَٱجْعَلْنَا بِهِمْ مُتَمَسِّكِينَ
And from those attaining safety and success through their guardianship	وَبِوِلَايَتِهِمْ مِنَ ٱلْفَائِزِينَ ٱلْآمِنِينَ
Those upon who there is no fear, nor will they grieve	ٱلَّذِينَ لَا خَوْفٌ عَلَيْهِمْ وَلَا هُمْ يَحْزَنُونَ

Sayedah Fatima (as)

"Everyone who loves us and befriends our friends and is hostile to our enemies and submissive with his heart and tongue to us. They are not from our Shias if they are still opposing our orders and prohibitions regarding all of the destructive sins. But they will still be in Paradise after being purified of their sins with afflictions and adversities, or in the plains of the Day of Qiyamah with the varieties of difficulties, or in the top layer of Hell with its punishments. Until we pick them out, due to their love for us, and bring them to our presence." – Sayedah Fatima (as)

(Bihar Al-Anwar Hub-e-Ali translation, vol 65, page 228)

On 20 Jumada II to celebrate her birth, and on 13 Jumada I and 3 Jumada II to commemorate her martyrdom you can recite the following ziyarah:

Peace be upon you oh daughter of the Messenger of Allah	اَلسَّلَامُ عَلَيْكِ يَا بِنْتَ رَسُولِ ٱللَّهِ
Peace be upon you oh daughter of the Prophet of Allah	اَلسَّلَامُ عَلَيْكِ يَا بِنْتَ نَبِيِّ ٱللَّهِ
Peace be upon you oh daughter of the beloved of Allah	اَلسَّلَامُ عَلَيْكِ يَا بِنْتَ حَبِيبِ ٱللَّهِ
Peace be upon you oh daughter of the close friend of Allah	اَلسَّلَامُ عَلَيْكِ يَا بِنْتَ خَلِيلِ ٱللَّهِ
Peace be upon you oh daughter of the Choice of Allah	اَلسَّلَامُ عَلَيْكِ يَا بِنْتَ صَفِيِّ ٱللَّهِ
Peace be upon you oh daughter of the Trustee of Allah	اَلسَّلَامُ عَلَيْكِ يَا بِنْتَ اَمِينِ ٱللَّهِ
Peace be upon you oh daughter of the best of Allah's creation	اَلسَّلَامُ عَلَيْكِ يَا بِنْتَ خَيْرِ خَلْقِ ٱللَّهِ
Peace be upon you oh daughter of the best of Allah's Prophets, Messengers, and angels	اَلسَّلَامُ عَلَيْكِ يَا بِنْتَ افْضَلِ أَنْبِيَاءِ ٱللَّهِ وَرُسُلِهِ وَمَلَائِكَتِهِ
Peace be upon you oh daughter of the best of all created beings	اَلسَّلَامُ عَلَيْكِ يَا بِنْتَ خَيْرِ ٱلْبَرِيَّةِ

Peace be upon you oh chief of the women of the worlds	اَلسَّلَامُ عَلَيْكِ يَا سَيِّدَةَ نِسَاءِ ٱلْعَالَمِينَ
From the earlier and later generations	مِنَ ٱلْأَوَّلِينَ وَٱلْآخِرِينَ
Peace be upon you oh wife of the guardian (over the believers) of Allah	اَلسَّلَامُ عَلَيْكِ يَا زَوْجَةَ وَلِيِّ ٱللَّهِ
And the best of creation after the Messenger of Allah	وَخَيْرِ ٱلْخَلْقِ بَعْدَ رَسُولِ ٱللَّهِ
Peace be upon you oh mother of Hasan and Husain	اَلسَّلَامُ عَلَيْكِ يَا اُمَّ ٱلْحَسَنِ وَٱلْحُسَيْنِ
The two chiefs of the youth of Paradise	سَيِّدَيْ شَبَابِ أَهْلِ ٱلْجَنَّةِ
Peace be upon you oh the truthful martyr	اَلسَّلَامُ عَلَيْكِ اَيَّتُهَا ٱلصِّدِّيقَةُ ٱلشَّهِيدَةُ
Peace be upon you oh content and contented with	اَلسَّلَامُ عَلَيْكِ اَيَّتُهَا ٱلرَّضِيَّةُ ٱلْمَرْضِيَّةُ
Peace be upon you oh virtuous and pure	اَلسَّلَامُ عَلَيْكِ اَيَّتُهَا ٱلْفَاضِلَةُ ٱلزَّكِيَّةُ
Peace be upon you oh heavenly lady	اَلسَّلَامُ عَلَيْكِ اَيَّتُهَا ٱلْحَوْرَاءُ ٱلْإِنْسِيَّةُ
Peace be upon you oh pious and immaculate	اَلسَّلَامُ عَلَيْكِ اَيَّتُهَا ٱلتَّقِيَّةُ ٱلنَّقِيَّةُ
Peace be upon you oh the narrated to and knowledgeable one	اَلسَّلَامُ عَلَيْكِ اَيَّتُهَا ٱلْمُحَدَّثَةُ ٱلْعَلِيمَةُ
Peace be upon you oh the oppressed one and usurped from	اَلسَّلَامُ عَلَيْكِ اَيَّتُهَا ٱلْمَظْلُومَةُ ٱلْمَغْصُوبَةُ
Peace be upon you oh persecuted and overwhelmed one	اَلسَّلَامُ عَلَيْكِ اَيَّتُهَا ٱلْمُضْطَهَدَةُ ٱلْمَقْهُورَةُ

Sayedah Fatima (as)

Peace be upon you oh Fatima the daughter of the Messenger of Allah	اَلسَّلَامُ عَلَيْكِ يَا فَاطِمَةُ بِنْتَ رَسُولِ ٱللَّهِ
And Allah's mercy and grace	وَرَحْمَةُ ٱللَّهِ وَبَرَكَاتُهُ
May Allah's blessings be upon you	صَلَّى ٱللَّهُ عَلَيْكِ
And on your soul, and your body	وَعَلَىٰ رُوحِكِ وَبَدَنِكِ
I bear witness that you passed away upon a clear proof from your Lord	أَشْهَدُ أَنَّكِ مَضَيْتِ عَلَىٰ بَيِّنَةٍ مِنْ رَبِّكِ
And that whoever pleases you has indeed pleased the Messenger of Allah	وَأَنَّ مَنْ سَرَّكِ فَقَدْ سَرَّ رَسُولَ ٱللَّهِ
May Allah's blessings be upon him and his family	صَلَّى ٱللَّهُ عَلَيْهِ وَآلِهِ
And whoever abandoned you has indeed abandoned the Messenger of Allah	وَمَنْ جَفَاكِ فَقَدْ جَفَا رَسُولَ ٱللَّهِ
May Allah's blessings be upon him and his family	صَلَّى ٱللَّهُ عَلَيْهِ وَآلِهِ
And whoever harms you has indeed harmed the Messenger of Allah	وَمَنْ آذَاكِ فَقَدْ آذَىٰ رَسُولَ ٱللَّهِ
May Allah's blessings be upon him and his family	صَلَّى ٱللَّهُ عَلَيْهِ وَآلِهِ
And whoever connects with you has indeed connected with the Messenger of Allah	وَمَنْ وَصَلَكِ فَقَدْ وَصَلَ رَسُولَ ٱللَّهِ
May Allah's blessings be upon him and his family	صَلَّى ٱللَّهُ عَلَيْهِ وَآلِهِ
And whoever cuts you off has indeed cut off the Messenger of Allah	وَمَنْ قَطَعَكِ فَقَدْ قَطَعَ رَسُولَ ٱللَّهِ
May Allah's blessings be upon him and his family	صَلَّى ٱللَّهُ عَلَيْهِ وَآلِهِ

Continuous Calling

For indeed you are a part of him	لِأَنَّكِ بِضْعَةٌ مِنْهُ
And his soul which is between his two sides	وَرُوحُهُ ٱلَّذِى بَيْنَ جَنْبَيْهِ
I call Allah and His angels to witness	أُشْهِدُ ٱللَّهَ وَمَلَائِكَتَهُ
That I am a friend to whoever is your friend	إِنِّى وَلِىٌّ لِمَنْ وَالَاكِ
And I am the enemy to whoever is your enemy	وَعَدُوٌّ لِمَنْ عَادَاكِ
And I am at war with whoever wages war against you	وَحَرْبٌ لِمَنْ حَارَبَكِ
Oh my master, I am with you, and with your father	أَنَا يَا مَوْلَاتِى بِكِ وَبِأَبِيكِ
And your husband, and the Imams from your offspring, with certainty	وَبَعْلِكِ وَٱلْأَئِمَّةِ مِنْ وُلْدِكِ مُوقِنٌ
I believe in their guardianship	وَبِوِلَايَتِهِمْ مُؤْمِنٌ
And I adhere to obedience to them	وَلِطَاعَتِهِمْ مُلْتَزِمٌ
I bear witness that the religion is their religion	أَشْهَدُ أَنَّ ٱلدِّينَ دِينُهُمْ
And the command is their command	وَٱلْحُكْمَ حُكْمُهُمْ
And they have indeed conveyed from Allah, the Mighty and Majestic	وَهُمْ قَدْ بَلَّغُوا عَنِ ٱللَّهِ عَزَّ وَجَلَّ
And invited to the path of Allah with wisdom and good preaching	وَدَعَوْا إِلَى سَبِيلِ ٱللَّهِ بِٱلْحِكْمَةِ وَٱلْمَوْعِظَةِ ٱلْحَسَنَةِ
No blame from any blamer impacts them regarding Allah	لَا تَأْخُذُهُمْ فِى ٱللَّهِ لَوْمَةُ لَائِمٍ
And may the blessings of Allah be upon you	وَصَلَوَاتُ ٱللَّهِ عَلَيْكِ
And upon your father and your husband	وَعَلَى أَبِيكِ وَبَعْلِكِ

Sayedah Fatima (as)

And your offspring, the pure Imams	وَذُرِّيَّتِكَ ٱلْأَئِمَّةَ ٱلطَّاهِرِينَ
Oh Allah, send blessings upon Muhammad and his Ahlul Bayt	اَللَّهُمَّ صَلِّ عَلَىٰ مُحَمَّدٍ وَأَهْلِ بَيْتِهِ
And send blessings upon the chaste, the pure	وَصَلِّ عَلَىٰ ٱلْبَتُولِ ٱلطَّاهِرَةِ
The truthful, the infallible	ٱلصِّدِّيقَةِ ٱلْمَعْصُومَةِ
The pious, the immaculate	ٱلتَّقِيَّةِ ٱلنَّقِيَّةِ
The contented, the contented with	ٱلرَّضِيَّةِ ٱلْمَرْضِيَّةِ
The impeccable, the rightly-guided one	ٱلزَّكِيَّةِ ٱلرَّشِيدَةِ
The oppressed, the overwhelmed one	ٱلْمَظْلُومَةِ ٱلْمَقْهُورَةِ
Wrongfully deprived of her right	ٱلْمَغْصُوبَةِ حَقُّهَا
Prevented from her inheritance	ٱلْمَمْنُوعَةِ إِرْثُهَا
Whose rib was broken,	ٱلْمَكْسُورَةِ ضِلْعُهَا
Whose husband was persecuted	ٱلْمَظْلُومِ بَعْلُهَا
Whose child was killed	ٱلْمَقْتُولِ وَلَدُهَا
Fatima, the daughter of Your Messenger	فَاطِمَةَ بِنْتِ رَسُولِكَ
And a part of his flesh	وَبَضْعَةَ لَحْمِهِ
And the essence of his heart	وَصَمِيمَ قَلْبِهِ
And the innermost part of him	وَفِلْذَةَ كَبِدِهِ
And the chosen one from You for him	وَٱلنُّخْبَةَ مِنْكَ لَهُ
And the gift You specifically granted to his successor	وَٱلتُّحْفَةَ خَصَصْتَ بِهَا وَصِيَّهُ
And the beloved of the Chosen One	وَحَبِيبَةَ ٱلْمُصْطَفَىٰ

And the spouse of the Approved One	وَقَرِينَةِ ٱلْمُرْتَضَى
And the chief of women	وَسَيِّدَةِ ٱلنِّسَاءِ
And the announcer of good news to the friends	وَمُبَشِّرَةِ ٱلْأَوْلِيَاءِ
The ally of piety and asceticism	حَلِيفَةِ ٱلْوَرَعِ وَٱلزُّهْدِ
And the Apple of the Heaven and Eternity	وَتُفَّاحَةِ ٱلْفِرْدَوْسِ وَٱلْخُلْدِ
She whose birth You have honoured the women of Paradise with	ٱلَّتِي شَرَّفْتَ مَوْلِدَهَا بِنِسَاءِ ٱلْجَنَّةِ
And derived from her the lights of the Imams	وَسَلَلْتَ مِنْهَا أَنْوَارَ ٱلْأَئِمَّةِ
And let down before her the veil of Prophethood	وَأَرْخَيْتَ دُونَهَا حِجَابَ ٱلنُّبُوَّةِ
Oh Allah, send blessings upon her	اَللَّهُمَّ صَلِّ عَلَيْهَا
A blessing that increases her station with You	صَلاةً تَزِيدُ فِي مَحَلِّهَا عِنْدَكَ
And her nobility with You,	وَشَرَفِهَا لَدَيْكَ
And her rank from Your pleasure	وَمَنْزِلَتِهَا مِنْ رِضَاكَ
And convey to her from us greetings and peace	وَبَلِّغْهَا مِنَّا تَحِيَّةً وَسَلَامًا
And grant us from Yourself, for loving her, virtue and excellence	وَآتِنَا مِنْ لَدُنْكَ فِي حُبِّهَا فَضْلاً وَإِحْسَاناً
And mercy and forgiveness	وَرَحْمَةً وَغُفْرَاناً
Indeed, You are the Generous pardoner	إِنَّكَ ذُو ٱلْعَفْوِ ٱلْكَرِيمِ

To lengthen this Ziyarah, I have added her Salawaat

Sayedah Fatima (as)

Oh Allah, send blessings upon the truthful Fatimah, the immaculate	اَللّٰهُمَّ صَلِّ عَلَى ٱلصِّدِّيقَةِ فَاطِمَةَ ٱلزَّكِيَّةِ
The beloved of Your beloved and Your Prophet	حَبِيبَةِ حَبِيبِكَ وَنَبِيِّكَ
And the mother of Your beloved ones and chosen ones	وَأُمِّ أَحِبَّائِكَ وَأَصْفِيَائِكَ
The one You selected and favoured	ٱلَّتِي ٱنْتَجَبْتَهَا وَفَضَّلْتَهَا
And chosen over the women of all the worlds	وَٱخْتَرْتَهَا عَلَىٰ نِسَاءِ ٱلْعَالَمِينَ
Oh Allah, be her advocate against those who wronged her	اَللّٰهُمَّ كُنِ ٱلطَّالِبَ لَهَا مِمَّنْ ظَلَمَهَا
And belittled her rights	وَٱسْتَخَفَّ بِحَقِّهَا
And be the Avenger, oh Allah, for the blood of her children	وَكُنِ ٱلثَّائِرَ ٱللّٰهُمَّ بِدَمِ أَوْلَادِهَا
Oh Allah, just as You made her the mother of the Imams of guidance	اَللّٰهُمَّ وَكَمَا جَعَلْتَهَا أُمَّ أَئِمَّةِ ٱلْهُدَىٰ
And the wife of the owner of the banner	وَحَلِيلَةَ صَاحِبِ ٱللِّوَاءِ
And the noble one in the presence of the highest assembly	وَٱلْكَرِيمَةَ عِنْدَ ٱلْمَلَإِ ٱلْأَعْلَىٰ
So send blessings upon her and her mother	فَصَلِّ عَلَيْهَا وَعَلَىٰ أُمِّهَا
Blessings that honour the face of her father	صَلَاةً تُكْرِمُ بِهَا وَجْهَ أَبِيهَا
Muhammad, may Allah's blessings be upon him and his family	مُحَمَّدٍ صَلَّى ٱللّٰهُ عَلَيْهِ وَآلِهِ
and delight the eyes of her progeny	وَتُقِرُّ بِهَا أَعْيُنَ ذُرِّيَّتِهَا
And convey to them from me, in this hour	وَأَبْلِغْهُمْ عَنِّي فِي هٰذِهِ ٱلسَّاعَةِ
The most excellent greetings and salutations	أَفْضَلَ ٱلتَّحِيَّةِ وَٱلسَّلَامِ

Continuous Calling

Imam Hassan (as)

A man said to Imam Hassan, "Oh son of the Messenger of Allah, I am from your Shias."

"Oh servant of Allah, if you are obedient to our orders and forbiddances, then you spoke the truth. But don't increase upon yourself by claiming a noble rank you are not deserving of. Do not say 'I am from your Shias' but rather say 'I am from those who befriend and love you, and I am hostile to your enemies,' and you would be in goodness, going towards goodness"
– Imam Hassan (as)

(Bihar Al-Anwar, Hub-e-Ali translation, vol 65, page 229)

On 15 Shahr Ramadan to celebrate his birth, and on 7 Safar to commemorate his martyrdom you can recite the following ziyarah.

Monday Ziyarah for Imam Hassan

Peace be on you, oh son of the Messenger of the Lord of the Worlds	اَلسَّلَامُ عَلَيْكَ يَا بْنَ رَسُولِ رَبِّ ٱلْعَالَمِينَ
Peace be on you, oh son of the commander of the faithful	اَلسَّلَامُ عَلَيْكَ يَا بْنَ أَمِيرِ ٱلْمُؤْمِنِينَ
Peace be on you, oh son of Fatima, the radiant	اَلسَّلَامُ عَلَيْكَ يَا بْنَ فَاطِمَةَ ٱلزَّهْرَاءِ
Peace be on you, oh beloved of Allah	اَلسَّلَامُ عَلَيْكَ يَا حَبِيبَ ٱللَّهِ
Peace be on you, oh choice of Allah	اَلسَّلَامُ عَلَيْكَ يَا صِفْوَةَ ٱللَّهِ
Peace be on you, oh trustee of Allah	اَلسَّلَامُ عَلَيْكَ يَا أَمِينَ ٱللَّهِ
Peace be on you, oh proof of Allah	اَلسَّلَامُ عَلَيْكَ يَا حُجَّةَ ٱللَّهِ
Peace be on you, oh light of Allah	اَلسَّلَامُ عَلَيْكَ يَا نُورَ ٱللَّهِ
Peace be on you, oh path of Allah	اَلسَّلَامُ عَلَيْكَ يَا صِرَاطَ ٱللَّهِ
Peace be on you, oh clarity of the judgement of Allah	اَلسَّلَامُ عَلَيْكَ يَا بَيَانَ حُكْمِ ٱللَّهِ

Imam Hassan (as)

Peace be on you, oh supporter of the religion of Allah	ٱلسَّلَامُ عَلَيْكَ يَا نَاصِرَ دِينِ ٱللَّهِ
Peace be on you, oh immaculate chief	ٱلسَّلَامُ عَلَيْكَ أَيُّهَا ٱلسَّيِّدُ ٱلزَّكِيُّ
Peace be on you, oh righteous and faithful	ٱلسَّلَامُ عَلَيْكَ أَيُّهَا ٱلْبَرُّ ٱلْوَفِيُّ
Peace be on you, oh established and trustworthy	ٱلسَّلَامُ عَلَيْكَ أَيُّهَا ٱلْقَائِمُ ٱلْأَمِينُ
Peace be on you, oh knowledgeable of the true interpretation	ٱلسَّلَامُ عَلَيْكَ أَيُّهَا ٱلْعَالِمُ بِٱلتَّأْوِيل
Peace be on you, oh guide and well-guided	ٱلسَّلَامُ عَلَيْكَ أَيُّهَا ٱلْهَادِى ٱلْمَهْدِىُّ
Peace be on you, oh pure and immaculate	ٱلسَّلَامُ عَلَيْكَ أَيُّهَا ٱلطَّاهِرُ ٱلزَّكِيُّ
Peace be on you, oh pious and immaculate	ٱلسَّلَامُ عَلَيْكَ أَيُّهَا ٱلتَّقِيُّ ٱلنَّقِيُّ
Peace be on you, oh authentic truth	ٱلسَّلَامُ عَلَيْكَ أَيُّهَا ٱلْحَقُّ ٱلْحَقِيقُ
Peace be on you, oh martyr and truthful	ٱلسَّلَامُ عَلَيْكَ أَيُّهَا ٱلشَّهِيدُ ٱلصِّدِّيقُ
Peace be on you, oh father of Muhammad, Hasan the son of Ali	ٱلسَّلَامُ عَلَيْكَ يَا أَبَا مُحَمَّدٍ ٱلْحَسَنَ بْنَ عَلِيٍّ
And the mercy of Allah and His blessings upon you	وَرَحْمَةُ ٱللَّهِ وَبَرَكَاتُهُ

From Kamilul Ziyarat

Peace be on you, oh son of the commander of the faithful	ٱلسَّلَامُ عَلَيْكَ يَا بْنَ أَمِيرِ ٱلْمُؤْمِنِينَ
And son of the first Muslim	وَٱبْنَ أَوَّلِ ٱلْمُسْلِمِينَ
And how can you not be like this	وَكَيْفَ لَا تَكُونُ كَذَلِكَ
And you are the descendant of guidance	وَأَنْتَ سَلِيلُ ٱلْهُدَى

Continuous Calling

And ally of piety	وَحَلِيفُ التَّقْوَى
And fifth of the People of the Cloak	وَخَامِسُ أَهْلِ الْكِسَاءِ
The hands of mercy nourished you	غَذَّتْكَ يَدُ الرَّحْمَةِ
And you were raised in the lap of Islam	وَرُبِّيتَ فِي حِجْرِ الْإِسْلَامِ
And nursed from the breast of faith	وَرُضِعْتَ مِنْ ثَدْيِ الْإِيْمَانِ
So you were pure in life	فَطِبْتَ حَيًّا
And pure in death	وَطِبْتَ مَيِّتًا
Except that the soul is not content with your separation	غَيْرَ أَنَّ النَّفْسَ غَيْرُ رَاضِيَةٍ بِفِرَاقِكَ
And not doubting in your life, may Allah have mercy on you	وَلَا شَاكَّةٍ فِي حَيَاتِكَ يَرْحَمُكَ اللَّهُ

Ziyarat Ameenullah

This can be recited for any Imam, simply change the name in the third line

Peace be upon you, oh trustee of Allah in His Earth	اَلسَّلَامُ عَلَيْكَ يَا أَمِينَ اللَّهِ فِي أَرْضِهِ
And His proof upon His servants	وَحُجَّتَهُ عَلَى عِبَادِهِ
Peace be on you oh Hasan the son of Ali, the well-chosen	اَلسَّلَامُ عَلَيْكَ يَا حَسَنَ بْنَ عَلِيٍّ الْمُجْتَبَى
I bear witness that you struggled for Allah, true to His struggle	أَشْهَدُ أَنَّكَ جَاهَدْتَ فِي اللَّهِ حَقَّ جِهَادِهِ
And you acted according to His book	وَعَمِلْتَ بِكِتَابِهِ
And you followed His Prophet's sunnah (way)	وَاتَّبَعْتَ سُنَنَ نَبِيِّهِ

Ziyarat Ameenullah

May Allah's blessings be upon him and his family	صَلَّى اللهُ عَلَيْهِ وَآلِهِ
Until Allah called you to His proximity	حَتَّى دَعَاكَ اللهُ إِلَى جِوَارِهِ
So He took you to Him by His choice	فَقَبَضَكَ إِلَيْهِ بِاخْتِيَارِهِ
And he imposed upon your enemies the proof	وَأَلْزَمَ أَعْدَاءَكَ الْحُجَّةَ
With what you have of the conclusive proofs over all His creation	مَعَ مَا لَكَ مِنَ الْحُجَجِ الْبَالِغَةِ عَلَى جَمِيعِ خَلْقِهِ
Oh Allah, so make my soul content with Your decree	اللَّهُمَّ فَاجْعَلْ نَفْسِي مُطْمَئِنَّةً بِقَدَرِكَ
Pleased with Your judgment	رَاضِيَةً بِقَضَائِكَ
Devoted to Your remembrance and Your supplication	مُولَعَةً بِذِكْرِكَ وَدُعَائِكَ
Loving to the chosen of Your friends	مُحِبَّةً لِصَفْوَةِ أَوْلِيَائِكَ
Beloved in Your earth and Your heaven	مَحْبُوبَةً فِي أَرْضِكَ وَسَمَائِكَ
Patient upon the descent of Your trials	صَابِرَةً عَلَى نُزُولِ بَلَائِكَ
Grateful for the excellence of Your bounties	شَاكِرَةً لِفَوَاضِلِ نَعْمَائِكَ
Mindful of the abundance of Your favours	ذَاكِرَةً لِسَوَابِغِ آلَائِكَ
Longing for the joy of meeting You	مُشْتَاقَةً إِلَى فَرْحَةِ لِقَائِكَ
Preparing piety for the day of Your recompense	مُتَزَوِّدَةً التَّقْوَى لِيَوْمِ جَزَائِكَ
Following the Sunnah (way) of Your friends	مُسْتَنَّةً بِسُنَنِ أَوْلِيَائِكَ
Departing from the manners of Your enemies	مُفَارِقَةً لِأَخْلَاقِ أَعْدَائِكَ

Continuous Calling

Distracted from the world by praising and glorifying You	مَشْغُولَةٌ عَنِ الدُّنْيَا بِحَمْدِكَ وَثَنَائِكَ
Oh Allah, indeed the hearts of the humble to You are overwhelmed with love	اللَّهُمَّ إِنَّ قُلُوبَ الْمُخْبِتِينَ إِلَيْكَ وَالِهَة
And the paths of those who desire You are open	وَسُبُلَ الرَّاغِبِينَ اِلَيْكَ شَارِعَة
And the signs for those who seek You are clear	وَأَعْلَامَ الْقَاصِدِينَ إِلَيْكَ وَاضِحَة
And the hearts of those who recognise You are fearful	وَأَفْئِدَةَ الْعَارِفِينَ مِنْكَ فَازِعَة
And the voices of those who call upon You are ascending	وَأَصْوَاتَ الدَّاعِينَ إِلَيْكَ صَاعِدَة
And the doors of response for them are opened	وَأَبْوَابَ الْإِجَابَةِ لَهُمْ مُفَتَّحَة
And the supplication of whoever confides in You is answered	وَدَعْوَةَ مَنْ نَاجَاكَ مُسْتَجَابَة
And the repentance of whoever turns to You is accepted	وَتَوْبَةَ مَنْ أَنَابَ إِلَيْكَ مَقْبُولَة
And the tear of whoever cries from fear of You is shown mercy	وَعَبْرَةَ مَنْ بَكَى مِنْ خَوْفِكَ مَرْحُومَة
And the relief for whoever seeks Your relief is available	وَالْإِغَاثَةَ لِمَنِ اسْتَغَاثَ بِكَ مَوْجُودَة
And the assistance for whoever seeks Your assistance is freely given	وَالْإِعَانَةَ لِمَنِ اسْتَعَانَ بِكَ مَبْذُولَة
And Your promises to Your servants are fulfilled	وَعِدَاتِكَ لِعِبَادِكَ مُنْجَزَة
And the slip of whoever seeks Your pardon is pardoned	وَزَلَلَ مَنِ اسْتَقَالَكَ مُقَالَة
And the deeds of the doers for You are preserved	وَأَعْمَالَ الْعَامِلِينَ لَدَيْكَ مَحْفُوظَة

Ziyarat Ameenullah

And Your provisions to the creation are descending from You	وَأَرْزَاقُكَ إِلَى الْخَلَائِقِ مِنْ لَدُنْكَ نَازِلَة
And the abundant returns are reaching them	وَعَوَائِدُ الْمَزِيدِ إِلَيْهِمْ وَاصِلَة
And the sins of those seeking forgiveness are forgiven	وَذُنُوبَ الْمُسْتَغْفِرِينَ مَغْفُورَة
And the needs of Your creation with You are fulfilled	وَحَوَائِجُ خَلْقِكَ عِنْدَكَ مَقْضِية
And the rewards of the askers with You are abundant	وَجَوَائِزُ السَّائِلِينَ عِنْدَكَ مُوَفَّرَة
And the returns of increase are continuous	وَعَوَائِدُ الْمَزِيدِ مُتَوَاتِرَة
And the tables of those seeking food are prepared	وَمَوَائِدُ الْمُسْتَطْعِمِينَ مُعَدَّة
And the springs of the thirsty are overflowing	وَمَنَاهِلُ الظِّمَاءِ مُتْرَعَة
Oh Allah, so answer my supplication	اللّٰهُمَّ فَاسْتَجِبْ دُعَائِي
And accept my praise	وَأَقْبَلْ ثَنَائِي
And gather between me and my guardians	وَأَجْمَعْ بَيْنِي وَبَيْنَ أَوْلِيَائِي
By the right of Muhammad and Ali	بِحَقِّ مُحَمَّدٍ وَّعَلِي
And Fatima and Hassan and Hussein	وَفَاطِمَةَ وَٱلْحَسَنِ وَٱلْحُسَيْنِ
Indeed You are the guardian of my bounties	إِنَّكَ وَلِيُّ نَعْمَائِي
And the ultimate goal of my wishes	وَمُنْتَهَىٰ مُنَايَ
And the end of my hope in my return and my abode	وَغَايَةُ رَجَائِي فِي مُنْقَلَبِي وَمَثْوَايَ
You are my God and my Chief and my Master	أَنْتَ إِلٰهِي وَسَيِّدِي وَمَوْلَايَ

Continuous Calling

Forgive our friends	إِغْفِرْ لِأَوْلِيَائِنَا
And restrain our enemies from us	وَكُفَّ عَنَّا أَعْدَائَنَا
And distract them from harming us	وَاشْغَلْهُمْ عَنْ أَذَانَا
And make manifest the word of truth	وَأَظْهِرْ كَلِمَةَ الْحَقِّ
And make it supreme	وَاجْعَلْهَا الْعُلْيَا
And nullify the word of falsehood	وَأَدْحِضْ كَلِمَةَ الْبَاطِلِ
And make it the lowest	وَاجْعَلْهَا السُّفْلَى
Indeed You have power over everything	إِنَّكَ عَلَى كُلِّ شَيْءٍ قَدِيرٌ

Imam Hussein (as)

"There is no servant whose eyes drops a drop regarding us, or his eye fills up with tears regarding us, except that Allah would settle him in Paradise forever" – Imam Hussein (as)

(Bihar Al-Anwar, Hub-e-Ali translation, vol 44, page 333)

On 3 Sha'ban to celebrate his birth, and on 10 Muharram to commemorate his martyrdom, and on every occasion, you can recite the following ziyarah. This is Ziyarah Nahiya, it is the Ziyarah of Imam Mahdi (afs) in Karbala.

Ziyarat Ashura is also available afterwards at the end of the chapter.

Peace be upon Adam, the chosen of Allah from His creation	اَلسَّلَامُ عَلَى آدَمَ صِفْوَةِ اللَّهِ مِنْ خَلِيقَتِهِ
Peace be upon Seth, the friend of Allah and His choice	اَلسَّلَامُ عَلَى شَيْثٍ وَلِيِّ اللَّهِ وَخِيَرَتِهِ
Peace be upon Enoch (Idris), who stood for Allah with His proof	اَلسَّلَامُ عَلَى إِدْرِيسَ الْقَائِمِ لِلَّهِ بِحُجَّتِهِ
Peace be upon Noah, whose call was answered	اَلسَّلَامُ عَلَى نُوحٍ الْمُجَابِ فِى دَعْوَتِهِ
Peace be upon Hud, supported by Allah with His assistance	اَلسَّلَامُ عَلَى هُودٍ الْمَمْدُودِ مِنَ اللَّهِ بِمَعُونَتِهِ
Peace be upon Salih, who Allah crowned with His nobility	اَلسَّلَامُ عَلَى صَالِحٍ الَّذِى تَوَّجَهُ اللَّهُ بِكَرَامَتِهِ
Peace be upon Abraham, who Allah bestowed with His friendship	اَلسَّلَامُ عَلَى إِبْرَاهِيمَ الَّذِى حَبَاهُ اللَّهُ بِخُلَّتِهِ
Peace be upon Ishmael, who Allah ransomed with a great sacrifice from His Paradise	اَلسَّلَامُ عَلَى إِسْمَاعِيلَ الَّذِى فَدَاهُ اللَّهُ بِذِبْحٍ عَظِيمٍ مِنْ جَنَّتِهِ

Peace be upon Isaac, in whose progeny Allah placed prophethood	اَلسَّلَامُ عَلَى إِسْحَاقَ الَّذِي جَعَلَ اللَّهُ النُّبُوَّةَ فِي ذُرِّيَّتِهِ
Peace be upon Jacob, who Allah restored his sight by His mercy	اَلسَّلَامُ عَلَى يَعْقُوبَ الَّذِي رَدَّ اللَّهُ عَلَيْهِ بَصَرَهُ بِرَحْمَتِهِ
Peace be upon Joseph, who Allah rescued from the well by His greatness	اَلسَّلَامُ عَلَى يُوسُفَ الَّذِي نَجَّاهُ اللَّهُ مِنَ الْجُبِّ بِعَظَمَتِهِ
Peace be upon Moses, the one Allah split the sea for him with His power	اَلسَّلَامُ عَلَى مُوسَى الَّذِي فَلَقَ اللَّهُ الْبَحْرَ لَهُ بِقُدْرَتِهِ
Peace be upon Aaron, who Allah distinguished with his prophethood	اَلسَّلَامُ عَلَى هَارُونَ الَّذِي خَصَّهُ اللَّهُ بِنُبُوَّتِهِ
Peace be upon Jethro (Shu'aib), who Allah supported against his nation	اَلسَّلَامُ عَلَى شُعَيْبٍ الَّذِي نَصَرَهُ اللَّهُ عَلَى أُمَّتِهِ
Peace be upon David, who Allah forgave his mistake (Quran 38:23-24)	اَلسَّلَامُ عَلَى دَاوُدَ الَّذِي تَابَ اللَّهُ عَلَيْهِ مِنْ خَطِيئَتِهِ
Peace be upon Solomon, who the Jinn were subdued for by His might	اَلسَّلَامُ عَلَى سُلَيْمَانَ الَّذِي ذَلَّتْ لَهُ الْجِنُّ بِعِزَّتِهِ
Peace be upon Job (Ayyub), who Allah cured from his illness	اَلسَّلَامُ عَلَى أَيُّوبَ الَّذِي شَفَاهُ اللَّهُ مِنْ عِلَّتِهِ
Peace be upon Jonah (Yunus), for who Allah fulfilled the promise He made	اَلسَّلَامُ عَلَى يُونُسَ الَّذِي أَنْجَزَ اللَّهُ لَهُ مَضْمُونَ عِدَتِهِ
Peace be upon Ezra (Uzair), who Allah brought to life after his death	اَلسَّلَامُ عَلَى عُزَيْرٍ الَّذِي أَحْيَاهُ اللَّهُ بَعْدَ مِيتَتِهِ

Imam Hussein (as)

Peace be upon Zechariah, the patient one in his tribulations	اَلسَّلَامُ عَلَى زَكَرِيَّا الصَّابِرِ فِى مِحْنَتِهِ
Peace be upon John (Yahya), who Allah brought near by his martyrdom	اَلسَّلَامُ عَلَى يَحْيَى الَّذِى أَزْلَفَهُ اللَّهُ بِشَهَادَتِهِ
Peace be upon Jesus, the spirit of Allah and His word	اَلسَّلَامُ عَلَى عِيسَى رُوحِ اللَّهِ وَكَلِمَتِهِ
Peace be upon Muhammad, beloved of Allah and His chosen one	اَلسَّلَامُ عَلَى مُحَمَّدٍ حَبِيبِ اللَّهِ وَصِفْوَتِهِ
Peace be upon the commander of the faithful, Ali the son of Abu Talib, distinguished by his brotherhood	اَلسَّلَامُ عَلَى أَمِيرِ الْمُؤْمِنِينَ عَلِيِّ بْنِ أَبِي طَالِبٍ الْمَخْصُوصِ بِأُخُوَّتِهِ
Peace be upon Fatima, the radiant, his daughter	اَلسَّلَامُ عَلَى فَاطِمَةَ الزَّهْرَاءِ ابْنَتِهِ
Peace be upon Abu Muhammad Hasan, the executor of his father, and his successor	اَلسَّلَامُ عَلَى أَبِي مُحَمَّدٍ الْحَسَنِ وَصِيِّ أَبِيهِ وَخَلِيفَتِهِ
Peace be upon al-Husain, who sacrificed himself by the blood of his heart	اَلسَّلَامُ عَلَى الْحُسَيْنِ الَّذِى سَمَحَتْ نَفْسُهُ بِمُهْجَتِهِ
Peace be upon him, who obeyed Allah secretly and openly	اَلسَّلَامُ عَلَى مَنْ أَطَاعَ اللَّهَ فِى سِرِّهِ وَعَلَانِيَتِهِ
Peace be upon him in whose soil Allah has placed the cure	اَلسَّلَامُ عَلَى مَنْ جَعَلَ اللَّهُ الشِّفَاءَ فِى تُرْبَتِهِ
Peace be upon the one under whose dome is answers (to supplications)	اَلسَّلَامُ عَلَى مَنِ الْإِجَابَةُ تَحْتَ قُبَّتِهِ
Peace be upon him whose descendants are the Imams	اَلسَّلَامُ عَلَى مَنِ الْأَئِمَّةُ مِنْ ذُرِّيَّتِهِ
Peace be upon the son of the seal of the prophets	اَلسَّلَامُ عَلَى ابْنِ خَاتَمِ الْأَنْبِيَاءِ

Continuous Calling

Peace be upon the son of the chief of the successors	اَلسَّلامُ عَلَى ابْنِ سَيِّدِ الأَوْصِياءِ
Peace be upon the son of Fatima, the radiant	اَلسَّلامُ عَلَى ابْنِ فاطِمَةَ الزَّهْراءِ
Peace be upon the son of Khadija, the great	اَلسَّلامُ عَلَى ابْنِ خَديجَةَ الْكُبْرى
Peace be upon the son of the Lote Tree of the Utmost Boundary	اَلسَّلامُ عَلَى ابْنِ سِدْرَةِ الْمُنْتَهى
Peace be upon the son of the Garden of refuge	اَلسَّلامُ عَلَى ابْنِ جَنَّةِ الْمَأْوى
Peace be upon the son of Zamzam and al-Safaa	اَلسَّلامُ عَلَى ابْنِ زَمْزَمَ وَالصَّفا
Peace be upon him, who was wrapped in blood	اَلسَّلامُ عَلَى الْمُرَمَّلِ بِالدِّماءِ
Peace be upon him, whose tents were gutted	اَلسَّلامُ عَلَى الْمَهْتُوكِ الْخِباءِ
Peace be upon the fifth of the companions of the Cloak	اَلسَّلامُ عَلَى خامِسِ أَصْحابِ الْكِساءِ
Peace be upon the strangest of the strangers	اَلسَّلامُ عَلَى غَريبِ الْغُرَباءِ
Peace be upon the martyr of the martyrs	اَلسَّلامُ عَلَى شَهيدِ الشُّهَداءِ
Peace be upon him, slain by the false claimants	اَلسَّلامُ عَلَى قَتيلِ الأَدْعِياءِ
Peace be upon the resident of Karbala	اَلسَّلامُ عَلَى ساكِنِ كَرْبَلاءَ
Peace be upon the one for who the heavenly Angels wept	اَلسَّلامُ عَلَى مَنْ بَكَتْهُ مَلائِكَةُ السَّماءِ
Peace be upon the one whose descendants are the pure	اَلسَّلامُ عَلَى مَنْ ذُرِّيَّتُهُ الأَزْكِياءُ
Peace be upon the leader of the religion	اَلسَّلامُ عَلَى يَعْسُوبِ الدّينِ

Imam Hussein (as)

Peace be upon the abode of the proofs	اَلسَّلامُ عَلَى مَنازِلِ الْبَراهينِ
Peace be upon the Imams, the masters	اَلسَّلامُ عَلَى الْأَئِمَّةِ السَّاداتِ
Peace be upon the bloodstained chests.	اَلسَّلامُ عَلَى الْجُيُوبِ الْمُضَرَّجاتِ
Peace be upon the withered lips	اَلسَّلامُ عَلَى الشِّفاهِ الذَّابِلاتِ
Peace be upon the uprooted souls	اَلسَّلامُ عَلَى النُّفُوسِ الْمُصْطَلَماتِ
Peace be upon the snatched spirits	اَلسَّلامُ عَلَى الْأَرْواحِ الْمُخْتَلَساتِ
Peace be upon the naked bodies	اَلسَّلامُ عَلَى الْأَجْسادِ الْعارِياتِ
Peace be upon the pale frames	اَلسَّلامُ عَلَى الْجُسُومِ الشَّاحِباتِ
Peace be upon the flowing blood	اَلسَّلامُ عَلَى الدِّماءِ السَّائِلاتِ
Peace be upon the severed limbs	اَلسَّلامُ عَلَى الْأَعْضاءِ الْمُقَطَّعاتِ
Peace be upon the heads raised upon spears	اَلسَّلامُ عَلَى الرُّؤُوسِ الْمُشالاتِ
Peace be upon the exposed women	اَلسَّلامُ عَلَى النِّسْوَةِ الْبارِزاتِ
Peace be upon the proof of the Lord of the worlds	اَلسَّلامُ عَلَى حُجَّةِ رَبِّ الْعالَمينَ
Peace be upon you and upon your pure fathers	اَلسَّلامُ عَلَيْكَ وَعَلَى آبائِكَ الطَّاهِرينَ
Peace be upon you and upon your martyred sons	اَلسَّلامُ عَلَيْكَ وَعَلَى أَبْنائِكَ الْمُسْتَشْهَدينَ
Peace be upon you and upon your supporting progeny	اَلسَّلامُ عَلَيْكَ وَعَلَى ذُرِّيَّتِكَ النَّاصِرينَ
Peace be upon you and upon the accompanying Angels	اَلسَّلامُ عَلَيْكَ وَعَلَى الْمَلائِكَةِ الْمُضاجِعينَ

Peace be upon the oppressed killed one	اَلسَّلَامُ عَلَى الْقَتِيلِ الْمَظْلُومِ
Peace be upon his poisoned brother	اَلسَّلَامُ عَلَى أَخِيهِ الْمَسْمُومِ
Peace be upon Ali al-Akbar	اَلسَّلَامُ عَلَى عَلِيٍّ الْكَبِيرِ
Peace be upon the suckling infant	اَلسَّلَامُ عَلَى الرَّضِيعِ الصَّغِيرِ
Peace be upon the stripped bodies	اَلسَّلَامُ عَلَى الْأَبْدَانِ السَّلِيبَةِ
Peace be upon the nearby (and estranged) family	اَلسَّلَامُ عَلَى الْعِتْرَةِ الْقَرِيبَةِ [الْغَرِيبَةِ]
Peace be upon those slain in the desert	اَلسَّلَامُ عَلَى الْمُجَدَّلِينَ فِي الْفَلَوَاتِ
Peace be upon those left far from their homeland	اَلسَّلَامُ عَلَى النَّازِحِينَ عَنِ الْأَوْطَانِ
Peace be upon those buried without shrouds	اَلسَّلَامُ عَلَى الْمَدْفُونِينَ بِلَا أَكْفَانٍ
Peace be upon the heads separated from the bodies	اَلسَّلَامُ عَلَى الرُّؤُوسِ الْمُفَرَّقَةِ عَنِ الْأَبْدَانِ
Peace be upon the steadfast, patient one	اَلسَّلَامُ عَلَى الْمُحْتَسِبِ الصَّابِرِ
Peace be upon the oppressed one without any supporter	اَلسَّلَامُ عَلَى الْمَظْلُومِ بِلَا نَاصِرٍ
Peace be upon the resident of the pure soil	اَلسَّلَامُ عَلَى سَاكِنِ التُّرْبَةِ الزَّاكِيَةِ
Peace be upon the possessor of the lofty dome	اَلسَّلَامُ عَلَى صَاحِبِ الْقُبَّةِ السَّامِيَةِ
Peace be upon him, who the Majestic purified	اَلسَّلَامُ عَلَى مَنْ طَهَّرَهُ الْجَلِيلُ
Peace be upon the one who Gabriel prided himself with	اَلسَّلَامُ عَلَى مَنِ افْتَخَرَ بِهِ جَبْرَئِيلُ
Peace be upon the one who Michael cooed to in the cradle	اَلسَّلَامُ عَلَى مَنْ نَاغَاهُ فِي الْمَهْدِ مِيكَائِيلُ

Imam Hussein (as)

Peace be upon the one whose security was violated	اَلسَّلامُ عَلَى مَنْ نُكِثَتْ ذِمَّتُهُ
Peace be upon the one whose sanctity was violated	اَلسَّلامُ عَلَى مَنْ هُتِكَتْ حُرْمَتُهُ
Peace be upon the one whose blood was unjustly shed	اَلسَّلامُ عَلَى مَنْ أُرِيقَ بِالظُّلْمِ دَمُهُ
Peace be upon the one washed with the blood of wounds	اَلسَّلامُ عَلَى الْمُغَسَّلِ بِدَمِ الْجِراحِ
Peace be upon the one made to drink from the cups of spears	اَلسَّلامُ عَلَى الْمُجَرَّعِ بِكَأْساتِ الرِّماحِ
Peace be upon the violated one whose blood was considered lawful	اَلسَّلامُ عَلَى الْمُضامِ الْمُسْتَباحِ
Peace be upon the one whose throat was slit among the people	اَلسَّلامُ عَلَى الْمَنْحُورِ فِي الْوَرى
Peace be upon the one who the villagers buried	اَلسَّلامُ عَلَى مَنْ دَفَنَهُ أَهْلُ الْقُرى
Peace be upon the one whose arteries were severed	اَلسَّلامُ عَلَى الْمَقْطُوعِ الْوَتِينِ
Peace be upon the defender without any helper	اَلسَّلامُ عَلَى الْمُحامِى بِلا مُعِينٍ
Peace be upon the dyed grey hair	اَلسَّلامُ عَلَى الشَّيْبِ الْخَضِيبِ
Peace be upon the dusty cheek	اَلسَّلامُ عَلَى الْخَدِّ التَّرِيبِ
Peace be upon the stripped body	اَلسَّلامُ عَلَى الْبَدَنِ السَّلِيبِ
Peace be upon the mouth struck with a rod	اَلسَّلامُ عَلَى الثَّغْرِ الْمَقْرُوعِ بِالْقَضِيبِ
Peace be upon the raised head	اَلسَّلامُ عَلَى الرَّأْسِ الْمَرْفُوعِ

Continuous Calling

Peace be upon the naked corpses in the desert, torn at by the prowling wolves, and visited by the ferocious beasts

ٱلسَّلَامُ عَلَى الْأَجْسَامِ الْعَارِيَةِ فِي الْفَلَوَاتِ تَنْهَشُهَا الذِّئَابُ الْعَادِيَاتُ وَتَخْتَلِفُ إِلَيْهَا السِّبَاعُ الضَّارِيَاتُ

Peace be upon you oh my master, and upon the Angels fluttering around your dome

ٱلسَّلَامُ عَلَيْكَ يَا مَوْلَايَ وَعَلَى الْمَلَائِكَةِ الْمُرَفْرِفِينَ حَوْلَ قُبَّتِكَ

Circling your soil, circumambulating your courtyard, and arrive for your visitation

الْحَاقِّينَ بِتُرْبَتِكَ الطَّائِفِينَ بِعَرْصَتِكَ الْوَارِدِينَ لِزِيَارَتِكَ

Peace be upon you for indeed I have aimed towards you and hoped for success with you

ٱلسَّلَامُ عَلَيْكَ فَإِنِّي قَصَدْتُ إِلَيْكَ وَرَجَوْتُ الْفَوْزَ لَدَيْكَ

Peace be upon you the greeting of one who recognizes your sanctity, is sincere in your allegiance, seeks nearness to Allah through love for you, and disavows your enemies

ٱلسَّلَامُ عَلَيْكَ سَلَامَ الْعَارِفِ بِحُرْمَتِكَ الْمُخْلِصِ فِي وِلَايَتِكَ الْمُتَقَرِّبِ إِلَى اللَّهِ بِمَحَبَّتِكَ الْبَرِيءِ مِنْ أَعْدَائِكَ

The greeting of one whose heart is wounded by your calamity, and whose tears pour when you are mentioned

سَلَامَ مَنْ قَلْبُهُ بِمُصَابِكَ مَقْرُوحٌ وَدَمْعُهُ عِنْدَ ذِكْرِكَ مَسْفُوحٌ

The greeting of the agonized, the grief-stricken, the dazed, the submissive

سَلَامَ الْمَفْجُوعِ الْحَزِينِ الْوَالِهِ الْمُسْتَكِينِ

The greeting of one who, had he been with you at Tufuf, would have shielded you with himself from the sharpness of the swords and sacrificed his entrails before you

سَلَامَ مَنْ لَوْ كَانَ مَعَكَ بِالطُّفُوفِ لَوَقَاكَ بِنَفْسِهِ حَدَّ السُّيُوفِ وَبَذَلَ حُشَاشَتَهُ دُونَكَ لِلْحُتُوفِ

And would have struggled between your hands, and supported you against those who transgressed against you, and ransomed for you with his soul, body, wealth, and children	وَجَاهَدَ بَيْنَ يَدَيْكَ وَنَصَرَكَ عَلَى مَنْ بَغَى عَلَيْكَ وَفَدَاكَ بِرُوحِهِ وَجَسَدِهِ وَمَالِهِ وَوَلَدِهِ
And his soul is a ransom for your soul	وَرُوحُهُ لِرُوحِكَ فِدَاءٌ
And his family is a shield for your family	وَأَهْلُهُ لِأَهْلِكَ وِقَاءٌ
So if the ages delay me and fate prevents me from supporting you	فَلَئِنْ أَخَّرَتْنِي الدُّهُورُ وَعَاقَنِي عَنْ نَصْرِكَ الْمَقْدُورُ
And as I could not fight those who fought you, nor show hostility to those who showed hostility to you	وَلَمْ أَكُنْ لِمَنْ حَارَبَكَ مُحَارِباً وَلِمَنْ نَصَبَ لَكَ الْعَدَاوَةَ مُنَاصِباً
Then I will lament for you morning and evening, and I will cry blood instead of tears in grief over you, and in regret over what befell you, and in yearning	فَلَأَنْدُبَنَّكَ صَبَاحاً وَمَسَاءً وَلَأَبْكِيَنَّ لَكَ بَدَلَ الدُّمُوعِ دَماً حَسْرَةً عَلَيْكَ وَتَأَسُّفاً عَلَى مَا دَهَاكَ وَتَلَهُّفاً
Until I die from the agony of the calamity and the choking depression	حَتَّى أَمُوتَ بِلَوْعَةِ الْمُصَابِ وَغُصَّةِ الِاكْتِئَابِ
I bear witness that you certainly established prayer, gave charity	أَشْهَدُ أَنَّكَ قَدْ أَقَمْتَ الصَّلَاةَ وَآتَيْتَ الزَّكَاةَ
Enjoined good and forbade evil and transgression	وَأَمَرْتَ بِالْمَعْرُوفِ وَنَهَيْتَ عَنِ الْمُنْكَرِ وَالْعُدْوَانِ
And you obeyed Allah and did not disobey Him, and you held fast to Him and His rope	وَأَطَعْتَ اللَّهَ وَمَا عَصَيْتَهُ وَتَمَسَّكْتَ بِهِ وَبِحَبْلِهِ

Continuous Calling

So you pleased Him, feared Him, were attentive and responded to Him	فَأَرْضَيْتَهُ وَخَشِيتَهُ وَرَاقَبْتَهُ وَاسْتَجَبْتَهُ
And you established the traditions and extinguished the discord	وَسَنَنْتَ السُّنَنَ وَأَطْفَأْتَ الْفِتَنَ
Called towards righteousness, clarified the paths of correctness, and truly struggled in the way of Allah	وَدَعَوْتَ إِلَى الرَّشَادِ وَأَوْضَحْتَ سُبُلَ السَّدَادِ وَجَاهَدْتَ فِي اللهِ حَقَّ الْجِهَادِ
And you were obedient to Allah	وَكُنْتَ للهِ طَائِعاً
And a follower of your grandfather Muhammad, peace be upon him and his family	وَلِجَدِّكَ مُحَمَّدٍ صَلَّى اللهُ عَلَيْهِ وَآلِهِ تَابِعاً
And a listener to the words of your father	وَلِقَوْلِ أَبِيكَ سَامِعاً
And one who rushed towards the will of your brother	وَإِلَى وَصِيَّةِ أَخِيكَ مُسَارِعاً
And an upholder of the religion, and a subduer of tyranny	وَلِعِمَادِ الدِّينِ رَافِعاً وَلِلطُّغْيَانِ قَامِعاً
And one who confronts the tyrants, and advises the community	وَلِلطُّغَاةِ مُقَارِعاً وَلِلْأُمَّةِ نَاصِحاً
And one who swims in the depths of death	وَفِي غَمَرَاتِ الْمَوْتِ سَابِحاً
And struggles against the wicked and upholds the arguments of Allah	وَلِلْفُسَّاقِ مُكَافِحاً وَبِحُجَجِ اللهِ قَائِماً
Merciful by Islam towards the Muslims	وَلِلْإِسْلَامِ وَالْمُسْلِمِينَ رَاحِماً
And a supporter of truth and patient in trials	وَلِلْحَقِّ نَاصِراً وَعِنْدَ الْبَلَاءِ صَابِراً
And a nourisher for the religion, and a defender of its domain	وَلِلدِّينِ كَالِئاً وَعَنْ حَوْزَتِهِ مُرَامِياً
You safeguard guidance and support it	تَحُوطُ الْهُدَى وَتَنْصُرُهُ
And you spread justice and propagate it	وَتَبْسُطُ الْعَدْلَ وَتَنْشُرُهُ

Imam Hussein (as)

And you support the religion and manifest it	وَتَنْصُرُ الدّينَ وَتُظْهِرُهُ
And you restrain the frivolous and deter him	وَتَكُفُّ الْعابِثَ وَتَزْجُرُهُ
And you take for the lowly from the noble	وَتَأْخُذُ لِلدَّنِيِّ مِنَ الشَّرِيفِ
And you equalise judgement between the strong and the weak	وَتُساوى فِى الْحُكْمِ بَيْنَ الْقَوِيِّ وَالضَّعِيفِ
You were the spring of the orphans, the protection of humanity, the honour of Islam	كُنْتَ رَبِيعَ الْأَيْتامِ وَعِصْمَةَ الْأَنامِ وَعِزَّ الْإِسْلامِ
And the essence of judgments and ally of blessings	وَمَعْدِنَ الْأَحْكامِ وَحَلِيفَ الْإِنْعامِ
Following the paths of your grandfather and father	سالِكاً طَرائِقَ [فى طريقَةِ] جَدِّكَ وَأَبِيكَ
Resembling your brother in will	مُشْبِهاً فِى الْوَصِيَّةِ لِأَخِيكَ
Faithful to covenants, praised in noble character traits	وَفِىَّ الذِّمَمِ رَضِىَّ الشِّيَمِ
Outwardly generous, spending the darkness in prayer	ظاهِرَ الْكَرَمِ مُتَهَجِّداً فِى الظُّلَمِ
Upright in ways, noble in manners, great in recorded deeds	قَوِيمَ الطَّرائِقِ كَرِيمَ الْخَلائِقِ عَظِيمَ السَّوابِقِ
Noble in lineage, lofty in ancestry, elevated in ranks	شَرِيفَ النَّسَبِ مُنِيفَ الْحَسَبِ رَفِيعَ الرُّتَبِ
Possessing many virtues, praiseworthy manners, abundant in gifts	كَثِيرَ الْمَناقِبِ مَحْمُودَ الضَّرائِبِ جَزِيلَ الْمَواهِبِ

Continuous Calling

Forbearing, rightly-guided, repentant, generous, knowledgeable, firm	حَلِيمٌ رَشِيدٌ مُنِيبٌ جَوادٌ عَلِيمٌ شَدِيدٌ
An Imam, a martyr, yearning, repentant, beloved, awe-inspiring	إمامٌ شَهِيدٌ أَوّاهٌ مُنِيبٌ حَبِيبٌ مَهِيبٌ
You were to the Messenger, peace be upon him and his family, a son,	كُنْتَ لِلرَّسُولِ صَلَّى اللَّهُ عَلَيْهِ وَآلِهِ وَلَدَاً
And for the Quran, a supporter [saviour]	وَلِلْقُرْءانِ سَنَداً [مُنْقِذاً]
And a pillar for the nation	وَلِلْأُمَّةِ عَضُداً
And diligent in obedience	وَفِي الطَّاعَةِ مُجْتَهِداً
Preserving the covenant and pledge	حَافِظاً لِلْعَهْدِ وَالْمِيثَاقِ
Shunning the paths of the immoral	نَاكِباً عَنْ سُبُلِ الْفُسَّاقِ
Expending your utmost effort	[وَ] بَاذِلاً لِلْمَجْهُودِ
Prolonging bowings and prostrations	طَوِيلَ الرُّكُوعِ وَالسُّجُودِ
Renouncing the world with the renunciation of one departing from it	زَاهِداً فِي الدُّنْيَا زُهْدَ الرَّاحِلِ عَنْها
Looking at it with the eyes of one estranged from it	نَاظِراً إِلَيْهَا بِعَيْنِ الْمُسْتَوْحِشِينَ مِنْها
Your hopes were restrained from it	آمَالُكَ عَنْها مَكْفُوفَةٌ
And your determination diverted from its adornments	وَهِمَّتُكَ عَنْ زِينَتِهَا مَصْرُوفَةٌ
And your glances were averted from its joys	وَأَلْحَاظُكَ عَنْ بَهْجَتِهَا مَطْرُوفَةٌ
And your desire for the Hereafter was well-known	وَرَغْبَتُكَ فِي الْآخِرَةِ مَعْرُوفَةٌ
Until oppression extended its arm	حَتَّى إِذَا الْجَوْرُ مَدَّ بَاعَهُ
And injustice removed its mask	وَأَسْفَرَ الظُّلْمُ قِنَاعَهُ

Imam Hussein (as)

And misguidance called its followers	وَدَعَا الْغَيُّ أَتْبَاعَهُ
While you were dwelling in the sanctuary of your grandfather	وَأَنْتَ فِى حَرَمِ جَدِّكَ قَاطِنٌ
And detached from the oppressors	وَلِلظَّالِمِينَ مُبَايِنٌ
Sitting in the house and the prayer niche	جَلِيسُ الْبَيْتِ وَالْمِحْرَابِ
Isolated from pleasures and desires	مُعْتَزِلٌ عَنِ اللَّذَّاتِ وَالشَّهَوَاتِ
Denouncing evil with your heart and tongue as much as you were able and was possible	تُنْكِرُ الْمُنْكَرَ بِقَلْبِكَ وَلِسَانِكَ عَلَى حَسَبِ طَاقَتِكَ وَإِمْكَانِكَ
Then knowledge required you due to its disavowal	ثُمَّ اقْتَضَاكَ الْعِلْمُ لِلْإِنْكَارِ
And it became necessary for you to struggle against the wicked	وَلَزِمَكَ [أَلْزَمَكَ] أَنْ تُجَاهِدَ الْفُجَّارَ
So you set out with your children, families, Shias, and friends	فَسِرْتَ فِى أَوْلَادِكَ وَأَهَالِيكَ وَشِيعَتِكَ وَمَوَالِيكَ
Proclaiming the truth and clear proofs	وَصَدَعْتَ بِالْحَقِّ وَالْبَيِّنَةِ
And invited towards Allah with wisdom and good advice	وَدَعَوْتَ إِلَى اللَّهِ بِالْحِكْمَةِ وَالْمَوْعِظَةِ الْحَسَنَةِ
And commanded the establishment of the limits, and obedience to the Worshipped One	وَأَمَرْتَ بِإِقَامَةِ الْحُدُودِ وَالطَّاعَةِ لِلْمَعْبُودِ
And you prohibited indecencies and transgression	وَنَهَيْتَ عَنِ الْخَبَائِثِ وَالطُّغْيَانِ
But, they confronted you with injustice and aggression	وَوَاجَهُوكَ بِالظُّلْمِ وَالْعُدْوَانِ
So you resisted them after hinting to them (warning them) and confirming the proofs against them	فَجَاهَدْتَهُمْ بَعْدَ الْإِيعَازِ لَهُمْ [الْإِيعَادِ إِلَيْهِمْ] وَتَأْكِيدِ الْحُجَّةِ عَلَيْهِمْ

Continuous Calling

But they violated your protection and their allegiance to you	فَنَكَثُوا ذِمَامَكَ وَبَيْعَتَكَ
And angered your Lord and your grandfather	وَأَسْخَطُوا رَبَّكَ وَجَدَّكَ
And they initiated war against you	وَبَدَؤُوكَ بِالْحَرْبِ
So you stood firm to stabs and strikes	فَثَبَتَّ لِلطَّعْنِ وَالضَّرْبِ
Crushed the troops of the wicked, and stormed the cloud of dust	وَطَحَنْتَ جُنُودَ الْفُجَّارِ وَاقْتَحَمْتَ قَسْطَلَ الْغُبَارِ
Fighting with Dhul-fiqar as if you were Ali, the chosen one	مُجَالِداً بِذِى الْفَقَارِ كَأَنَّكَ عَلِيٌّ الْمُخْتَارُ
So when they saw you firm, neither afraid nor nervous	فَلَمَّا رَأَوْكَ ثَابِتَ الْجَأْشِ غَيْرَ خَائِفٍ وَلَا خَاشٍ
They set up deceitful traps, and fought you with their scheming and evil	نَصَبُوا لَكَ غَوَائِلَ مَكْرِهِمْ وَقَاتَلُوكَ بِكَيْدِهِمْ وَشَرِّهِمْ
And the accursed one commanded his troops, and prevented you from water and its access	وَأَمَرَ اللَّعِينُ جُنُودَهُ فَمَنَعُوكَ الْمَاءَ وَوُرُودَهُ
They rushed to battle you and descended swiftly upon you	وَنَاجَزُوكَ الْقِتَالَ وَعَاجَلُوكَ النِّزَالَ
And showered you with arrows and spears	وَرَشَقُوكَ بِالسِّهَامِ وَالنِّبَالِ
And extended towards you the violent hands	وَبَسَطُوا إِلَيْكَ أَكُفَّ الِاصْطِلَامِ
They neither respected any obligation to you, nor did they consider it a sin to kill your friends or loot your possessions	وَلَمْ يَرْعَوْا لَكَ ذِمَاماً وَلَا رَاقَبُوا فِيكَ أَثَاماً فِى قَتْلِهِمْ أَوْلِيَاءَكَ وَنَهْبِهِمْ رِحَالَكَ

Imam Hussein (as)

You were in the front line of the dusty chaos and enduring harm	وَأَنْتَ مُقَدَّمٌ فِي الْهَبَوَاتِ وَمُحْتَمِلٌ لِلْأَذِيَاتِ
Indeed the angels of the heavens were astonished by your patience	قَدْ عَجِبَتْ مِنْ صَبْرِكَ مَلَائِكَةُ السَّمَاوَاتِ
So they surrounded you from every side	فَأَحْدَقُوا بِكَ مِنْ كُلِّ الْجِهَاتِ
And afflicted you with wounds	وَأَثْخَنُوكَ بِالْجِرَاحِ
And prevented you from returning	وَحَالُوا بَيْنَكَ وَبَيْنَ الرَّوَاحِ
And you had no supporter remaining	وَلَمْ يَبْقَ لَكَ نَاصِرٌ
And you were expectant and patient	وَأَنْتَ مُحْتَسِبٌ صَابِرٌ
Defending your women and children	تَذُبُّ عَنْ نِسْوَتِكَ وَأَوْلَادِكَ
Until they knocked you from your horse	حَتَّى نَكَسُوكَ عَنْ جَوَادِكَ
So you fell to the ground, wounded	فَهَوَيْتَ إِلَى الْأَرْضِ جَرِيحاً
Horses trampled you with their hooves	تَطَؤُكَ الْخُيُولُ بِحَوَافِرِهَا
And tyrants overpowered you with their swords	وَتَعْلُوكَ الطُّغَاةُ بِبَوَاتِرِهَا
Your forehead was already drenched in sweat for death	قَدْ رَشَحَ لِلْمَوْتِ جَبِينُكَ
And your left and right were clenching and unclenching	وَاخْتَلَفَتْ بِالْإِنْقِبَاضِ وَالْإِنْبِسَاطِ شِمَالُكَ وَيَمِينُكَ
Secretly glancing upon your caravan and home	تُدِيرُ طَرْفاً خَفِيّاً إِلَى رَحْلِكَ وَبَيْتِكَ
While you were preoccupied, away from your children and families	وَقَدْ شُغِلْتَ بِنَفْسِكَ عَنْ وُلْدِكَ وَأَهَالِيكَ

Continuous Calling

And your horse darted away aimlessly, headed towards your tents, neighing and weeping	وَأَسْرَعَ فَرَسُكَ شارِداً إلى خِيامِكَ قاصِداً مُحَمْحِماً باكِياً
So when the women saw your horse disgraced	فَلَمَّا رَأَيْنَ النِّساءُ جَوادَكَ مُخْزِياً
And saw your saddle twisted on it	وَنَظَرْنَ سَرْجَكَ عَلَيْهِ مَلْوِيّاً
They emerged from the tents	بَرَزْنَ مِنَ الخُدُورِ
Dishevelling their hair	ناشِراتِ الشُّعُورِ
Striking their faces and cheeks, unveiled	عَلَى الخُدُودِ لاطِماتِ الْوُجُوهِ سافِراتٍ
Wailing and lamenting	وَبِالعَويلِ داعِياتٍ
After honour, humiliated	وَبَعْدَ الْعِزِّ مُذَلَّلاتٍ
And rushing towards your fatal spot	وَإلى مَصْرَعِكَ مُبادِراتٍ
And Shimr was sitting on your chest	وَالشِّمْرُ جالِسٌ عَلى صَدْرِكَ
Plunging his sword into your throat	وَمُولِغٌ سَيْفَهُ عَلى نَحْرِكَ
Grasping your grey hair with his hand	قابِضٌ عَلى شَيْبَتِكَ بِيَدِهِ
Slaughtering you with his blade	ذابِحٌ لَكَ بِمُهَنَّدِهِ
Your senses had become still	قَدْ سَكَنَتْ حَواسُّكَ
And your breaths faint	وَخَفِيَتْ أَنْفاسُكَ
And your head raised upon a spear	وَرُفِعَ عَلَى الْقَناةِ رَأْسُكَ
And your family captured like slaves	وَسُبِيَ أَهْلُكَ كالْعَبِيدِ
Shackled in iron chains, upon the humps of camels	وَصُفِّدُوا فِي الحَدِيدِ فَوْقَ أَقْتابِ الْمَطِيّاتِ
Their faces scorched by the burning noon heat	تَلْفَحُ وُجُوهَهُمْ حَرُّ الْهاجِراتِ

Imam Hussein (as)

Driven through deserts and wastelands	يُساقُونَ فِي الْبَرارِي وَالْفَلَواتِ
Their hands bound to their necks	أَيْديهِمْ مَغْلُولَةٌ إِلَى الْأَعْناقِ
Paraded through the markets	يُطافُ بِهِمْ فِي الْأَسْواقِ
So woe to the disobedient wicked ones!	فَالْوَيْلُ لِلْعُصاةِ الْفُسَّاقِ
Indeed, by killing you they killed Islam	لَقَدْ قَتَلُوا بِقَتْلِكَ الْإِسْلامَ
And suspended prayer and fasting	وَعَطَّلُوا الصَّلاةَ وَالصِّيامَ
And violated the traditions and judgments	وَنَقَضُوا السُّنَنَ وَالْأَحْكامَ
And demolished the foundations of faith	وَهَدَمُوا قَواعِدَ الْإِيمانِ
And distorted the verses of the Quran	وَحَرَّفُوا آياتِ الْقُرْآنِ
And rushed into tyranny and aggression	وَهَمْلَجُوا فِي الْبَغْيِ وَالْعُدْوانِ
Indeed, the Messenger of Allah, peace be upon him and his family, has become severed	لَقَدْ أَصْبَحَ رَسُولُ اللَّهِ صَلَّى اللَّهُ عَلَيْهِ وَآلِهِ مَوْتُوراً
And the Book of Allah, the Mighty and Majestic, was again abandoned	وَعادَ كِتابُ اللَّهِ عَزَّوَجَلَّ مَهْجُوراً
And truth was betrayed when you were forcibly overcome	وَغُودِرَ الْحَقُّ إِذْ قُهِرْتَ مَقْهُوراً
And with your loss, Takbir (God is great) and Tahlil (There is no god but Allah) were lost	وَفُقِدَ بِفَقْدِكَ التَّكْبيرُ وَالتَّهْليلُ
As well as the making lawful and unlawful, the revelation and interpretation	وَالتَّحْريمُ وَالتَّحْليلُ وَالتَّنْزيلُ وَالتَّأْويلُ
After you, alteration, distortion, atheism, nullification, whims, misguidance, trials, and falsehood appeared	وَظَهَرَ بَعْدَكَ التَّغْييرُ وَالتَّبْديلُ وَالْإِلْحادُ وَالتَّعْطيلُ وَالْأَهْواءُ وَالْأَضاليلُ وَالْفِتَنُ وَالْأَباطيلُ

Continuous Calling

So your mourner stood by the grave of your grandfather the Messenger, peace be upon him and his family	فَقَامَ نَاعِيكَ عِنْدَ قَبْرِ جَدِّكَ الرَّسُولِ صَلَّى اللّٰهُ عَلَيْهِ وَآلِهِ
Lamenting you to him with streaming tears, saying;	فَنَعَاكَ إِلَيْهِ بِالدَّمْعِ الْهُطُولِ قَائِلًا:
"Oh Messenger of Allah, your grandson and youth has been killed	يَا رَسُولَ اللّٰهِ قُتِلَ سِبْطُكَ وَفَتَاكَ
And your family and sanctuary have been violated	وَاسْتُبِيحَ أَهْلُكَ وَحِمَاكَ
And after you, your progeny were captured	وَسُبِيَتْ بَعْدَكَ ذَرَارِيكَ
And the dreaded calamity befell your family and relatives"	وَوَقَعَ الْمَحْذُورُ بِعِتْرَتِكَ وَذَوِيكَ
So the Messenger was disturbed, and his grieving heart wept	فَأَنْزَعَجَ الرَّسُولُ وَبَكَى قَلْبُهُ الْمَهُولُ
The angels and prophets consoled him	وَعَزَّاهُ بِكَ الْمَلَائِكَةُ وَالْأَنْبِيَاءُ
And your mother, the radiant one, was devastated for you	وَفُجِعَتْ بِكَ أُمُّكَ الزَّهْرَاءُ
Legions of the close Angels gathered to console your father, the commander of the faithful	وَاخْتَلَفَتْ جُنُودُ الْمَلَائِكَةِ الْمُقَرَّبِينَ تُعَزِّي أَبَاكَ أَمِيرَ الْمُؤْمِنِينَ
Mourning commemorations were held for you in the highest of the high	وَأُقِيمَتْ لَكَ الْمَآتِمُ فِى أَعْلَا عِلِّيِّينَ
And the Maidens of heaven struck their faces in grief	وَلَطَمَتْ عَلَيْكَ الْحُورُ الْعِينُ
The skies and their inhabitants wept	وَبَكَتِ السَّمَاءُ وَسُكَّانُهَا
As did Paradise and its keepers	وَالْجِنَانُ وَخُزَّانُهَا
And the hills and their surroundings	وَالْهِضَابُ وَأَقْطَارُهَا
And the oceans and their creatures	وَالْبِحَارُ وَحِيتَانُهَا

Imam Hussein (as)

And the heavens and their youths	وَالْجِنَانُ وَوِلْدَانُهَا
And the House, and the Station	وَالْبَيْتُ وَالْمَقَامُ
And the Sacred Monument	وَالْمَشْعَرُ الْحَرَامُ
And the sacred precincts and the state of ihram	وَالْحِلُّ وَالْإِحْرَامُ
Oh Allah, so by the sanctity of this Noble Place	اَللّٰهُمَّ فَبِحُرْمَةِ هٰذَا الْمَكَانِ الْمُنِيفِ
Send blessings upon Muhammad and the family of Muhammad	صَلِّ عَلَىٰ مُحَمَّدٍ وَآلِ مُحَمَّدٍ
And gather me in their company	وَاحْشُرْنِي فِي زُمْرَتِهِمْ
And admit me to Paradise by their intercession	وَأَدْخِلْنِي الْجَنَّةَ بِشَفَاعَتِهِمْ
Oh Allah, I certainly connect to you oh Swiftest of Reckoners	اَللّٰهُمَّ إِنِّي أَتَوَسَّلُ إِلَيْكَ يَا أَسْرَعَ الْحَاسِبِينَ
And Most Generous of the Generous, and Most Just of Judges	وَيَا أَكْرَمَ الْأَكْرَمِينَ وَيَا أَحْكَمَ الْحَاكِمِينَ
By Muhammad, seal of the prophets, Your Messenger to all the worlds	بِمُحَمَّدٍ خَاتَمِ النَّبِيِّينَ رَسُولِكَ إِلَى الْعَالَمِينَ أَجْمَعِينَ
And by his brother and cousin, the uprooter, the deep, the knowledgeable, and the firm Ali, commander of the faithful	وَبِأَخِيهِ وَابْنِ عَمِّهِ الْأَنْزَعِ الْبَطِينِ الْعَالِمِ الْمَكِينِ عَلِيٍّ أَمِيرِ الْمُؤْمِنِينَ
And by Fatima, chief of the women of the worlds	وَبِفَاطِمَةَ سَيِّدَةِ نِسَاءِ الْعَالَمِينَ
And by Hasan, the immaculate protection of the pious	وَبِالْحَسَنِ الزَّكِيِّ عِصْمَةِ الْمُتَّقِينَ
And by Abi Abdillah, Husain, the most noble of the martyrs	وَبِأَبِي عَبْدِ اللّٰهِ الْحُسَيْنِ أَكْرَمِ الْمُسْتَشْهَدِينَ

And by his slain children and oppressed family	وَبِأَوْلَادِهِ الْمَقْتُولِينَ وَبِعِتْرَتِهِ الْمَظْلُومِينَ
And by Ali ibn Husain, adornment of the worshippers	وَبِعَلِيِّ بْنِ الْحُسَيْنِ زَيْنِ الْعَابِدِينَ
And by Muhammad ibn Ali, direction of the repentant	وَبِمُحَمَّدِ بْنِ عَلِيٍّ قِبْلَةِ الْأَوَّابِينَ
And Ja'far ibn Muhammad, most truthful of the truthful	وَجَعْفَرِ بْنِ مُحَمَّدٍ أَصْدَقِ الصَّادِقِينَ
And Musa ibn Ja'far, manifester of the proofs	وَمُوسَى بْنِ جَعْفَرٍ مُظْهِرِ الْبَرَاهِينَ
And Ali ibn Musa, supporter of the religion	وَعَلِيِّ بْنِ مُوسَى نَاصِرِ الدِّينِ
And Muhammad ibn Ali, guide of the rightly guided	وَمُحَمَّدِ بْنِ عَلِيٍّ قُدْوَةِ الْمُهْتَدِينَ
And Ali ibn Muhammad, most ascetic of the ascetics	وَعَلِيِّ بْنِ مُحَمَّدٍ أَزْهَدِ الزَّاهِدِينَ
And al-Hasan ibn Ali, inheritor of the successors	وَالْحَسَنِ بْنِ عَلِيٍّ وَارِثِ الْمُسْتَخْلَفِينَ
And the Proof over all creation	وَالْحُجَّةِ عَلَى الْخَلْقِ أَجْمَعِينَ
That you bless Muhammad and the family of Muhammad	أَنْ تُصَلِّيَ عَلَى مُحَمَّدٍ وَآلِ مُحَمَّدٍ
The truthful, the righteous, the family of Taha and Yaseen	الصَّادِقِينَ الْأَبْرَارِينَ آلِ طٰهٰ وَيس
And that you make me on the Day of Resurrection from the secure and calm	وَأَنْ تَجْعَلَنِي فِي الْقِيَامَةِ مِنَ الْآمِنِينَ الْمُطْمَئِنِّينَ
The successful, happy, and rejoicing	الْفَائِزِينَ الْفَرِحِينَ الْمُسْتَبْشِرِينَ
Oh Allah, write me among the Muslims	اَللَّهُمَّ اكْتُبْنِي فِي الْمُسْلِمِينَ
And join me with the righteous	وَأَلْحِقْنِي بِالصَّالِحِينَ

Imam Hussein (as)

And grant me a truthful tongue among the latter ones	وَاجْعَلْ لِى لِسَانَ صِدْقٍ فِى الْآخِرِينَ
And support me against the transgressors	وَانْصُرْنِى عَلَى الْبَاغِينَ
And suffice me against the plots of the envious	وَاكْفِنِى كَيْدَ الْحَاسِدِينَ
And ward off from me the schemes of the schemers	وَاصْرِفْ عَنِّى مَكْرَ الْمَاكِرِينَ
And withhold from me the hands of the oppressors	وَاقْبِضْ عَنِّى أَيْدِىَ الظَّالِمِينَ
And gather me with the blessed chiefs in the highest of the high	وَاجْمَعْ بَيْنِى وَبَيْنَ السَّادَةِ الْمَيَامِينِ فِى أَعْلَى عِلِّيِّينَ
With those You bestowed upon from the prophets, the truthful, the martyrs, and the righteous	مَعَ الَّذِينَ أَنْعَمْتَ عَلَيْهِمْ مِنَ النَّبِيِّينَ وَالصِّدِّيقِينَ وَالشُّهَدَاءِ وَالصَّالِحِينَ
By Your mercy, oh Most Merciful of the merciful	بِرَحْمَتِكَ يَا أَرْحَمَ الرَّاحِمِينَ
Oh Allah, I implore You by Your infallible Prophet	اَللّٰهُمَّ إِنِّى أُقْسِمُ عَلَيْكَ بِنَبِيِّكَ الْمَعْصُومِ
And by Your sealed judgment, and Your concealed prohibition	وَبِحُكْمِكَ الْمَحْتُومِ وَنَهْيِكَ [نَهْيِكَ] الْمَكْتُومِ
And by this gathered grave where the infallible, slain, oppressed Imam rests	وَبِهٰذَا الْقَبْرِ الْمَلْمُومِ الْمُوَسَّدِ فِى كَنَفِهِ الْإِمَامُ الْمَعْصُومُ الْمَقْتُولُ الْمَظْلُومُ
That You relieve me of my distress	أَنْ تَكْشِفَ مَا بِى مِنَ الْغُمُومِ
And repel from me the evil of the sealed decree	وَتَصْرِفَ عَنِّى شَرَّ الْقَدَرِ الْمَحْتُومِ

Continuous Calling

And grant me refuge from the Fire of scorching winds.	وَتُجِيرَنِي مِنَ النَّارِ ذَاتِ السَّمُومِ
Oh Allah, cover me in Your grace	اَللَّهُمَّ جَلِّلْنِي بِنِعْمَتِكَ
And make me content with Your apportionment	وَرَضِّنِي بِقَسْمِكَ
And envelop me in Your benevolence and generosity	وَتَغَمَّدْنِي بِجُودِكَ وَكَرَمِكَ
And distance me from Your plot and wrath	وَبَاعِدْنِي مِنْ مَكْرِكَ وَنِقْمَتِكَ
Oh Allah, protect me from errors	اَللَّهُمَّ اعْصِمْنِي مِنَ الزَّلَلِ
And direct me in speech and action	وَسَدِّدْنِي فِي الْقَوْلِ وَالْعَمَلِ
And expand my lifespan	وَافْسَحْ لِي فِي مُدَّةِ الْأَجَلِ
And spare me from pain and illness	وَاعْفِنِي مِنَ الْأَوْجَاعِ وَالْعِلَلِ
And make me attain, through my masters and Your grace, the best of hope	وَبَلِّغْنِي بِمَوَالِيَّ وَبِفَضْلِكَ أَفْضَلَ الْأَمَلِ
Oh Allah, bless Muhammad and the family of Muhammad, and accept my repentance	اَللَّهُمَّ صَلِّ عَلَى مُحَمَّدٍ وَآلِ مُحَمَّدٍ وَاقْبَلْ تَوْبَتِي
And have mercy on my tears	وَارْحَمْ عَبْرَتِي
And pardon my slips	وَأَقِلْنِي عَثْرَتِي
And relieve my distress	وَنَفِّسْ كُرْبَتِي
And forgive me my sin	وَاغْفِرْ لِي خَطِيئَتِي
And set right for me my offspring	وَأَصْلِحْ لِي فِي ذُرِّيَّتِي

Imam Hussein (as)

Oh Allah, do not leave for me in this great gathering and noble place any sin except that You forgive it	اَللّٰهُمَّ لَا تَدَعْ لِى فِى هٰذَا الْمَشْهَدِ الْمُعَظَّمِ وَالْمَحَلِّ الْمُكَرَّمِ ذَنْباً إِلاَّ غَفَرْتَهُ
And no flaw except that You conceal	وَلَا عَيْباً إِلاَّ سَتَرْتَهُ
And no distress except that You remove	وَلَا غَمّاً إِلاَّ كَشَفْتَهُ
And no provision except that You extend	وَلَا رِزْقاً إِلاَّ بَسَطْتَهُ
And no dignity except that You elevate	وَلَا جَاهاً إِلاَّ عَمَرْتَهُ
And no corruption except that You rectify	وَلَا فَسَاداً إِلاَّ أَصْلَحْتَهُ
And no hope except that You fulfill	وَلَا أَمَلاً إِلاَّ بَلَّغْتَهُ
And no supplication except that You answer	وَلَا دُعَاءً إِلاَّ أَجَبْتَهُ
And no difficulty except that You relieve	وَلَا مَضِيقاً إِلاَّ فَرَّجْتَهُ
And no separation except that You reunite	وَلَا شَمْلاً إِلاَّ جَمَعْتَهُ
And no matter except that You complete	وَلَا أَمْراً إِلاَّ أَتْمَمْتَهُ
And no wealth except that You increase	وَلَا مَالاً إِلاَّ كَثَّرْتَهُ
And no character except that You beautify	وَلَا خُلُقاً إِلاَّ حَسَّنْتَهُ
And no spending except that You compensate	وَلَا إِنْفَاقاً إِلاَّ أَخْلَفْتَهُ
And no state except that You set it aright	وَلَا حَالاً إِلاَّ عَمَرْتَهُ
And no envier except that You subdue	وَلَا حَسُوداً إِلاَّ قَمَعْتَهُ
And no enemy except that You destroy	وَلَا عَدُوّاً إِلاَّ أَرْدَيْتَهُ
And no evil except that You suffice	وَلَا شَرّاً إِلاَّ كَفَيْتَهُ

Continuous Calling

And no illness except that You cure	وَلا مَرَضاً إِلاّ شَفَيْتَهُ
And no distant except that You bring near	وَلا بَعِيداً إِلاّ أَدْنَيْتَهُ
And no scattering except that You gather	وَلا شَعَثاً إِلاّ لَمَمْتَهُ
And no request except that You grant	وَلا سُؤالاً [سُؤْلاً] إِلاّ أَعْطَيْتَهُ
Oh Allah, I ask You for the good of the immediate	اَللّهُمَّ إِنِّي أَسْئَلُكَ خَيْرَ الْعاجِلَةِ
And the reward of the delayed	وَثَوابَ الآجِلَةِ
Oh Allah, enrich me with Your lawful over the unlawful	اَللّهُمَّ أَغْنِنِي بِحَلالِكَ عَنِ الْحَرامِ
And through Your grace over all people	وَبِفَضْلِكَ عَنْ جَمِيعِ الْأَنامِ
Oh Allah, I ask You for beneficial knowledge	اَللّهُمَّ إِنِّي أَسْئَلُكَ عِلْماً نافِعاً
And a humble heart	وَقَلْباً خاشِعاً
And a healing certainty	وَيَقِيناً شافِياً
And purifying deeds	وَعَمَلاً زاكِياً
And beautiful patience	وَصَبْراً جَمِيلاً
And abundant reward	وَأَجْراً جَزِيلاً
Oh Allah, provide me with gratitude for Your blessings upon me	اَللّهُمَّ ارْزُقْنِي شُكْرَ نِعْمَتِكَ عَلَيَّ
And increase in Your favour and generosity towards me	وَزِدْ فِي إِحْسانِكَ وَكَرَمِكَ إِلَيَّ
And make my speech among people well-received	وَاجْعَلْ قَوْلِي فِي النّاسِ مَسْمُوعاً
And my deeds raised up before You	وَعَمَلِي عِنْدَكَ مَرْفُوعاً
And my legacy in good deeds followed	وَأَثَرِي فِي الْخَيْراتِ مَتْبُوعاً

Imam Hussein (as)

And my enemy subdued	وَعَدُوّى مَقْمُوعاً
Oh Allah, send blessings upon Muhammad and the family of Muhammad, the virtuous ones, during the hours of night and periods of day	اَللّهُمَّ صَلِّ عَلَى مُحَمَّدٍ وَآلِ مُحَمَّدٍ الأَخْيارِ فى آناءِ اللَّيْلِ وَأَطرافِ النَّهارِ
And suffice me against the evil of the wicked	وَاكْفِنى شَرَّ الأَشْرارِ
And purify me from sins and burdens	وَطَهِّرْنى مِنَ الذُّنُوبِ وَالأَوْزارِ
And grant me refuge from the Fire	وَأَجِرْنى مِنَ النّارِ
And admit me to the abode of permanence	وَأَحِلَّنى دارَالْقَرارِ
And forgive me and all my brothers and sisters among the believing men and believing women	وَاغْفِرْ لى وَلِجَميعِ إخْوانى فيكَ وَأَخَواتِى الْمُؤْمِنينَ وَالْمُؤْمِناتِ
By Your mercy, oh Most Merciful of the merciful	بِرَحْمَتِكَ يا أَرْحَمَ الرّاحِمينَ.

Ziyarat Ashura

Peace be upon you oh Aba-Abdullah	اَلسَّلَامُ عَلَيْكَ يَا أَبَا عَبْدِ ٱللَّهِ
Peace be upon you oh son of Allah's Messenger	اَلسَّلَامُ عَلَيْكَ يَا بْنَ رَسُولِ ٱللَّهِ
Peace be upon you oh chosen of Allah and son of His choice	اَلسَّلَامُ عَلَيْكَ يَا خِيَرَةَ ٱللَّهِ وَٱبْنَ خِيَرَتِهِ
Peace be upon you oh son of the commander of the faithful	اَلسَّلَامُ عَلَيْكَ يَا بْنَ أَمِيرِ ٱلْمُؤْمِنِينَ
And son of the chief of the successors	وَٱبْنَ سَيِّدِ ٱلْوَصِيِّينَ
Peace be upon you oh son of Fatima	اَلسَّلَامُ عَلَيْكَ يَا بْنَ فَاطِمَةَ
The chief of the women of the worlds	سَيِّدَةِ نِسَاءِ ٱلْعَالَمِينَ
Peace be upon you oh vengeance of Allah, son of His vengeance, and the severed unique one	اَلسَّلَامُ عَلَيْكَ يَا ثَارَ ٱللَّهِ وَٱبْنَ ثَارِهِ وَٱلْوِتْرَ ٱلْمَوْتُورَ
Peace be upon you and upon the souls that settled in your courtyard	اَلسَّلَامُ عَلَيْكَ وَعَلَى ٱلْأَرْوَاحِ ٱلَّتِي حَلَّتْ بِفِنَائِكَ
Peace of Allah be upon all of you from me forever	عَلَيْكُمْ مِنِّي جَمِيعاً سَلَامُ ٱللَّهِ أَبَداً
As long as I remain and the night and day remain	مَا بَقِيتُ وَبَقِيَ ٱللَّيْلُ وَٱلنَّهَارُ
Oh Aba-Abdullah	يَا أَبَا عَبْدِ ٱللَّهِ
Indeed the calamity has become great	لَقَدْ عَظُمَتِ ٱلرَّزِيَّةُ
And the affliction has become tremendous and great through you	وَجَلَّتْ وَعَظُمَتِ ٱلْمُصِيبَةُ بِكَ
Upon us and upon all the people of Islam	عَلَيْنَا وَعَلَى جَمِيعِ أَهْلِ ٱلْإِسْلَامِ

And your affliction has become tremendous and great	وَجَلَّتْ وَعَظُمَتْ مُصِيبَتُكَ
In the heavens upon all the people of the heavens	فِي ٱلسَّمَاوَاتِ عَلَىٰ جَمِيعِ أَهْلِ ٱلسَّمَاوَاتِ
So may Allah curse the nation that laid the foundation of oppression and tyranny upon you oh Ahlul Bayt	فَلَعَنَ ٱللَّهُ أُمَّةً أَسَّسَتْ أَسَاسَ ٱلظُّلْمِ وَٱلْجَوْرِ عَلَيْكُمْ أَهْلَ ٱلْبَيْتِ
And may Allah curse the nation that pushed you away from your station	وَلَعَنَ ٱللَّهُ أُمَّةً دَفَعَتْكُمْ عَنْ مَقَامِكُمْ
And removed you from your ranks which Allah had arranged you in	وَأَزَالَتْكُمْ عَنْ مَرَاتِبِكُمُ ٱلَّتِي رَتَّبَكُمُ ٱللَّهُ فِيهَا
And may Allah curse the nation that killed you	وَلَعَنَ ٱللَّهُ أُمَّةً قَتَلَتْكُمْ
And may Allah curse those who paved the way for them	وَلَعَنَ ٱللَّهُ ٱلْمُمَهِّدِينَ لَهُمْ
By enabling them to fight against you	بِالتَّمْكِينِ مِنْ قِتَالِكُمْ
I dissociate myself to Allah and to you from them	بَرِئْتُ إِلَىٰ ٱللَّهِ وَإِلَيْكُمْ مِنْهُمْ
And from their partisans and followers and allies	وَمِنْ أَشْيَاعِهِمْ وَأَتْبَاعِهِمْ وَأَوْلِيَائِهِمْ
Oh Aba-Abdullah	يَا أَبَا عَبْدِ ٱللَّهِ
I am at peace with whoever makes peace with you	إِنِّي سِلْمٌ لِمَنْ سَالَمَكُمْ
And at war with whoever fights you until the Day of Resurrection	وَحَرْبٌ لِمَنْ حَارَبَكُمْ إِلَىٰ يَوْمِ ٱلْقِيَامَةِ
And may Allah curse the family of Ziyad and the family of Marwan	وَلَعَنَ ٱللَّهُ آلَ زِيَادٍ وَآلَ مَرْوَانَ
And may Allah curse the Bani Umayyah entirely	وَلَعَنَ ٱللَّهُ بَنِي أُمَيَّةَ قَاطِبَةً
And may Allah curse Ibn Marjanah	وَلَعَنَ ٱللَّهُ ٱبْنَ مَرْجَانَةَ

And may Allah curse Umar ibn Sa'd	وَلَعَنَ ٱللَّهُ عُمَرَ بْنَ سَعْدٍ
And may Allah curse Shimr	وَلَعَنَ ٱللَّهُ شِمْراً
And may Allah curse a nation that saddled and bridled	وَلَعَنَ ٱللَّهُ أُمَّةً أَسْرَجَتْ وَأَلْجَمَتْ
And veiled themselves for fighting you	وَتَنَقَّبَتْ لِقِتَالِكَ
May my father and mother be sacrificed for you	بِأَبِي أَنْتَ وَأُمِّي
Indeed great has become my affliction through you	لَقَدْ عَظُمَ مُصَابِي بِكَ
So I ask Allah, who honoured your station and honoured me through you	فَأَسْأَلُ ٱللَّهَ ٱلَّذِي أَكْرَمَ مَقَامَكَ وَأَكْرَمَنِي بِكَ
That He grants me seeking your blood revenge	أَنْ يَرْزُقَنِي طَلَبَ ثَأْرِكَ
With a supported Imam from the Ahlul Bayt of Muhammad	مَعَ إِمَامٍ مَنْصُورٍ مِنْ أَهْلِ بَيْتِ مُحَمَّدٍ
May Allah bless him and his family	صَلَّى ٱللَّهُ عَلَيْهِ وَآلِهِ
Oh Allah make me respected with You	اَللَّهُمَّ اجْعَلْنِي عِنْدَكَ وَجِيهاً
Through Hussein, peace be upon him, in this world and the hereafter	بِٱلْحُسَيْنِ عَلَيْهِ ٱلسَّلَامُ فِي ٱلدُّنْيَا وَٱلْآخِرَةِ
Oh Aba-Abdullah	يَا أَبَا عَبْدِ ٱللَّهِ
Indeed I seek nearness to Allah and to His Messenger	إِنِّي أَتَقَرَّبُ إِلَى ٱللَّهِ وَإِلَى رَسُولِهِ
And to the commander of the faithful and to Fatimah	وَإِلَى أَمِيرِ ٱلْمُؤْمِنِينَ وَإِلَى فَاطِمَةَ
And to Hassan and to you through loyalty to you	وَإِلَى ٱلْحَسَنِ وَإِلَيْكَ بِمُوَالَاتِكَ

And through dissociation from whoever fought you	وَبِٱلْبَرَاءَةِ مِمَّنْ قَاتَلَكَ
And set up war against you	وَنَصَبَ لَكَ ٱلْحَرْبَ
And through dissociation from whoever laid the foundation of oppression and tyranny upon you	وَبِٱلْبَرَاءَةِ مِمَّنْ أَسَّسَ أَسَاسَ ٱلظُّلْمِ وَٱلْجَوْرِ عَلَيْكُمْ
And I dissociate to Allah and to His Messenger	وَأَبْرَأُ إِلَى ٱللَّهِ وَإِلَى رَسُولِهِ
From those who laid the foundation of that	مِمَّنْ أَسَّسَ أَسَاسَ ذَلِكَ
And built upon it his structure	وَبَنَى عَلَيْهِ بُنْيَانَهُ
And continued in his oppression and tyranny upon you and upon your partisans	وَجَرَى فِي ظُلْمِهِ وَجَوْرِهِ عَلَيْكُمْ وَعَلَى أَشْيَاعِكُمْ
I dissociate to Allah and to you from them	بَرِئْتُ إِلَى ٱللَّهِ وَإِلَيْكُمْ مِنْهُمْ
And I seek nearness to Allah then to you	وَأَتَقَرَّبُ إِلَى ٱللَّهِ ثُمَّ إِلَيْكُمْ
Through loyalty to you and loyalty to your allies	بِمُوَالَاتِكُمْ وَمُوَالَاةِ وَلِيِّكُمْ
And through dissociation from your enemies	وَبِٱلْبَرَاءَةِ مِنْ أَعْدَائِكُمْ
And those who set up war against you	وَٱلنَّاصِبِينَ لَكُمُ ٱلْحَرْبَ
And through dissociation from their partisans and their followers	وَبِٱلْبَرَاءَةِ مِنْ أَشْيَاعِهِمْ وَأَتْبَاعِهِمْ
I am at peace with whoever makes peace with you	إِنِّي سِلْمٌ لِمَنْ سَالَمَكُمْ
And at war with whoever fights you	وَحَرْبٌ لِمَنْ حَارَبَكُمْ
And ally for whoever allies with you	وَوَلِيٌّ لِمَنْ وَالَاكُمْ

And enemy for whoever shows enmity to you	وَعَدُوٌّ لِمَنْ عَادَاكُمْ
So I ask Allah who honoured me with recognition of you	فَأَسْأَلُ ٱللَّهَ ٱلَّذِى أَكْرَمَنِى بِمَعْرِفَتِكُمْ
And recognition of your allies	وَمَعْرِفَةِ أَوْلِيَائِكُمْ
And granted me dissociation from your enemies	وَرَزَقَنِى ٱلْبَرَاءَةَ مِنْ أَعْدَائِكُمْ
That He makes me with you in this world and the hereafter	أَنْ يَجْعَلَنِى مَعَكُمْ فِى ٱلدُّنْيَا وَٱلْآخِرَة
And that He establishes for me a truthful footing with you	وَأَنْ يُثَبِّتَ لِى عِنْدَكُمْ قَدَمَ صِدْقٍ
In this world and the hereafter	فِى ٱلدُّنْيَا وَٱلْآخِرَة
And I ask Him that He makes me reach your praised station with Allah	وَأَسْأَلُهُ أَنْ يُبَلِّغَنِى ٱلْمَقَامَ ٱلْمَحْمُودَ لَكُمْ عِنْدَ ٱللَّهِ
And that He grants me seeking my blood revenge	وَأَنْ يَرْزُقَنِى طَلَبَ ثَأْرِى
With a guiding imam who is apparent	مَعَ إِمَامِ هُدًى ظَاهِرٍ
Speaking with truth, from you	نَاطِقٍ بِٱلْحَقِّ مِنْكُمْ
And I ask Allah by your right	وَأَسْأَلُ ٱللَّهَ بِحَقِّكُمْ
And by the affair which you have with Him	وَبِٱلشَّأْنِ ٱلَّذِى لَكُمْ عِنْدَهُ
That He give me, through my affliction for you	أَنْ يُعْطِيَنِى بِمُصَابِى بِكُمْ
The best of what He gives to one afflicted by their calamity	أَفْضَلَ مَا يُعْطِى مُصَاباً بِمُصِيبَتِهِ
A calamity how great it is	مُصِيبَةٍ مَا أَعْظَمَهَا
And greatest is its tragedy in Islam	وَأَعْظَمَ رَزِيَّتَهَا فِى ٱلْإِسْلَامِ

And in all the heavens and the earth	وَفِي جَمِيعِ ٱلسَّمَاوَاتِ وَٱلْأَرْضِ
Oh Allah make me in this station of mine	اَللَّهُمَّ ٱجْعَلْنِي فِي مَقَامِي هٰذَا
From those who receive from You blessings and mercy and forgiveness	مِمَّنْ تَنَالُهُ مِنْكَ صَلَوَاتٌ وَرَحْمَةٌ وَمَغْفِرَةٌ
Oh Allah make my life the life of Muhammad and the family of Muhammad	اَللَّهُمَّ ٱجْعَلْ مَحْيَايَ مَحْيَا مُحَمَّدٍ وَآلِ مُحَمَّدٍ
And my death the death of Muhammad and the family of Muhammad	وَمَمَاتِي مَمَاتَ مُحَمَّدٍ وَآلِ مُحَمَّدٍ
Oh Allah indeed this is a day	اَللَّهُمَّ إِنَّ هٰذَا يَوْمٌ
Which the Bani Umayyah considered blessed	تَبَرَّكَتْ بِهِ بَنُو أُمَيَّةَ
And the son of the liver eater woman	وَٱبْنُ آكِلَةِ ٱلْأَكْبَادِ
The cursed son of the cursed	ٱللَّعِينُ ٱبْنُ ٱللَّعِينِ
Upon Your tongue and the tongue of Your Prophet	عَلَىٰ لِسَانِكَ وَلِسَانِ نَبِيِّكَ
May Allah bless him and his family	صَلَّىٰ ٱللَّهُ عَلَيْهِ وَآلِهِ
In every place and position	فِي كُلِّ مَوْطِنٍ وَمَوْقِفٍ
Where Your Prophet stood, may Allah bless him and his family	وَقَفَ فِيهِ نَبِيُّكَ صَلَّىٰ ٱللَّهُ عَلَيْهِ وَآلِهِ
Oh Allah curse Abu Sufyan and Muawiyah and Yazid ibn Muawiyah	اَللَّهُمَّ ٱلْعَنْ أَبَا سُفْيَانَ وَمُعَاوِيَةَ وَيَزِيدَ بْنَ مُعَاوِيَةَ
Upon them from You the curse forever and ever	عَلَيْهِمْ مِنْكَ ٱللَّعْنَةُ أَبَدَ ٱلْآبِدِينَ
And this is a day which the family of Ziyad and the family of Marwan rejoiced in	وَهٰذَا يَوْمٌ فَرِحَتْ بِهِ آلُ زِيَادٍ وَآلُ مَرْوَانَ

By their killing of Hussein, may Allah's blessings be upon him	بِقَتْلِهِمُ ٱلْحُسَيْنَ صَلَوَاتُ ٱللَّهِ عَلَيْهِ
Oh Allah so multiply upon them the curse from You	اَللَّهُمَّ فَضَاعِفْ عَلَيْهِمُ ٱللَّعْنَ مِنْكَ
And the painful punishment	وَٱلْعَذَابَ ٱلْأَلِيمَ
Oh Allah indeed I seek nearness to You on this day	اَللَّهُمَّ إِنِّي أَتَقَرَّبُ إِلَيْكَ فِي هَذَا ٱلْيَوْمِ
And in this position of mine	وَفِي مَوْقِفِي هَذَا
And the days of my life	وَأَيَّامِ حَيَاتِي
Through dissociation from them and cursing them	بِٱلْبَرَاءَةِ مِنْهُمْ وَٱللَّعْنَةِ عَلَيْهِمْ
And through loyalty to Your Prophet and the family of Your Prophet	وَبِٱلْمُوَالَاةِ لِنَبِيِّكَ وَآلِ نَبِيِّكَ
Upon him and upon them peace	عَلَيْهِ وَعَلَيْهِمُ ٱلسَّلَامُ

You may then repeat the following 100 times:

Oh Allah curse the first oppressor	اَللَّهُمَّ ٱلْعَنْ أَوَّلَ ظَالِمٍ
Who oppressed the right of Muhammad and the family of Muhammad	ظَلَمَ حَقَّ مُحَمَّدٍ وَآلِ مُحَمَّدٍ
And the last follower of him in that	وَآخِرَ تَابِعٍ لَهُ عَلَى ذَلِكَ
Oh Allah curse the band that struggled against Hussein	اَللَّهُمَّ ٱلْعَنِ ٱلْعِصَابَةَ ٱلَّتِي جَاهَدَتِ ٱلْحُسَيْنَ
And allied and pledged allegiance and followed in his killing	وَشَايَعَتْ وَبَايَعَتْ وَتَابَعَتْ عَلَى قَتْلِهِ
Oh Allah curse them all	اَللَّهُمَّ ٱلْعَنْهُمْ جَمِيعاً

Ziyarat Ashura

You may then repeat the following 100 times:

Peace be upon you oh Aba-Abdullah	اَلسَّلَامُ عَلَيْكَ يَا أَبَا عَبْدِ ٱللَّهِ
And upon the souls that settled in your courtyard	وَعَلَى ٱلْأَرْوَاحِ ٱلَّتِي حَلَّتْ بِفِنَائِكَ
Upon you from me the peace of Allah forever	عَلَيْكَ مِنِّي سَلَامُ ٱللَّهِ أَبَداً
As long as I remain and the night and day remain	مَا بَقِيتُ وَبَقِيَ ٱللَّيْلُ وَٱلنَّهَارُ
And may Allah not make it the last pledge from me for visiting you	وَلَا جَعَلَهُ ٱللَّهُ آخِرَ ٱلْعَهْدِ مِنِّي لِزِيَارَتِكُمْ
Peace be upon Hussein	اَلسَّلَامُ عَلَى ٱلْحُسَيْنِ
And upon Ali ibn Hussein	وَعَلَى عَلِيِّ بْنِ ٱلْحُسَيْنِ
And upon the sons of Hussein	وَعَلَى أَوْلَادِ ٱلْحُسَيْنِ
And upon the companions of Hussein	وَعَلَى أَصْحَابِ ٱلْحُسَيْنِ

Then continue:

Oh Allah single out You the first oppressor with curse from me	اَللَّهُمَّ خُصَّ أَنْتَ أَوَّلَ ظَالِمٍ بِٱللَّعْنِ مِنِّي
And begin with him first	وَٱبْدَأْ بِهِ أَوَّلاً
Then curse the second and the third and the fourth	ثُمَّ ٱلْعَنِ ٱلثَّانِيَ وَٱلثَّالِثَ وَٱلرَّابِعَ
Oh Allah curse Yazid fifth	اَللَّهُمَّ ٱلْعَنْ يَزِيدَ خَامِساً
And curse Ubayd Allah ibn Ziyad and Ibn Marjanah	وَٱلْعَنْ عُبَيْدَ ٱللَّهِ بْنَ زِيَادٍ وَٱبْنَ مَرْجَانَةَ
And Umar ibn Sa'd and Shimr	وَعُمَرَ بْنَ سَعْدٍ وَشِمْراً

And the family of Abu Sufyan and the family of Ziyad and the family of Marwan	وَآلِ أَبِي سُفْيَانَ وَآلِ زِيَادٍ وَآلِ مَرْوَانَ
Until the Day of Resurrection	إِلَى يَوْمِ ٱلْقِيَامَةِ

Then go into prostration and say:

Oh Allah for You is praise	اَللَّهُمَّ لَكَ ٱلْحَمْدُ
The praise of those grateful to You for their affliction	حَمْدَ ٱلشَّاكِرِينَ لَكَ عَلَى مُصَابِهِمْ
Praise be to Allah for my great tragedy	ٱلْحَمْدُ لِلَّهِ عَلَى عَظِيمِ رَزِيَّتِي
Oh Allah grant me the intercession of Hussein on the Day of Arrival	اَللَّهُمَّ ٱرْزُقْنِي شَفَاعَةَ ٱلْحُسَيْنِ يَوْمَ ٱلْوُرُودِ
And establish for me a truthful footing with You	وَثَبِّتْ لِي قَدَمَ صِدْقٍ عِنْدَكَ
With Hussein and the companions of Hussein	مَعَ ٱلْحُسَيْنِ وَأَصْحَابِ ٱلْحُسَيْنِ
Those who sacrificed their souls for Hussein peace be upon him	ٱلَّذِينَ بَذَلُوا مُهَجَهُمْ دُونَ ٱلْحُسَيْنِ عَلَيْهِ ٱلسَّلَامُ

Imam Zeinul Abideen (as)

"Whoever loves us for the sake of Allah our love will benefit him, even if he were in the mountains of Deylam." – Imam Zeinul Abideen (as)

(Bihar Al-Anwar, Hub-e-Ali translation, vol 65, page 169)

On 5 Sha'ban to celebrate his birth, and on 25 Muharram to commemorate his martyrdom you can recite the following ziyarah.

Peace be upon you oh adornment of the worshippers	السَّلامُ عَلَيْكَ يَا زَيْنَ العَابِدِينَ
Peace be upon you oh adornment of those who pray at night	السَّلامُ عَلَيْكَ يَا زَيْنَ المُتَهَجِّدِينَ
Peace be upon you oh Imam of the pious	السَّلامُ عَلَيْكَ يَا إِمَامَ المُتَّقِينَ
Peace be upon you oh pearl of the righteous	السَّلامُ عَلَيْكَ يَا دُرَّةَ الصَّالِحِينَ
Peace be upon you oh guardian of the Muslims	السَّلامُ عَلَيْكَ يَا وَلِيَّ المُسْلِمِينَ
Peace be upon you oh delight of the eyes of the seers and recognisers	السَّلامُ عَلَيْكَ يَا قُرَّةَ عَيْنِ النَّاظِرِينَ العَارِفِينَ
Peace be upon you oh successor of the predecessors	السَّلامُ عَلَيْكَ يَا خَلَفَ السَّابِقِينَ
Peace be upon you oh successor of the successors	السَّلامُ عَلَيْكَ يَا وَصِيَّ الوَصِيِّينَ
Peace be upon you oh keeper of the wills of the Messengers	السَّلامُ عَلَيْكَ يَا خَازِنَ وَصَايَا المُرْسَلِينَ
Peace be upon you oh light of the lonely	السَّلامُ عَلَيْكَ يَا ضَوْءَ المُسْتَوْحِشِينَ
Peace be upon you oh light of the diligent	السَّلامُ عَلَيْكَ يَا نُورَ المُجْتَهِدِينَ

Peace be upon you oh lamp of the travellers	السَّلَامُ عَلَيْكَ يَا سِرَاجَ المُرْتَاضِينَ
Peace be upon you oh treasure of the worshippers	السَّلَامُ عَلَيْكَ يَا ذُخْرَ المُتَعَبِّدِينَ
Peace be upon you oh lantern of the worlds	السَّلَامُ عَلَيْكَ يَا مِصْبَاحَ العَالَمِينَ
Peace be upon you oh ship of knowledge	السَّلَامُ عَلَيْكَ يَا سَفِينَةَ العِلْمِ
Peace be upon you oh tranquillity of clemency	السَّلَامُ عَلَيْكَ يَا سَكِينَةَ الحِلْمِ
Peace be upon you oh scale of retaliation	السَّلَامُ عَلَيْكَ يَا مِيزَانَ القِصَاصِ
Peace be upon you oh ship of deliverance	السَّلَامُ عَلَيْكَ يَا سَفِينَةَ الخَلَاصِ
Peace be upon you oh ocean of generosity	السَّلَامُ عَلَيْكَ يَا بَحْرَ النَّدَى
Peace be upon you oh full moon in the darkness	السَّلَامُ عَلَيْكَ بَدْرَ الدُّجَى
Peace be upon you oh sighing forbearing one	السَّلَامُ عَلَيْكَ أَيُّهَا الأَوَّاهُ الحَلِيمُ
Peace be upon you oh patient, wise one	السَّلَامُ عَلَيْكَ أَيُّهَا الصَّابِرُ الحَكِيمُ
Peace be upon you oh head of the weepers	السَّلَامُ عَلَيْكَ يَا رَئِيسَ البَكَّائِينَ
Peace be upon you oh lantern of the believers	السَّلَامُ عَلَيْكَ يَا مِصْبَاحَ المُؤْمِنِينَ
Peace be upon you oh my master, oh Aba Muhammad	السَّلَامُ عَلَيْكَ يَا مَوْلَايَ يَا أَبَا مُحَمَّدٍ
I bear witness that you are the proof of Allah	أَشْهَدُ أَنَّكَ حُجَّةُ اللَّهِ
And the son of His proof	وَابْنُ حُجَّتِهِ

Imam Zeinul Abideen (as)

And the father of His proofs, and the son of His trustee	وَأَبُو حُجَجِهِ وَابْنُ أَمِينِهِ
And the father of His trustees	وَأَبُو أُمَنَائِهِ
And that you advised sincerely in the worship of your Lord	وَأَنَّكَ نَاصَحْتَ فِي عِبَادَةِ رَبِّكَ
And hastened in His pleasure	وَسَارَعْتَ فِي مَرْضَاتِهِ
And disappointed His enemies	وَخَيَّبْتَ أَعْدَاءَهُ
And delighted His friends	وَسَرَرْتَ أَوْلِيَاءَهُ
I bear witness that you worshipped Allah with true worship	أَشْهَدُ أَنَّكَ قَدْ عَبَدْتَ اللَّهَ حَقَّ عِبَادَتِهِ
And feared Him as He should be feared	وَاتَّقَيْتَهُ حَقَّ تُقَاتِهِ
And obeyed Him with true obedience until certainty came to you	وَأَطَعْتَهُ حَقَّ طَاعَتِهِ حَتَّى أَتَاكَ الْيَقِينُ
So upon you, oh my master, oh son of the Messenger of Allah, be the best greetings	فَعَلَيْكَ يَا مَوْلَايَ يَا بْنَ رَسُولِ اللَّهِ أَفْضَلُ التَّحِيَّةِ
And peace be upon you, and the mercy of Allah and His blessings	وَالسَّلَامُ عَلَيْكَ وَرَحْمَةُ اللَّهِ وَبَرَكَاتُهُ

Another ziarat

Peace be upon you, oh Imam of guidance	ٱلسَّلَامُ عَلَيْكَ يَا إِمَامَ الْهُدَى
Peace be upon you, oh full moon in the darkness	ٱلسَّلَامُ عَلَيْكَ يَا بَدْرَ الدُّجَى
Peace be upon you, oh refuge of piety	ٱلسَّلَامُ عَلَيْكَ يَا كَهْفَ التُّقَى
Peace be upon you, oh leader of the people of piety	ٱلسَّلَامُ عَلَيْكَ يَا قَائِدَ أَهْلِ التَّقْوَى

Peace be upon you, oh splitter of the knowledge of Prophets	اَلسَّلَامُ عَلَيْكَ يَا بَاقِرَ عَلْمِ النَّبِيِّينَ
Peace be upon you, oh adornment of the heavens and the earths	اَلسَّلَامُ عَلَيْكَ يَا زَيْنَ السَّمٰوٰاتِ وَالْأَرْضِينَ
Oh Allah, just as you have made him a landmark for your servants and a repository of Your forbearance, and an interpreter of Your revelation	اَللّٰهُمَّ كَمَا جَعَلْتَهُ عَلَماً لِعِبَادِكَ وَمُسْتَوْدَعاً لِحِلْمِكَ وَمُتَرْجِماً لِوَحْيِكَ
Then send blessings on him, the best that You blessed upon anyone from the progeny of Your prophets, Your chosen ones, Your messengers, and Your trustees, oh Lord of the Worlds	فَصَلِّ عَلَيْهِ أَفْضَلَ مَا صَلَّيْتَ عَلَىٰ أَحَدٍ مِنْ ذُرِّيَّةِ أَنْبِيَائِكَ وَأَصْفِيَائِكَ وَرُسُلِكَ وَأُمَنَائِكَ يَا رَبَّ الْعَالَمِينَ

Imam Baqir (as)

"Do you have secluded meetings and discuss among yourselves what you like?"

"Yes, we indeed talk about the excellences of the family of Muhammad in private."

"I would very much like to be present in those gatherings. By Allah, I like your fragrances and your souls. Indeed you are following the religion of Allah and His angels, and you help it through piety and effort". – Imam Baqir (as)

(Mikyal Al-Makaarim, Sayyid Rizvi translation, page 642)

On 1 Rajab to celebrate his birth, and on 7 Dhul-Hijjah to commemorate his martyrdom you can recite the following ziyarah.

Peace be upon you oh splitter of the knowledge of Allah	السَّلامُ عَلَيْكَ أَيُّهَا البَاقِرُ لِعِلْمِ اللَّهِ
Peace be upon you oh investigator for the religion of Allah	السَّلامُ عَلَيْكَ أَيُّهَا الفَاحِصُ عَنْ دِينِ اللَّهِ
Peace be upon you oh clarifier of the rulings of Allah	السَّلامُ عَلَيْكَ أَيُّهَا المُبَيِّنُ لِحُكْمِ اللَّهِ
Peace be upon you oh upholder of the justice of Allah	السَّلامُ عَلَيْكَ أَيُّهَا القَائِمُ بِقِسْطِ اللَّهِ
Peace be upon you oh advisor to the servants of Allah	السَّلامُ عَلَيْكَ أَيُّهَا النَّاصِحُ لِعِبَادِ اللَّهِ
Peace be upon you oh caller towards Allah	السَّلامُ عَلَيْكَ أَيُّهَا الدَّاعِى إِلَى اللَّهِ
Peace be upon you oh who leads towards Allah	السَّلامُ عَلَيْكَ أَيُّهَا الدَّلِيلُ إِلَى اللَّهِ
Peace be upon you oh manifest grace	السَّلامُ عَلَيْكَ أَيُّهَا الفَضْلُ المُبِينُ

Continuous Calling

Peace be upon you oh shining light	السَّلَامُ عَلَيْكَ أَيُّهَا النُّورُ السَّاطِعُ
Peace be upon you oh brilliant full moon	السَّلَامُ عَلَيْكَ أَيُّهَا البَدْرُ اللَّامِعُ
Peace be upon you oh vivid truth	السَّلَامُ عَلَيْكَ أَيُّهَا الحَقُّ الأَبْلَجُ
Peace be upon you oh bright lamp	السَّلَامُ عَلَيْكَ أَيُّهَا السِّرَاجُ الأَسْرَجُ
Peace be upon you oh shining star	السَّلَامُ عَلَيْكَ أَيُّهَا النَّجْمُ الأَزْهَرُ
Peace be upon you oh dazzling planet	السَّلَامُ عَلَيْكَ أَيُّهَا الكَوْكَبُ الأَبْهَرُ
Peace be upon you oh the one free from unsolvable complexities	السَّلَامُ عَلَيْكَ أَيُّهَا المُنَزَّهُ عَنِ المُعْضِلَاتِ
Peace be upon you oh one protected from slips	السَّلَامُ عَلَيْكَ أَيُّهَا المَعْصُومُ مِنَ الزَّلَّاتِ
Peace be upon you oh immaculate in lineage	السَّلَامُ عَلَيْكَ أَيُّهَا الزَّكِيُّ فِي الحَسَبِ
Peace be upon you oh the one raised in ancestry	السَّلَامُ عَلَيْكَ أَيُّهَا الرَّفِيعُ فِي النَّسَبِ
Peace be upon you oh compassionate Imam	السَّلَامُ عَلَيْكَ أَيُّهَا الإِمَامُ الشَّفِيقُ
Peace be upon you oh well built fortress	السَّلَامُ عَلَيْكَ أَيُّهَا القَصْرُ المَشِيدُ
Peace be upon you oh Proof of Allah over all creation	السَّلَامُ عَلَيْكَ يَا حُجَّةَ اللهِ عَلَى الخَلْقِ أَجْمَعِينَ

Imam Baqir (as)

I bear witness, oh my master, that you proclaimed the truth loudly	أَشْهَدُ يَا مَوْلَايَ أَنَّكَ قَدْ صَدَعْتَ الْحَقَّ صَدْعاً
And extracted knowledge deeply	وَبَقَرْتَ الْعِلْمَ بَقْراً
And scattered it widely	وَنَثَرْتَهُ نَثْراً
You were not taken in the way of Allah by the blame of any blamer	لَمْ تَأْخُذْكَ فِي اللَّهِ لَوْمَةُ لَائِمٍ
And you were a keeper of the religion of Allah	وَكُنْتَ لِدِينِ اللَّهِ مُكَاتِماً
And you fulfilled what was upon you	وَقَضَيْتَ مَا كَانَ عَلَيْكَ
And you brought out your friends from allegiance to other than Allah to allegiance to Allah	وَأَخْرَجْتَ أَوْلِيَاءَكَ مِنْ وِلَايَةِ غَيْرِ اللَّهِ إِلَى وِلَايَةِ اللَّهِ
And you commanded obedience to Allah	وَأَمَرْتَ بِطَاعَةِ اللَّهِ
And you prohibited disobedience to Allah	وَنَهَيْتَ عَنْ مَعْصِيَةِ اللَّهِ
Until Allah took you to His pleasure	حَتَّى قَبَضَكَ اللَّهُ إِلَى رِضْوَانِهِ
And made you go to the abode of His nobility	وَذَهَبَ بِكَ إِلَى دَارِ كَرَامَتِهِ
And the dwellings of His chosen ones	وَإِلَى مَسَاكِنِ أَصْفِيَائِهِ
And the neighborhood of His friends	وَمُجَاوَرَةِ أَوْلِيَائِهِ
And peace be upon you and the mercy of Allah and His blessings	وَالسَّلَامُ عَلَيْكَ وَرَحْمَةُ اللَّهِ وَبَرَكَاتُهُ

Imam Sadiq (as)

"By Allah! I love your aromas, and your souls, and seeing you, and visiting you, and I am on the religion of Allah and the religion of His angels, so assist me in that with devotion." – Imam Sadiq (as)

(Bihar Al-Anwar, Hub-e-Ali translation, vol 65, page 40)

On 17 Rabiul Awal to celebrate his birth, and on 25 Shawwal to commemorate his martyrdom you can recite the following ziyarah.

Peace be upon you oh truthful Imam	السَّلامُ عَلَيكَ أَيُّها الإِمامُ الصَّادِقُ
Peace be upon you oh articulate successor	السَّلامُ عَلَيكَ أَيُّها الوَصِي النَّاطِقُ
Peace be upon you oh destroyer and rebuilder	السَّلامُ عَلَيكَ أَيُّها الفَاتِقُ الرَّاتِقُ
Peace be upon you oh the greatest peak	السَّلامُ عَلَيكَ أَيُّها السَّنَامُ الأَعْظَمُ
Peace be upon you oh most upright path	السَّلامُ عَلَيكَ أَيُّها الصِّراطُ الأَقْوَمُ
Peace be upon you oh key to goodness	السَّلامُ عَلَيكَ يا مِفْتاحَ الخَيراتِ
Peace be upon you oh essence of blessings	السَّلامُ عَلَيكَ يا مَعْدِنَ البَرَكاتِ
Peace be upon you oh possessor of proofs and evidences	السَّلامُ عَلَيكَ يا صاحِبَ الحُجَجِ وَالدَّلالاتِ
Peace be upon you oh possessor of clear proofs	السَّلامُ عَلَيكَ يا صاحِبَ البَراهِينِ الواضِحاتِ
Peace be upon you oh supporter of the religion of Allah	السَّلامُ عَلَيكَ يا ناصِرَ دِينِ اللهِ
Peace be upon you oh propagator of the rulings of Allah	السَّلامُ عَلَيكَ يا ناشِرَ حُكْمِ اللهِ
Peace be upon you oh decisive in rhetoric	السَّلامُ عَلَيكَ يا فاصِلَ الخِطاباتِ

Imam Sadiq (as)

Peace be upon you oh remover of distresses	السَّلامُ عَلَيْكَ يا كاشِفَ الكُرُباتِ
Peace be upon you oh dean of the truthful	السَّلامُ عَلَيْكَ يا عَمِيدَ الصَّادِقِينَ
Peace be upon you oh tongue of the articulate	السَّلامُ عَلَيْكَ يا لِسانَ النَّاطِقِينَ
Peace be upon you oh successor of the fearful	السَّلامُ عَلَيْكَ يا خَلَفَ الخائِفِينَ
Peace be upon you oh leader of the righteous	السَّلامُ عَلَيْكَ يا زَعِيمَ الصَّالِحِينَ
Peace be upon you oh chief of the Muslims	السَّلامُ عَلَيْكَ يا سَيِّدَ المُسْلِمِينَ
Peace be upon you oh cave of the believers	السَّلامُ عَلَى يا كَهْفَ المُؤْمِنِينَ
Peace be upon you oh guide of the misguided	السَّلامُ عَلَيْكَ يا هادِيَ المُضِلِّينَ
Peace be upon you oh tranquillity of the obedient	السَّلامُ عَلَيْكَ يا سَكَنَ الطَّائِعِينَ
I bear witness, oh my master, that you are the landmark of guidance	أَشْهَدُ يا مَوْلايَ أَنَّكَ عَلَمُ الهُدَى
And the firmest handhold, and the morning sun, and the graceful ocean	وَالعُرْوَةُ الوُثْقَى وَشَمْسُ الضُّحَى وَبَحْرُ النَّدَى
And the cave of humanity, and the highest exemplar	وَكَهْفُ الوَرَى وَالمَثَلُ الأَعْلَى
And may Allah's blessings be upon your soul and body	وَصَلَّى اللهُ عَلَى رُوحِكَ وَبَدَنِكَ
And peace be upon you and upon Al-Abbas, the uncle of the Messenger of Allah	وَالسَّلامُ عَلَيْكَ وَعَلَى العَبَّاسِ عَمِّ رَسُولِ اللهِ
And the mercy of Allah and His blessings	وَآلِهِ وَرَحْمَةُ اللهِ وَبَرَكاتُه

Imam Kadhem (as)

"By Allah! Our friend does not exit the world except that Allah, His Messenger, and we are pleased with him. Allah will resurrect him with what sins he has, his face whitened, his nakedness covered, safe of his dread. There is no fear on him nor will he grieve, and that is because he does not exit the world until he is cleansed of his sins, either by calamity in wealth, himself, children, or illness." – Imam Kadhem (as)

(Bihar Al-Anwar, Hub-e-Ali translation, vol 65, page 216)

On 7 Safar to celebrate his birth, and on 25 Rajab to commemorate his martyrdom you can recite the following ziyarah.

Peace be upon you oh friend of Allah and son of His friend	اَلسَّلَامُ عَلَيْكَ يَا وَلِيَّ ٱللَّهِ وَٱبْنَ وَلِيِّهِ
Peace be upon you oh proof of Allah and son of His proof	اَلسَّلَامُ عَلَيْكَ يَا حُجَّةَ ٱللَّهِ وَٱبْنَ حُجَّتِهِ
Peace be upon you oh chosen by Allah and son of His choice	اَلسَّلَامُ عَلَيْكَ يَا صَفِيَّ ٱللَّهِ وَٱبْنَ صَفِيِّهِ
Peace be upon you oh trustee of Allah and son of His trustee	اَلسَّلَامُ عَلَيْكَ يَا أَمِينَ ٱللَّهِ وَٱبْنَ أَمِينِهِ
Peace be upon you oh light of Allah in the darkness of the earth	اَلسَّلَامُ عَلَيْكَ يَا نُورَ ٱللَّهِ فِي ظُلُمَاتِ ٱلْأَرْضِ
Peace be upon you oh Imam of guidance	اَلسَّلَامُ عَلَيْكَ يَا إِمَامَ ٱلْهُدَى
Peace be upon you oh landmark of the religion and piety	اَلسَّلَامُ عَلَيْكَ يَا عَلَمَ ٱلدِّينِ وَٱلتُّقَى
Peace be upon you oh treasurer of the knowledge of the Prophets	اَلسَّلَامُ عَلَيْكَ يَا خَازِنَ عِلْمِ ٱلنَّبِيِّينَ
Peace be upon you oh treasurer of the knowledge of the Messengers	اَلسَّلَامُ عَلَيْكَ يَا خَازِنَ عِلْمِ ٱلْمُرْسَلِينَ

Imam Kadhem (as)

Peace be upon you oh representative of the preceding successors	اَلسَّلَامُ عَلَيْكَ يَا نَائِبَ ٱلْأَوْصِيَاءِ ٱلسَّابِقِينَ
Peace be upon you oh essence of the clear revelation	اَلسَّلَامُ عَلَيْكَ يَا مَعْدِنَ ٱلْوَحْيِ ٱلْمُبِينِ
Peace be upon you oh possessor of certain knowledge	اَلسَّلَامُ عَلَيْكَ يَا صَاحِبَ ٱلْعِلْمِ ٱلْيَقِينِ
Peace be upon you oh repository of the knowledge of the Messengers	اَلسَّلَامُ عَلَيْكَ يَا عَيْبَةَ عِلْمِ ٱلْمُرْسَلِينَ
Peace be upon you oh righteous Imam	اَلسَّلَامُ عَلَيْكَ أَيُّهَا ٱلْإِمَامُ ٱلصَّالِحُ
Peace be upon you oh ascetic Imam	اَلسَّلَامُ عَلَيْكَ أَيُّهَا ٱلْإِمَامُ ٱلزَّاهِدُ
Peace be upon you oh worshipping Imam	اَلسَّلَامُ عَلَيْكَ أَيُّهَا ٱلْإِمَامُ ٱلْعَابِدُ
Peace be upon you oh rightly-guided Imam and chief	اَلسَّلَامُ عَلَيْكَ أَيُّهَا ٱلْإِمَامُ ٱلسَّيِّدُ ٱلرَّشِيدُ
Peace be upon you oh martyred and killed one	اَلسَّلَامُ عَلَيْكَ أَيُّهَا ٱلْمَقْتُولُ ٱلشَّهِيدُ
Peace be upon you oh son of Allah's Messenger and son of his successor	اَلسَّلَامُ عَلَيْكَ يَا بْنَ رَسُولِ ٱللَّهِ وَٱبْنَ وَصِيِّهِ
Peace be upon you oh my master Musa ibn Ja'far	اَلسَّلَامُ عَلَيْكَ يَا مَوْلَايَ مُوسَىٰ بْنَ جَعْفَرٍ
And the mercy of Allah and His blessings	وَرَحْمَةُ ٱللَّهِ وَبَرَكَاتُهُ
I bear witness that you certainly conveyed from Allah what He entrusted you with	أَشْهَدُ أَنَّكَ قَدْ بَلَّغْتَ عَنِ ٱللَّهِ مَا حَمَّلَكَ

And preserved what He deposited with you	وَحَفِظْتَ مَا ٱسْتَوْدَعَكَ
And made lawful the lawful of Allah	وَحَلَّلْتَ حَلَالَ ٱللَّهِ
And made unlawful the unlawful of Allah	وَحَرَّمْتَ حَرَامَ ٱللَّهِ
And established the laws of Allah	وَأَقَمْتَ أَحْكَامَ ٱللَّهِ
And recited the Book of Allah	وَتَلَوْتَ كِتَابَ ٱللَّهِ
And endured harm in the cause of Allah	وَصَبَرْتَ عَلَى ٱلْأَذَى فِي جَنْبِ ٱللَّهِ
And struggled for Allah, true to His struggle	وَجَاهَدْتَ فِي ٱللَّهِ حَقَّ جِهَادِهِ
Until certainty came to you	حَتَّى أَتَاكَ ٱلْيَقِينُ
And I bear witness that you proceeded on what your pure fathers proceeded	وَأَشْهَدُ أَنَّكَ مَضَيْتَ عَلَى مَا مَضَى عَلَيْهِ آبَاؤُكَ ٱلطَّاهِرُونَ
And good forefathers	وَأَجْدَادُكَ ٱلطَّيِّبُونَ
The successors, the guides	ٱلْأَوْصِيَاءُ ٱلْهَادُونَ
The rightly guided Imams	ٱلْأَئِمَّةُ ٱلْمَهْدِيُّونَ
You did not prefer blindness over guidance	لَمْ تُؤْثِرْ عَمًى عَلَى هُدًى
And did not incline from truth towards falsehood	وَلَمْ تَمِلْ مِنْ حَقٍّ إِلَى بَاطِلٍ
I also bear witness that you advised for Allah	وَأَشْهَدُ أَنَّكَ نَصَحْتَ لِلَّهِ
And His Messenger, and the commander of the faithful	وَلِرَسُولِهِ وَلِأَمِيرِ ٱلْمُؤْمِنِينَ
And you fulfilled the trust	وَأَنَّكَ أَدَّيْتَ ٱلْأَمَانَةَ
And avoided betrayal	وَٱجْتَنَبْتَ ٱلْخِيَانَةَ
And established the prayers	وَأَقَمْتَ ٱلصَّلَاةَ

Imam Kadhem (as)

And gave charity	وَآتَيْتَ ٱلزَّكَاةَ
And enjoined good	وَأَمَرْتَ بِٱلْمَعْرُوفِ
And forbade evil	وَنَهَيْتَ عَنِ ٱلْمُنْكَرِ
And worshipped Allah sincerely	وَعَبَدْتَ ٱللَّهَ مُخْلِصاً
Struggling, seeking reward	مُجْتَهِداً مُحْتَسِباً
Until certainty came to you	حَتَّىٰ أَتَاكَ ٱلْيَقِينُ
So may Allah reward you on behalf of Islam and its people	فَجَزَاكَ ٱللَّهُ عَنِ ٱلْإِسْلَامِ وَأَهْلِهِ
With the best and noblest reward	أَفْضَلَ ٱلْجَزَاءِ وَأَشْرَفَ ٱلْجَزَاءِ
I have come to you, oh son of the Messenger of Allah, as a visitor	أَتَيْتُكَ يَا بْنَ رَسُولِ ٱللَّهِ زَائِراً
Recognizing your right	عَارِفاً بِحَقِّكَ
Acknowledging your virtue	مُقِرّاً بِفَضْلِكَ
Bearing your knowledge	مُحْتَمِلاً لِعِلْمِكَ
Seeking protection through your covenant	مُحْتَجِباً بِذِمَّتِكَ
Taking refuge at your grave	عَائِذاً بِقَبْرِكَ
Seeking shelter at your shrine	لَائِذاً بِضَرِيحِكَ
Seeking your intercession with Allah	مُسْتَشْفِعاً بِكَ إِلَىٰ ٱللَّهِ
Being loyal to your loyalists	مُوَالِياً لِأَوْلِيَائِكَ
Being hostile to your enemies	مُعَادِياً لِأَعْدَائِكَ
Insightful regarding your matter	مُسْتَبْصِراً بِشَأْنِكَ
And with the guidance you are on	وَبِٱلْهُدَىٰ ٱلَّذِي أَنْتَ عَلَيْهِ

Knowing the misguidance of whoever opposed you	عَالِماً بِضَلَالَةِ مَنْ خَالَفَكَ
And the blindness which they are on	وَبِالْعَمَىٰ ٱلَّذِي هُمْ عَلَيْهِ
May my father and mother be sacrificed for you	بِأَبِي أَنْتَ وَأُمِّي
And myself and my family	وَنَفْسِي وَأَهْلِي
And my wealth and my children	وَمَالِي وَوَلَدِي
Oh son of Allah's Messenger	يَا بْنَ رَسُولِ ٱللَّه
I came seeking closeness to Allah the Exalted by visiting you	أَتَيْتُكَ مُتَقَرِّباً بِزِيَارَتِكَ إِلَى ٱللَّهِ تَعَالَىٰ
And seeking your intercession with Him	وَمُسْتَشْفِعاً بِكَ إِلَيْهِ
So intercede for me with your Lord	فَٱشْفَعْ لِي عِنْدَ رَبِّكَ
That He may forgive my sins	لِيَغْفِرَ لِي ذُنُوبِي
And pardon my offenses	وَيَعْفُوَ عَنْ جُرْمِي
And overlook my evildoings	وَيَتَجَاوَزَ عَنْ سَيِّئَاتِي
And erase my mistakes from me	وَيَمْحُوَ عَنِّي خَطِيئَاتِي
And admit me into Paradise	وَيُدْخِلَنِي ٱلْجَنَّةَ
And bestow upon me with what suits Him	وَيَتَفَضَّلَ عَلَيَّ بِمَا هُوَ أَهْلُهُ
And to forgive me, and my parents	وَيَغْفِرَ لِي وَلِآبَائِي
And my brothers and sisters	وَلِإِخْوَانِي وَأَخَوَاتِي
And all the believing men and women	وَلِجَمِيعِ ٱلْمُؤْمِنِينَ وَٱلْمُؤْمِنَاتِ
In the easts of the earth and its wests	فِي مَشَارِقِ ٱلْأَرْضِ وَمَغَارِبِهَا
By His grace, generosity, and favour	بِفَضْلِهِ وَجُودِهِ وَمَنِّهِ

Imam Kadhem (as)

Peace be upon you oh my master	اَلسَّلَامُ عَلَيْكَ يَا مَوْلَايَ
Oh Musa ibn Ja'far	يَا مُوسَىٰ بْنَ جَعْفَرٍ
And the mercy of Allah and His blessings	وَرَحْمَةُ ٱللَّهِ وَبَرَكَاتُهُ
I bear witness that you are the guiding Imam	أَشْهَدُ أَنَّكَ ٱلْإِمَامُ ٱلْهَادِى
And the intimate guiding master	وَٱلْوَلِىُّ ٱلْمُرْشِدُ
And you are the essence of revelation	وَأَنَّكَ مَعْدِنُ ٱلتَّنْزِيلِ
And possessor of true interpretation	وَصَاحِبُ ٱلتَّأْوِيلِ
And carrier of the Torah and the Gospel	وَحَامِلُ ٱلتَّوْرَاةِ وَٱلْإِنْجِيلِ
And knowledgeable, the just	وَٱلْعَالِمُ ٱلْعَادِلُ
And the truthful, working one	وَٱلصَّادِقُ ٱلْعَامِلُ
Oh my master, I disassociate myself to Allah from your enemies	يَا مَوْلَايَ أَنَا أَبْرَأُ إِلَى ٱللَّهِ مِنْ أَعْدَائِكَ
And I seek closeness to Allah through loyalty to you	وَأَتَقَرَّبُ إِلَى ٱللَّهِ بِمُوَالَاتِكَ
So may Allah send blessings upon you	فَصَلَّى ٱللَّهُ عَلَيْكَ
And upon your fathers and your forefathers and your sons	وَعَلَىٰ آبَائِكَ وَأَجْدَادِكَ وَأَبْنَائِكَ
And your Shia, and those who love you	وَشِيعَتِكَ وَمُحِبِّيكَ
And the mercy of Allah and His blessings	وَرَحْمَةُ ٱللَّهِ وَبَرَكَاتُهُ

Imam Redha (as)

"Oh Musa bin Sayyar, you don't know that the deeds of our Shias are presented to us, Imams, every morning and evening. Then for each of their shortcomings we beg the Almighty Allah to forgive them, and for each of their good deeds we pray to the Almighty to reward them." – Imam Redha (as)

(Mikyal Al-Makaarim, Sayyid Rizvi translation, page 101)

On 11 Dhul-Qidah to celebrate his birth, and on 29 Safar to commemorate his martyrdom you can recite the following ziyarah.

Peace be upon you oh friend of Allah and son of His friends	اَلسَّلَامُ عَلَيْكَ يَا وَلِيَّ اللَّهِ وَابْنَ أَوْلِيَآئِهِ
Peace be upon you oh ambassador of Allah and the son of His ambassadors	اَلسَّلَامُ عَلَيْكَ يَا سَفِيْرَ اللَّهِ وَابْنَ سُفَرَآئِهِ
Peace be upon you oh proof of Allah and son of His proofs	اَلسَّلَامُ عَلَيْكَ يَا حُجَّةَ اللَّهِ وَابْنَ حُجَجِهِ
Peace be upon you oh light of Allah in the darkness of Earth and the son of His lights	اَلسَّلَامُ عَلَيْكَ يَا نُوْرَ اللَّهِ فِيْ ظُلُمَاتِ الْأَرْضِ وَابْنَ أَنْوَارِهِ
Peace be upon you oh pillar of religion	اَلسَّلَامُ عَلَيْكَ يَا عَمُوْدَ الدِّيْنِ
Peace be upon you oh inheritor of the Prophets and Messengers	اَلسَّلَامُ عَلَيْكَ يَا وَارِثَ الْأَنْبِيَآءِ وَالْمُرْسَلِيْنَ
Peace be upon you oh inheritor of Adam, chosen one of Allah	اَلسَّلَامُ عَلَيْكَ يَا وَارِثَ آدَمَ صَفْوَةِ اللَّهِ
Peace be upon you oh inheritor of Nuh, confidant of Allah	اَلسَّلَامُ عَلَيْكَ يَا وَارِثَ نُوْحٍ نَجِيِّ اللَّهِ

Peace be upon you oh inheritor of Ibrahim, friend of Allah	اَلسَّلَامُ عَلَيْكَ يَا وَارِثَ إِبْرَاهِيمَ خَلِيلِ اللهِ
Peace be upon you oh inheritor of Ismail, the sacrifice to Allah	اَلسَّلَامُ عَلَيْكَ يَا وَارِثَ إِسْمَاعِيلَ ذَبِيحِ اللهِ
Peace be upon you oh inheritor of Musa, who spoke with Allah	اَلسَّلَامُ عَلَيْكَ يَا وَارِثَ مُوسَىٰ كَلِيمِ اللهِ
Peace be upon you oh inheritor of Issa, the spirit of Allah	اَلسَّلَامُ عَلَيْكَ يَا وَارِثَ عِيْسَىٰ رُوْحِ اللهِ
Peace be upon you oh inheritor of Muhammad, (the beloved of Allah and) the Messenger of Allah	اَلسَّلَامُ عَلَيْكَ يَا وَارِثَ مُحَمَّدٍ (حَبِيْبِ اللهِ وَ) رَسُوْلِ اللهِ
Peace be upon you oh inheritor of the commander of the faithful, Ali Ibn Abu Talib	اَلسَّلَامُ عَلَيْكَ يَا وَارِثَ أَمِيْرِ الْمُؤْمِنِيْنَ عَلِيِّ بْنِ أَبِيْ طَالِبٍ
Peace of Allah be upon him, guardian (over the believers) of Allah, and successor of the Messenger of Allah	عَلَيْهِ السَّلَامُ وَلِيِّ اللهِ وَوَصِيِّ رَسُوْلِ اللهِ
Peace be upon you oh inheritor of Fatima, the radiant, chief of the women of the worlds, daughter of the Messenger of Allah	اَلسَّلَامُ عَلَيْكَ يَا وَارِثَ فَاطِمَةَ الزَّهْرَاءِ سَيِّدَةِ نِسَاءِ الْعَالَمِيْنَ بِنْتِ رَسُوْلِ اللهِ
Peace be upon you oh inheritor of Hasan and Husain, chiefs of the youths of Paradise (and grandsons of the Messenger of Allah)	اَلسَّلَامُ عَلَيْكَ يَا وَارِثَ الْحَسَنِ وَالْحُسَيْنِ سَيِّدَيْ شَبَابِ أَهْلِ الْجَنَّةِ (وَسِبْطَيْ رَسُوْلِ اللهِ)

Peace be upon you oh inheritor of Ali ibn Husain, chief of the prostrators and adornment of the worshippers	اَلسَّلَامُ عَلَيْكَ يَا وَارِثَ عَلِيِّ ابْنِ الْحُسَيْنِ سَيِّدِ السَّاجِدِيْنَ وَزَيْنِ الْعَابِدِيْنَ
Peace be upon you oh inheritor of Muhammad ibn Ali, splitter of knowledge of the first and last ones	اَلسَّلَامُ عَلَيْكَ يَا وَارِثَ مُحَمَّدِ بْنِ عَلِيٍّ بَاقِرِ عِلْمِ الْأَوَّلِيْنَ وَالْآخِرِيْنَ
Peace be upon you oh inheritor of Ja'far ibn Muhammad, the truthful, righteous, pious, and trustworthy	اَلسَّلَامُ عَلَيْكَ يَا وَارِثَ جَعْفَرِ بْنِ مُحَمَّدٍ الصَّادِقِ الْبَارِّ التَّقِيِّ الْأَمِيْنِ
Peace be upon you oh inheritor of Musa ibn Ja'far the knowledgeable, suppressor (of rage), kind, forbearing	اَلسَّلَامُ عَلَيْكَ يَا وَارِثَ مُوْسَى بْنِ جَعْفَرٍ الْعَالِمِ الْكَاظِمِ الْحَفِيِّ الْحَلِيْمِ
Peace be upon you oh truthful martyr	اَلسَّلَامُ عَلَيْكَ أَيُّهَا الصِّدِّيْقُ الشَّهِيْدُ
Peace be upon you oh satisfied, righteous, pious, and loyal successor	اَلسَّلَامُ عَلَيْكَ أَيُّهَا الْوَصِيُّ الرَّضِيُّ الْبَرُّ التَّقِيُّ الْوَفِيُّ
I bear witness that you established prayer, gave zakat,	أَشْهَدُ أَنَّكَ قَدْ أَقَمْتَ الصَّلَاةَ وَآتَيْتَ الزَّكَاةَ
Enjoined good and forbade evil, and worshipped Allah sincerely until certainty came to you	وَأَمَرْتَ بِالْمَعْرُوْفِ وَنَهَيْتَ عَنِ الْمُنْكَرِ وَعَبَدْتَ اللهَ مُخْلِصًا حَتَّى أَتَاكَ الْيَقِيْنُ
Peace be upon you oh great Imam and noble Imam, the far close Imam, and the poisoned stranger Imam	اَلسَّلَامُ عَلَيْكَ يَا إِمَامَ قَصِيْبٍ وَإِمَامَ نَجِيْبٍ وَإِمَامَ بَعِيْدٍ قَرِيْبٍ وَإِمَامَ مَسْمُوْمٍ غَرِيْبٍ

Imam Redha (as)

Peace be upon you oh insightful scholar and noble eminence, departed from soil of his grandfather, and father	اَلسَّلامُ عَلَيْكَ أَيُّهَا الْعَالِمُ النَّبِيهُ وَالْقَدْرُ الْوَجِيهُ النَّازِحُ عَنْ تُرْبَةِ جَدِّهِ وَأَبِيهِ
Peace be upon the one who commanded his children and family to mourn him before he was killed	اَلسَّلامُ عَلَى مَنْ أَمَرَ أَوْلادَهُ وَعِيَالَهُ بِالنِّيَاحَةِ عَلَيْهِ قَبْلَ وُصُولِ الْقَتْلِ إِلَيْهِ
Peace be upon your desolate dwellings, just as Mina and Arafat have become desolate without you	اَلسَّلامُ عَلَى دِيَارِكُمُ الْمُوحِشَاتِ كَمَا أَسْتَوْحَشَتْ مِنْكُمْ مِنًى وَعَرَفَاتٌ
Peace be upon the chiefs of the servants, promise of threat, the unused well, and the lofty palace	اَلسَّلامُ عَلَى سَادَاتِ الْعَبِيدِ وَعُدَّةِ الْوَعِيدِ وَالْبِئْرِ الْمُعَطَّلَةِ وَالْقَصْرِ الْمَشِيدِ
Peace be upon the help of the desperate and the one who elevated the land of Khorasan	اَلسَّلامُ عَلَى غَوْثِ اللَّهْفَانِ وَمَنْ صَارَتْ بِهِ أَرْضُ خُرَاسَانَ
Peace be upon the one who has few visitors, and the delight of the eye of Fatima, chief of the women of the worlds	اَلسَّلامُ عَلَى قَلِيلِ الزَّائِرِينَ وَقُرَّةِ عَيْنِ فَاطِمَةَ سَيِّدَةِ نِسَاءِ الْعَالَمِينَ
Peace be upon the joyful pleasure, pleasing manners, and branches from the tree of Ahmad	اَلسَّلامُ عَلَى الْبَهْجَةِ الرَّضَوِيَّةِ وَالْأَخْلاقِ الرَّضِيَّةِ وَالْغُصُونِ الْمُتَفَرِّعَةِ مِنَ الشَّجَرَةِ الْأَحْمَدِيَّةِ
Peace be upon the one to who the leadership of the greatest kingdom reached, and knowledge of everything for completion of the decided matter	اَلسَّلامُ عَلَى مَنْ أَنْتَهَى إِلَيْهِ رِئَاسَةُ الْمُلْكِ الْأَعْظَمِ وَعِلْمُ كُلِّ شَيْءٍ لِتَمَامِ الْأَمْرِ الْمُحْكَمِ

Continuous Calling

Peace be upon those whose names are a means for the askers, their shrines a sanctuary for the creatures, their proofs nullify the doubts of deviators

اَلسَّلَامُ عَلَى مَنْ اَسْمَآؤُهُمْ وَسِيْلَةُ السَّآئِلِيْنَ وَهَيَاكِلُهُمْ أَمَانُ الْمَخْلُوقِيْنَ وَحُجَجُهُمْ إِبْطَالُ شُبَهِ الْمُلْحِدِيْنَ

Peace be upon the one who's father's speaking cushion was made available, the commander of the faithful, until he debated the People of the Book and established the foundations of the religion

اَلسَّلَامُ عَلَى مَنْ كُسِرَتْ لَهُ وِسَادَةُ وَالِدِهِ أَمِيْرِ الْمُؤْمِنِيْنَ حَتَّى خَصَمَ أَهْلَ الْكُتُبِ وَثَبَّتَ قَوَاعِدَ الدِّيْنِ

Peace be upon the standard of standards, the hearts of his followers are broken due to his estrangement until the Day of Resurrection

اَلسَّلَامُ عَلَى عَلَمِ الْأَعْلَامِ وَمَنْ كُسِرَتْ قُلُوْبُ شِيْعَتِهِ بِغُرْبَتِهِ إِلَى يَوْمِ الْقِيَامَةِ

Peace be upon the blazing lamp and turbulent ocean whose soil became the descent and ascent of angels

اَلسَّلَامُ عَلَى السِّرَاجِ الْوَهَّاجِ وَالْبَحْرِ الْعَجَّاجِ الَّذِيْ صَارَتْ تُرْبَتُهُ مَهْبَطَ الْأَمْلَاكِ وَالْمِعْرَاجِ

Peace be upon the leaders of Islam and kings of faith

اَلسَّلَامُ عَلَى أُمَرَآءِ الْإِسْلَامِ وَمُلُوْكِ الْإِيْمَانِ

Peace be upon the astonishing light, the pure births, and those for who Allah revealed the knowledge of the unseen and the witnessed, and made them, by His grace, the spring of guidance and essence of happiness

اَلسَّلَامُ عَلَى بَاهِرِيْ النُّوْرِ وَطَاهِرِي الْوِلَادَةِ وَمَنْ أَطْلَعَهُمُ اللَّهُ عَلَى عُلُوْمِ الْغَيْبِ وَالشَّهَادَةِ وَجَعَلَهُمْ بِإِفْضَالِهِ مَنْبِعَ الْهُدَى وَمَعْدِنَ السَّعَادَةِ

Peace be upon the one the landmarks of Tus rejoiced for where he settled

اَلسَّلَامُ عَلَى مَنِ ابْتَهَجَتْ بِهِ مَعَالِمُ طُوْسٍ حَيْثُ حَلَّ بِرَبْعِهَا

Peace be upon the pride of the righteous one, and whose shrine is far, and the condition for entering Paradise and Hellfire

اَلسَّلَامُ عَلَى مُفْتَخَرِ الْأَبْرَارِ وَنَائِي الْمَزَارِ وَشَرْطِ دُخُولِ الْجَنَّةِ وَالنَّارِ

Peace be upon the one who Allah does not cut off His blessings at all hours, and through them stillness settled and movement moved

اَلسَّلَامُ عَلَى مَنْ لَمْ يَقْطَعِ اللَّهُ عَنْهُمْ صَلَوَاتِهِ فِي آنَاءِ السَّاعَاتِ وَبِهِمْ سَكَنَتِ السَّوَاكِنُ وَتَحَرَّكَتِ الْمُتَحَرِّكَاتِ

Peace be upon those whose leadership is a distinguisher between the two groups, as the people of two horizons worshipped through their allegiance

اَلسَّلَامُ عَلَى مَنْ جَعَلَ إِمَامَتَهُمْ مُمَيِّزَةً بَيْنَ الْفَرِيقَيْنِ كَمَا تَعَبَّدَ بِوَلَايَتِهِمْ أَهْلُ الْخَافِقَيْنِ

Peace be upon the one through who Allah has revived the decaying wisdom of the Prophets, and sent them with their guardianship, to perfect the word of Allah, Lord of the Worlds

اَلسَّلَامُ عَلَى مَنْ أَحْيَى اللَّهُ بِهِمْ دَارِسَ حِكَمِ النَّبِيِّينَ وَابْتَعَثَهُمْ بِوَلَايَتِهِمْ لِتَمَامِ كَلِمَةِ اللَّهِ رَبِّ الْعَالَمِينَ

Peace be upon the months of the year, and the number of hours, and the number of 'There is no god but Allah' in the inscribed records

اَلسَّلَامُ عَلَى شُهُورِ الْحَوْلِ وَعَدَدِ السَّاعَاتِ وَعَدَدِ لَا إِلَهَ إِلَّا اللَّهُ فِي رُقُومِ (الرُّقُومِ) الْمُسَطَّرَاتِ

Peace be upon the arrival and rising of the world, and those who when asked about the word of monotheism, they said "By Allah, we are from its conditions."

اَلسَّلَامُ عَلَى إِقْبَالِ الدُّنْيَا وَسُعُودِهَا وَمَنْ سُئِلُوا عَنْ كَلِمَةِ التَّوْحِيدِ فَقَالُوا نَحْنُ وَاللَّهِ مِنْ شُرُوطِهَا

Peace be upon those who justify the existence of every creation through their guardianship and about who the preachers have preached

اَلسَّلَامُ عَلَى مَنْ يُعَلَّلُ وُجُودُ كُلِّ مَخْلُوقٍ بِوَلَايَتِهِمْ وَمَنْ خَطَبَتْ لَهُمُ الْخُطَبَاءُ

Peace be upon those whose glory and praise is lofty, and who surpassed, with their fathers and sons, the earlier and later generations	اَلسَّلَامُ عَلَى مَنْ عَلَا مَجْدُهُمْ وَثَنَاؤُهُمْ وَفَاقَ الْأَوَّلِينَ وَالْآخِرِينَ أَبَاؤُهُمْ وَأَبْنَاؤُهُمْ
Peace be upon those by whose pride, pride boasts, elevated by the mandatory sending of blessings upon them, and the purity of their clothes	اَلسَّلَامُ عَلَى مَنِ افْتَخَرَ الْفَخْرُ بِفَخْرِهِمْ وَعَلَا بِهِمْ بِوُجُوبِ الصَّلَاةِ عَلَيْهِمْ وَطَهَارَةِ ثِيَابِهِمْ
Peace be upon the moon of moons, pride of the righteous, and the speaker of every language with its people, that said to his followers "Allah would not appoint an Imam on a community until He teaches him their languages and religions"	اَلسَّلَامُ عَلَى قَمَرِ الْأَقْمَارِ وَفَخْرِ الْأَبْرَارِ الْمُتَكَلِّمِ مَعَ كُلِّ لُغَةٍ بِلِسَانِهِمُ الْقَابِلِ لِشِيعَتِهِ مَا كَانَ اللَّهُ لِيُوَلِّيَ إِمَامًا عَلَى أُمَّةٍ حَتَّى يُعَرِّفَهُ بِلُغَاتِهِمْ وَأَدْيَانِهِمْ
Peace be upon the happiness of the heart, relief of the distressed, and noble of nobles and the pride of Abd Manaf	اَلسَّلَامُ عَلَى فَرْحَةِ الْقُلُوبِ وَفَرَجِ الْمَكْرُوبِ وَشَرِيفِ الْأَشْرَافِ وَمَفْخَرِ عَبْدِ مَنَافٍ
If only I was from the circulators in the courtyard of his presence, witness to the joy of his companionship	يَا لَيْتَنِي كُنْتُ مِنَ الطَّائِفِينَ بِعَرْصَةِ حَضْرَتِهِ مُسْتَشْهِدًا لِبَهْجَةِ مُؤَانَسَتِهِ
Peace be upon the compassionate Imam, who stirred the sorrows of the Day of At-Tufuf	اَلسَّلَامُ عَلَى الْإِمَامِ الرَّؤُوفِ الَّذِي هَيَّجَ أَحْزَانَ يَوْمِ الطُّفُوفِ

Imam Redha (as)

I swear by Allah and by your pure fathers and your chosen righteous sons, had the journey to your abode not been made far, I would have fulfilled some of the obligation of your right by frequently visiting	بِاللَّهِ أُقْسِمُ وَبِآبَائِكَ الْأَطْهَارِ وَبِأَبْنَائِكَ الْمُنْتَجَبِينَ الْأَبْرَارِ لَوْ لَا بُعْدُ الشُّقَّةِ حَيْثُ شَطَّتْ بِكُمُ الدَّارِ لَقَضَيْتُ بَعْضَ وَاجِبِ حَقِّكُمْ بِتَكْرَارِ الْمَزَارِ
Peace be upon you oh the protectors of the religion, children of the Prophets, and chiefs of the created, and may Allah's mercy and blessings be upon you	اَلسَّلَامُ عَلَيْكُمْ يَا حُمَاةَ الدِّينِ وَأَوْلَادَ النَّبِيِّينَ وَسَادَةَ الْمَخْلُوقِينَ وَرَحْمَةُ اللَّهِ وَبَرَكَاتُهُ

Imam Jawad (as)

Writing to a man who lost his son:

"May Allah increase your reward, comfort you, and strengthen your heart, He is Mighty, Powerful. May Allah give you a descendant soon and I hope that He has done so God willing." – Imam Jawad (as)

(The Life of Imam Jawad by Baqir Shareef al-Qurashi, Abdullah al-Shahin translation, page 80)

On 10 Rajab to celebrate his birth, and on 30 Dhul-Qidah to commemorate his martyrdom you can recite the following ziyarah.

Peace be upon you oh Abu-Ja'far	اَلسَّلَامُ عَلَيْكَ يَا أَبَا جَعْفَرٍ
Muhammad ibn Ali	مُحَمَّدُ بْنَ عَلِيٍّ
The righteous, the pious	ٱلْبَرُّ ٱلتَّقِيُّ
The faithful Imam	ٱلْإِمَامُ ٱلْوَفِيُّ
Peace be upon you oh content and immaculate	اَلسَّلَامُ عَلَيْكَ أَيُّهَا ٱلرَّضِيُّ ٱلزَّكِيُّ
Peace be upon you oh guardian of Allah (over the believers)	اَلسَّلَامُ عَلَيْكَ يَا وَلِيَّ ٱللَّهِ
Peace be upon you oh confidant of Allah	اَلسَّلَامُ عَلَيْكَ يَا نَجِيَّ ٱللَّهِ
Peace be upon you oh representative of Allah	اَلسَّلَامُ عَلَيْكَ يَا سَفِيرَ ٱللَّهِ
Peace be upon you oh secret of Allah	اَلسَّلَامُ عَلَيْكَ يَا سِرَّ ٱللَّهِ
Peace be upon you oh light of Allah	اَلسَّلَامُ عَلَيْكَ يَا ضِيَاءَ ٱللَّهِ
Peace be upon you oh radiance of Allah	اَلسَّلَامُ عَلَيْكَ يَا سَنَاءَ ٱللَّهِ
Peace be upon you oh word of Allah	اَلسَّلَامُ عَلَيْكَ يَا كَلِمَةَ ٱللَّهِ
Peace be upon you oh Allah's mercy	اَلسَّلَامُ عَلَيْكَ يَا رَحْمَةَ ٱللَّهِ
Peace be upon you oh shining light	اَلسَّلَامُ عَلَيْكَ أَيُّهَا ٱلنُّورُ ٱلسَّاطِعُ

Imam Jawad (as)

Peace be upon you oh rising full moon	اَلسَّلَامُ عَلَيْكَ أَيُّهَا ٱلْبَدْرُ ٱلطَّالِعُ
Peace be upon you oh pure one from the pure	اَلسَّلَامُ عَلَيْكَ أَيُّهَا ٱلطَّيِّبُ مِنَ ٱلطَّيِّبِينَ
Peace be upon you oh purified from the purified	اَلسَّلَامُ عَلَيْكَ أَيُّهَا ٱلطَّاهِرُ مِنَ ٱلْمُطَهَّرِينَ
Peace be upon you oh greatest sign	اَلسَّلَامُ عَلَيْكَ أَيُّهَا ٱلْآيَةُ ٱلْعُظْمَىٰ
Peace be upon you oh grandest proof	اَلسَّلَامُ عَلَيْكَ أَيُّهَا ٱلْحُجَّةُ ٱلْكُبْرَىٰ
Peace be upon you oh purified from slips	اَلسَّلَامُ عَلَيْكَ أَيُّهَا ٱلْمُطَهَّرُ مِنَ ٱلزَّلَّاتِ
Peace be upon you oh free from difficulties	اَلسَّلَامُ عَلَيْكَ أَيُّهَا ٱلْمُنَزَّهُ عَنِ ٱلْمُعْضِلَاتِ
Peace be upon you oh exalted above the deficiency of descriptions	اَلسَّلَامُ عَلَيْكَ أَيُّهَا ٱلْعَلِيُّ عَنْ نَقْصِ ٱلْأَوْصَافِ
Peace be upon you oh content among the noble ones	اَلسَّلَامُ عَلَيْكَ أَيُّهَا ٱلرَّضِيُّ عِنْدَ ٱلْأَشْرَافِ
Peace be upon you oh pillar of the religion	اَلسَّلَامُ عَلَيْكَ يَا عَمُودَ ٱلدِّينِ
I bear witness that you are the guardian (over the believers) of Allah	أَشْهَدُ أَنَّكَ وَلِيُّ ٱللَّهِ
And His proof on His Earth	وَحُجَّتُهُ فِي أَرْضِهِ
And you are the side of Allah and the choice of Allah	وَأَنَّكَ جَنْبُ ٱللَّهِ وَخِيَرَةُ ٱللَّهِ
And the repository of the knowledge of Allah and the Prophets	وَمُسْتَوْدَعُ عِلْمِ ٱللَّهِ وَعِلْمِ ٱلْأَنْبِيَاءِ

And the pillar of faith and interpreter of the Qur'an	وَرُكْنُ ٱلْإِيمَانِ وَتَرْجُمَانُ ٱلْقُرْآنِ
And I bear witness that whoever follows you is on truth and guidance	وَأَشْهَدُ أَنَّ مَنِ ٱتَّبَعَكَ عَلَى ٱلْحَقِّ وَٱلْهُدَى
And whoever denies you and shows hostility towards you	وَأَنَّ مَنْ أَنْكَرَكَ وَنَصَبَ لَكَ ٱلْعَدَاوَةَ
Is upon misguidance and ruin	عَلَى ٱلضَّلَالَةِ وَٱلرَّدَى
I disassociate to Allah and to you from them in this world and the Hereafter	أَبْرَأُ إِلَى ٱللَّهِ وَإِلَيْكَ مِنْهُمْ فِي ٱلدُّنْيَا وَٱلْآخِرَةِ
Peace be upon you as long as I remain alive, and as long as night and day remain	وَٱلسَّلَامُ عَلَيْكَ مَا بَقِيتُ وَبَقِيَ ٱللَّيْلُ وَٱلنَّهَارُ
Oh Allah, send blessings upon Muhammad and his Ahlul Bayt	ٱللَّهُمَّ صَلِّ عَلَى مُحَمَّدٍ وَأَهْلِ بَيْتِهِ
And send blessings upon Muhammad ibn Ali	وَصَلِّ عَلَى مُحَمَّدِ بْنِ عَلِيٍّ
The immaculate, the pious	ٱلزَّكِيِّ ٱلتَّقِيِّ
The righteous, the faithful	وَٱلْبَرِّ ٱلْوَفِيِّ
The refined, the pure	وَٱلْمُهَذَّبِ ٱلنَّقِيِّ
Guide of the nation	هَادِي ٱلْأُمَّةِ
And inheritor of the Imams	وَوَارِثِ ٱلْأَئِمَّةِ
And keeper of mercy	وَخَازِنِ ٱلرَّحْمَةِ
And spring of wisdom	وَيَنْبُوعِ ٱلْحِكْمَةِ
And leader of blessings	وَقَائِدِ ٱلْبَرَكَةِ
And match of the Qur'an in obedience	وَعَدِيلِ ٱلْقُرْآنِ فِي ٱلطَّاعَةِ

Imam Jawad (as)

And unique among the successors in sincerity and worship	وَوَاحِدِ ٱلْأَوْصِيَاءِ فِي ٱلْإِخْلَاصِ وَٱلْعِبَادَةِ
Your supreme proof	وَحُجَّتِكَ ٱلْعُلْيَا
And Your highest example	وَمَثَلِكَ ٱلْأَعْلَىٰ
And Your best Word	وَكَلِمَتِكَ ٱلْحُسْنَىٰ
And the caller to You	ٱلدَّاعِي إِلَيْكَ
And the director to You	وَٱلدَّالِّ عَلَيْكَ
The one You appointed as a landmark for Your servants	ٱلَّذِي نَصَبْتَهُ عَلَماً لِعِبَادِكَ
And interpreter of Your Book	وَمُتَرْجِماً لِكِتَابِكَ
And proclaimer of Your command	وَصَادِعاً بِأَمْرِكَ
And supporter of Your religion	وَنَاصِراً لِدِينِكَ
And proof against Your creation	وَحُجَّةً عَلَىٰ خَلْقِكَ
And light with which you pierce darkness	وَنُوراً تَخْرُقُ بِهِ ٱلظُّلَمَ
And a model by which guidance is attained	وَقُدْوَةً تُدْرَكُ بِهَا ٱلْهِدَايَةُ
And an intercessor by whom Paradise is obtained	وَشَفِيعاً تُنَالُ بِهِ ٱلْجَنَّةُ
Oh Allah, just as he took his share through his humility to You	اَللَّهُمَّ وَكَمَا أَخَذَ فِي خُشُوعِهِ لَكَ حَظَّهُ
And fulfilled, through fear of You, his share	وَٱسْتَوْفَىٰ مِنْ خَشْيَتِكَ نَصِيبَهُ
So send blessings upon him multiples of what You have sent upon any friend	فَصَلِّ عَلَيْهِ أَضْعَافَ مَا صَلَّيْتَ عَلَىٰ وَلِيٍّ

Continuous Calling

Whose obedience You have approved	اَرْتَضَيْتَ طَاعَتَهُ
And whose service You have accepted	وَقَبِلْتَ خِدْمَتَهُ
And convey to him from us greetings and peace	وَبَلِّغْهُ مِنَّا تَحِيَّةً وَسَلَاماً
And grant us, in our friendship with him, grace and excellence from You	وَآتِنَا فِي مُوَالَاتِهِ مِنْ لَدُنْكَ فَضْلًا وَإِحْسَاناً
And forgiveness and pleasure	وَمَغْفِرَةً وَرِضْوَاناً
You are possessor of the ancient grace	إِنَّكَ ذُو ٱلْمَنِّ ٱلْقَدِيمِ
And the beautiful pardoning	وَٱلصَّفْحِ ٱلْجَمِيلِ

Imam Hadi (as)

Comforting his companion who was struggling with poverty:

"Oh Abu Hashim, which blessing of Allah, Mighty and Majestic, is on you that you wanted to fulfill its gratitude? He provided you with faith, forbade your body from the Fire, provided you good health, assisted you with obedience, provided you with contentment, and protected you from extravagance." And then he gave him some money without him asking.
– Imam Hadi (as)

(Bihar Al-Anwar Hub-e-Ali translation, vol 50, page 155)

On 15 Dhul-Hijjah to celebrate his birth, and on 3 Rajab to commemorate his martyrdom you can recite the following ziyarah.

Peace be upon you oh Abul-Hasan	اَلسَّلَامُ عَلَيْكَ يَا اَبَا الْحَسَنِ
Ali the son of Muhammad	عَلِيُّ بْنَ مُحَمَّدٍ
The immaculate, the rightly-guided	اَلزَّكِيُّ الرَّاشِدُ
The piercing light	اَلنُّورُ الثَّاقِبُ
And the mercy of Allah and His blessings	وَرَحْمَةُ اللَّهِ وَبَرَكَاتُهُ
Peace be upon you oh chosen by Allah	اَلسَّلَامُ عَلَيْكَ يَا صَفِيَّ اللَّهِ
Peace be upon you oh secret of Allah	اَلسَّلَامُ عَلَيْكَ يَا سِرَّ اللَّهِ
Peace be upon you oh rope of Allah	اَلسَّلَامُ عَلَيْكَ يَا حَبْلَ اللَّهِ
Peace be upon you oh family of Allah	اَلسَّلَامُ عَلَيْكَ يَا آلَ اللَّهِ
Peace be upon you oh select of Allah	اَلسَّلَامُ عَلَيْكَ يَا خِيَرَةَ اللَّهِ
Peace be upon you oh choice of Allah	اَلسَّلَامُ عَلَيْكَ يَا صَفْوَةَ اللَّهِ
Peace be upon you oh trustee of Allah	اَلسَّلَامُ عَلَيْكَ يَا أَمِينَ اللَّهِ
Peace be upon you oh truth of Allah	اَلسَّلَامُ عَلَيْكَ يَا حَقَّ اللَّهِ
Peace be upon you oh beloved by Allah	اَلسَّلَامُ عَلَيْكَ يَا حَبِيبَ اللَّهِ

Peace be upon you oh light of the lights	ٱلسَّلَامُ عَلَيْكَ يَا نُورَ ٱلْأَنْوَارِ
Peace be upon you oh ornament of the righteous	ٱلسَّلَامُ عَلَيْكَ يَا زَيْنَ ٱلْأَبْرَارِ
Peace be upon you oh descendant of the select	ٱلسَّلَامُ عَلَيْكَ يَا سَلِيلَ ٱلْأَخْيَارِ
Peace be upon you oh essence of the pure	ٱلسَّلَامُ عَلَيْكَ يَا عُنْصُرَ ٱلْأَطْهَارِ
Peace be upon you oh proof of the Compassionate	ٱلسَّلَامُ عَلَيْكَ يَا حُجَّةَ ٱلرَّحْمٰنِ
Peace be upon you oh pillar of faith	ٱلسَّلَامُ عَلَيْكَ يَا رُكْنَ ٱلْإِيمَانِ
Peace be upon you oh master of the believers	ٱلسَّلَامُ عَلَيْكَ يَا مَوْلَى ٱلْمُؤْمِنِينَ
Peace be upon you oh guardian of the righteous	ٱلسَّلَامُ عَلَيْكَ يَا وَلِيَّ ٱلصَّالِحِينَ
Peace be upon you oh landmark of guidance	ٱلسَّلَامُ عَلَيْكَ يَا عَلَمَ ٱلْهُدَىٰ
Peace be upon you oh ally of piety	ٱلسَّلَامُ عَلَيْكَ يَا حَلِيفَ ٱلتُّقَىٰ
Peace be upon you oh pillar of the religion	ٱلسَّلَامُ عَلَيْكَ يَا عَمُودَ ٱلدِّينِ
Peace be upon you oh son of the seal of the Prophets	ٱلسَّلَامُ عَلَيْكَ يَا بْنَ خَاتِمِ ٱلنَّبِيِّينَ
Peace be upon you oh son of the chief of the successors	ٱلسَّلَامُ عَلَيْكَ يَا بْنَ سَيِّدِ ٱلْوَصِيِّينَ
Peace be upon you oh son of Fatimah the radiant	ٱلسَّلَامُ عَلَيْكَ يَا بْنَ فَاطِمَةَ ٱلزَّهْرَاءِ
Chief of the women of the worlds	سَيِّدَةِ نِسَاءِ ٱلْعَالَمِينَ
Peace be upon you oh faithful trustee	ٱلسَّلَامُ عَلَيْكَ أَيُّهَا ٱلْأَمِينُ ٱلْوَفِيُّ
Peace be upon you oh content banner	ٱلسَّلَامُ عَلَيْكَ أَيُّهَا ٱلْعَلَمُ ٱلرَّضِيُّ
Peace be upon you oh ascetic and pious	ٱلسَّلَامُ عَلَيْكَ أَيُّهَا ٱلزَّاهِدُ ٱلتَّقِيُّ

Imam Hadi (as)

Peace be upon you oh proof against all creation	اَلسَّلَامُ عَلَيْكَ أَيُّهَا ٱلْحُجَّةُ عَلَى ٱلْخَلْقِ أَجْمَعِينَ
Peace be upon you oh equivalent of the Quran	اَلسَّلَامُ عَلَيْكَ أَيُّهَا ٱلتَّالِي لِلْقُرْآنِ
Peace be upon you oh clarifier of the lawful from the unlawful	اَلسَّلَامُ عَلَيْكَ أَيُّهَا ٱلْمُبَيِّنُ لِلْحَلَالِ مِنَ ٱلْحَرَامِ
Peace be upon you oh sincere guardian	اَلسَّلَامُ عَلَيْكَ أَيُّهَا ٱلْوَلِيُّ ٱلنَّاصِحُ
Peace be upon you oh clear path	اَلسَّلَامُ عَلَيْكَ أَيُّهَا ٱلطَّرِيقُ ٱلْوَاضِحُ
Peace be upon you oh shining star	اَلسَّلَامُ عَلَيْكَ أَيُّهَا ٱلنَّجْمُ ٱللَّائِحُ
I bear witness oh my master oh Abul-Hasan	أَشْهَدُ يَا مَوْلَاىَ يَا أَبَا ٱلْحَسَنِ
That you are indeed the Proof of Allah over His creation	أَنَّكَ حُجَّةُ ٱللَّهِ عَلَى خَلْقِهِ
And His successor among His creatures	وَخَلِيفَتُهُ فِي بَرِيَّتِهِ
And His trustee in His lands	وَأَمِينُهُ فِي بِلَادِهِ
And His witness over His servants	وَشَاهِدُهُ عَلَى عِبَادِهِ
And I bear witness that you are the word of piety	وَأَشْهَدُ أَنَّكَ كَلِمَةُ ٱلتَّقْوَى
And the door of guidance	وَبَابُ ٱلْهُدَى
And the firmest handhold	وَٱلْعُرْوَةُ ٱلْوُثْقَى
And the proof over those above the Earth	وَٱلْحُجَّةُ عَلَى مَنْ فَوْقَ ٱلْأَرْضِ
And whoever is beneath the soil	وَمَنْ تَحْتَ ٱلثَّرَى
And I bear witness that you are purified from sins	وَأَشْهَدُ أَنَّكَ ٱلْمُطَهَّرُ مِنَ ٱلذُّنُوبِ
Absolved from faults	ٱلْمُبَرَّأُ مِنَ ٱلْعُيُوبِ

Continuous Calling

And favoured with the honour of Allah	وَٱلْمُخْتَصُّ بِكَرَامَةِ ٱللَّهِ
And granted the proof of Allah	وَٱلْمَحْبُوُّ بِحُجَّةِ ٱللَّهِ
And gifted with the word of Allah	وَٱلْمَوْهُوبُ لَهُ كَلِمَةُ ٱللَّهِ
And the pillar to which the servants resort	وَٱلرُّكْنُ ٱلَّذِى يَلْجَأُ إِلَيْهِ ٱلْعِبَادُ
And by whom the lands are revived	وَتُحْيَىٰ بِهِ ٱلْبِلَادُ
And I bear witness oh my master	وَأَشْهَدُ يَا مَوْلَاىَ
That I am, with you and your forefathers and your sons, certain and acknowledging	أَنِّى بِكَ وَبِآبَائِكَ وَأَبْنَائِكَ مُوقِنٌ مُقِرٌّ
And following you in my very self	وَلَكُمْ تَابِعٌ فِى ذَاتِ نَفْسِى
And the laws of my religion	وَشَرَايِعِ دِينِى
And the conclusion of my deeds	وَخَاتِمَةِ عَمَلِى
And my return and my place of rest	وَمُنْقَلَبِى وَمَثْوَاىَ
And I am friendly to your friends	وَأَنِّى وَلِىٌّ لِمَنْ وَالَاكُمْ
And an enemy to your enemies	وَعَدُوٌّ لِمَنْ عَادَاكُمْ
A believer in your secrecy and openness	مُؤْمِنٌ بِسِرِّكُمْ وَعَلَانِيَتِكُمْ
And your first and last	وَأَوَّلِكُمْ وَآخِرِكُمْ
May my father and mother be sacrificed for you	بِأَبِى أَنْتَ وَأُمِّى
And peace be upon you, and the mercy of Allah and His blessings	وَٱلسَّلَامُ عَلَيْكَ وَرَحْمَةُ ٱللَّهِ وَبَرَكَاتُهُ

Imam Askari (as)

Abu Hashim wrote to Imam Askari (as) complaining about the oppressiveness of prison. The Imam (as) wrote back "You will pray the Dhuhr prayer in your own house." This occurred but Abu Hashim was still distressed from poverty after a lengthy stay in prison, however, he felt ashamed to ask the Imam (as) again.

The Imam sent him some money without him asking, writing "When you are in need, do not be ashamed and do not refrain. Ask for it and you will be given what you need, God willing." – Imam Askari (as)

(Kitab al-Irshad Al-Buraq translation, page 487)

On 8 Rabiul Thani to celebrate his birth, and on 8 Rabiul Awal to commemorate his martyrdom you can recite the following ziyarah.

Peace be upon you oh my Master	اَلسَّلَامُ عَلَيْكَ يَا مَوْلَاىَ
Oh Abu-Muhammad Hasan the son of Ali	يَا أَبَا مُحَمَّدٍ الْحَسَنُ بْنَ عَلِيٍّ
The guide and the well-guided	اَلْهَادِىَ اَلْمُهْتَدِى
And Allah's mercy and blessings	وَرَحْمَةُ اللَّهِ وَبَرَكَاتُهُ
Peace be upon you oh guardian (over the believers) of Allah and son of His guardians	اَلسَّلَامُ عَلَيْكَ يَا وَلِيَّ اللَّهِ وَابْنَ أَوْلِيَائِهِ
Peace be upon you oh proof of Allah and son of His proofs	اَلسَّلَامُ عَلَيْكَ يَا حُجَّةَ اللَّهِ وَابْنَ حُجَجِهِ
Peace be upon you oh choice of Allah and son of His chosen ones	اَلسَّلَامُ عَلَيْكَ يَا صَفِيَّ اللَّهِ وَابْنَ أَصْفِيَائِهِ
Peace be upon you oh successor of Allah and son of His successors and father of His successor	اَلسَّلَامُ عَلَيْكَ يَا خَلِيفَةَ اللَّهِ وَابْنَ خُلَفَائِهِ وَأَبَا خَلِيفَتِهِ
Peace be upon you son of the seal of the prophets	اَلسَّلَامُ عَلَيْكَ يَا بْنَ خَاتَمِ النَّبِيِّينَ

Continuous Calling

Peace be upon you oh son of the chief of the successors	ٱلسَّلَامُ عَلَيْكَ يَا بْنَ سَيِّدِ ٱلْوَصِيِّينَ
Peace be upon you oh son of the commander of the faithful	ٱلسَّلَامُ عَلَيْكَ يَا بْنَ أَمِيرِ ٱلْمُؤْمِنِينَ
Peace be upon you oh son of the Chief of the women of the worlds	ٱلسَّلَامُ عَلَيْكَ يَا بْنَ سَيِّدَةِ نِسَاءِ ٱلْعَالَمِينَ
Peace be upon you oh son of the guiding Imams	ٱلسَّلَامُ عَلَيْكَ يَا بْنَ ٱلْأَئِمَّةِ ٱلْهَادِينَ
Peace be upon you oh son of the rightly guided successors	ٱلسَّلَامُ عَلَيْكَ يَا بْنَ ٱلْأَوْصِيَاءِ ٱلرَّاشِدِينَ
Peace be upon you oh protection of the pious	ٱلسَّلَامُ عَلَيْكَ يَا عِصْمَةَ ٱلْمُتَّقِينَ
Peace be upon you oh leader of the successful	ٱلسَّلَامُ عَلَيْكَ يَا إِمَامَ ٱلْفَائِزِينَ
Peace be upon you oh pillar of the believers	ٱلسَّلَامُ عَلَيْكَ يَا رُكْنَ ٱلْمُؤْمِنِينَ
Peace be upon you oh relief of the distressed	ٱلسَّلَامُ عَلَيْكَ يَا فَرَجَ ٱلْمَلْهُوفِينَ
Peace be upon you oh inheritor of the selected prophets	ٱلسَّلَامُ عَلَيْكَ يَا وَارِثَ ٱلْأَنْبِيَاءِ ٱلْمُنْتَجَبِينَ
Peace be upon you oh treasurer of the knowledge of the successor of the Messenger of Allah	ٱلسَّلَامُ عَلَيْكَ يَا خَازِنَ عِلْمِ وَصِيِّ رَسُولِ ٱللَّهِ
Peace be upon you oh caller to the judgment of Allah	ٱلسَّلَامُ عَلَيْكَ أَيُّهَا ٱلدَّاعِي بِحُكْمِ ٱللَّهِ
Peace be upon you oh speaker through the Book of Allah	ٱلسَّلَامُ عَلَيْكَ أَيُّهَا ٱلنَّاطِقُ بِكِتَابِ ٱللَّهِ

Imam Askari (as)

Peace be upon you oh proof of proofs	اَلسَّلَامُ عَلَيْكَ يَا حُجَّةَ الْحُجَجِ
Peace be upon you oh guide of nations	اَلسَّلَامُ عَلَيْكَ يَا هَادِيَ الْأُمَمِ
Peace be upon you oh guardian of blessings	اَلسَّلَامُ عَلَيْكَ يَا وَلِيَّ النِّعَمِ
Peace be upon you oh repository of knowledge	اَلسَّلَامُ عَلَيْكَ يَا عَيْبَةَ الْعِلْمِ
Peace be upon you oh ship of forbearance	اَلسَّلَامُ عَلَيْكَ يَا سَفِينَةَ الْحِلْمِ
Peace be upon you oh father of the awaited Imam	اَلسَّلَامُ عَلَيْكَ يَا أَبَا الْإِمَامِ الْمُنْتَظَرِ
Whose proof is apparent to the rational	اَلظَّاهِرَةِ لِلْعَاقِلِ حُجَّتُهُ
And whose recognition is firm in certainty	وَالثَّابِتَةِ فِي الْيَقِينِ مَعْرِفَتُهُ
Hidden from the eyes of the oppressors	الْمُحْتَجَبِ عَنْ أَعْيُنِ الظَّالِمِينَ
And concealed from the rule of the transgressors	وَالْمُغَيَّبِ عَنْ دَوْلَةِ الْفَاسِقِينَ
And through whom our Lord will renew Islam anew after its obliteration	وَالْمُعِيدِ رَبُّنَا بِهِ الْإِسْلَامَ جَدِيداً بَعْدَ الْإِنْطِمَاسِ
And the Quran fresh after its fading	وَالْقُرْآنَ غَضّاً بَعْدَ الْإِنْدِرَاسِ
I bear witness, oh my master, that you established prayer	أَشْهَدُ يَامَوْلَايَ أَنَّكَ أَقَمْتَ الصَّلَاةَ
And gave charity	وَآتَيْتَ الزَّكَاةَ
And enjoined good	وَأَمَرْتَ بِالْمَعْرُوفِ
And forbade evil	وَنَهَيْتَ عَنِ الْمُنْكَرِ
And called to the path of your Lord	وَدَعَوْتَ إِلَى سَبِيلِ رَبِّكَ
With wisdom and good advice	بِالْحِكْمَةِ وَالْمَوْعِظَةِ الْحَسَنَةِ
And worshipped Allah sincerely	وَعَبَدْتَ اللَّهَ مُخْلِصاً

Until certainty came to you	حَتَّىٰ أَتَاكَ ٱلْيَقِينُ
I ask Allah by the status that you have with Him	أَسْأَلُ ٱللَّهَ بِٱلشَّأْنِ ٱلَّذِى لَكُمْ عِنْدَهُ
To accept my visitation to you	أَنْ يَتَقَبَّلَ زِيَارَتِى لَكُمْ
And to appreciate my effort towards you	وَيَشْكُرَ سَعْيِى إِلَيْكُمْ
And answer my supplication by you	وَيَسْتَجِيبَ دُعَائِى بِكُمْ
And make me from the supporters of truth	وَيَجْعَلَنِى مِنْ أَنْصَارِ ٱلْحَقِّ
And its followers and its adherents	وَأَتْبَاعِهِ وَأَشْيَاعِهِ
And its allies and lovers	وَمَوَالِيهِ وَمُحِبِّيهِ
And peace be upon you and the mercy of Allah and His blessings	وَٱلسَّلَامُ عَلَيْكَ وَرَحْمَةُ ٱللَّهِ وَبَرَكَاتُهُ
Oh Allah, send blessings upon our chief Muhammad and his household	اَللَّهُمَّ صَلِّ عَلَىٰ سَيِّدِنَا مُحَمَّدٍ وَأَهْلِ بَيْتِهِ
And send blessings upon Hasan son of Ali	وَصَلِّ عَلَىٰ ٱلْحَسَنِ بْنِ عَلِيٍّ
The guide to Your religion	ٱلْهَادِى إِلَىٰ دِينِكَ
And the caller to Your path	وَٱلدَّاعِى إِلَىٰ سَبِيلِكَ
The banner of guidance	عَلَمِ ٱلْهُدَىٰ
And the beacon of piety	وَمَنَارِ ٱلتُّقَىٰ
And the essence of intelligence	وَمَعْدِنِ ٱلْحِجَىٰ
And the shelter of understanding	وَمَأْوَىٰ ٱلنُّهَىٰ
And the rain of creation	وَغَيْثِ ٱلْوَرَىٰ
And the cloud of wisdom	وَسَحَابِ ٱلْحِكْمَةِ

Imam Askari (as)

And the ocean of advice	وَبَحْرُ ٱلْمَوْعِظَةِ
And the inheritor of the Imams	وَوَارِثِ ٱلْأَئِمَّةِ
And the witness over the nation	وَٱلشَّهِيدِ عَلَى ٱلْأُمَّةِ
The infallible, the refined	ٱلْمَعْصُومِ ٱلْمُهَذَّبِ
And the virtuous, the close	وَٱلْفَاضِلِ ٱلْمُقَرَّبِ
And the purified from impurity	وَٱلْمُطَهَّرِ مِنَ ٱلرِّجْسِ
The one whom You made inherit the knowledge of the Book	ٱلَّذِي وَرَّثْتَهُ عِلْمَ ٱلْكِتَابِ
And inspired him with decisive speech	وَأَلْهَمْتَهُ فَصْلَ ٱلْخِطَابِ
And appointed him as a banner for the people of Your qibla	وَنَصَبْتَهُ عَلَماً لِأَهْلِ قِبْلَتِكَ
And linked obedience to him with obedience to You	وَقَرَنْتَ طَاعَتَهُ بِطَاعَتِكَ
And You made his love obligatory upon all Your creation	وَفَرَضْتَ مَوَدَّتَهُ عَلَى جَمِيعِ خَلِيقَتِكَ
Oh Allah, as he turned to You with good sincerity in Your oneness	اَللَّهُمَّ فَكَمَا أَنَابَ بِحُسْنِ ٱلْإِخْلَاصِ فِي تَوْحِيدِكَ
And repelled those who delved into comparing You	وَأَرْدَىٰ مَنْ خَاضَ فِي تَشْبِيهِكَ
And defended the people of faith for You	وَحَامَىٰ عَنْ أَهْلِ ٱلْإِيمَانِ بِكَ
So send, oh my Lord, blessings upon him	فَصَلِّ يَا رَبِّ عَلَيْهِ صَلَاةً
By which he reaches the station of the humble ones	يَلْحَقُ بِهَا مَحَلَّ ٱلْخَاشِعِينَ
And rises in Paradise	وَيَعْلُو فِي ٱلْجَنَّةِ
To the rank of his grandfather, the seal of the prophets	بِدَرَجَةِ جَدِّهِ خَاتَمِ ٱلنَّبِيِّينَ

And convey from us to him greetings and peace	وَبَلِّغْهُ مِنَّا تَحِيَّةً وَسَلاماً
And grant us from You in his loyalty	وَآتِنَا مِنْ لَدُنْكَ فِي مُوَالاتِهِ
Grace and excellence	فَضْلاً وَإِحْسَاناً
And forgiveness and contentment	وَمَغْفِرَةً وَرِضْوَاناً
Indeed, You are the possessor of great grace	إِنَّكَ ذُو فَضْلٍ عَظِيمٍ
And immense favour	وَمَنٍّ جَسِيمٍ

Imam Mahdi (as)

> "We are not neglectful of your affairs and we do not forsake your remembrance, otherwise your enemies would have destroyed you."
> – Imam Mahdi (as)

(Mikyal Al-Makaarim, Sayyid Rizvi translation, page 57)

On 15 Shaaban to celebrate his birth, and whenever you want to visit and greet your Imam. This is the famous Ziyarat Alee Yaaseen, which comes from a Hadith Qudsi (Holy Hadith – from Allah (swt)).

Peace be upon the family of Yasin	سَلَامٌ عَلَىٰ آلِ يٰـسٓ
Peace be upon you oh caller to Allah and His most divine signs	اَلسَّلَامُ عَلَيْكَ يَا دَاعِيَ ٱللَّهِ وَرَبَّانِيَّ آيَاتِهِ
Peace be upon you oh door of Allah and judge of His religion	اَلسَّلَامُ عَلَيْكَ يَا بَابَ ٱللَّهِ وَدَيَّانَ دِينِهِ
Peace be upon you oh successor of Allah and supporter of His truth	اَلسَّلَامُ عَلَيْكَ يَا خَلِيفَةَ ٱللَّهِ وَنَاصِرَ حَقِّهِ
Peace be upon you oh proof of Allah and guide to His will	اَلسَّلَامُ عَلَيْكَ يَا حُجَّةَ ٱللَّهِ وَدَلِيلَ إِرَادَتِهِ
Peace be upon you oh equivalent of Allah's Book and its interpreter	اَلسَّلَامُ عَلَيْكَ يَا تَالِيَ كِتَابِ ٱللَّهِ وَتَرْجُمَانَهُ
Peace be upon you in the hours of your night and the ends of your day	اَلسَّلَامُ عَلَيْكَ فِي آنَاءِ لَيْلِكَ وَأَطْرَافِ نَهَارِكَ
Peace be upon you oh remainder of Allah in His Earth	اَلسَّلَامُ عَلَيْكَ يَا بَقِيَّةَ ٱللَّهِ فِي أَرْضِهِ
Peace be upon you oh covenant of Allah which He took and emphasized	اَلسَّلَامُ عَلَيْكَ يَا مِيثَاقَ ٱللَّهِ ٱلَّذِي أَخَذَهُ وَوَكَّدَهُ

Continuous Calling

Peace be upon you oh promise of Allah which He guaranteed	اَلسَّلَامُ عَلَيْكَ يَا وَعْدَ ٱللَّهِ ٱلَّذِى ضَمِنَهُ
Peace be upon you oh raised banner	اَلسَّلَامُ عَلَيْكَ أَيُّهَا ٱلْعَلَمُ ٱلْمَنْصُوبُ
And poured knowledge	وَٱلْعِلْمُ ٱلْمَصْبُوبُ
And aid and vast mercy	وَٱلْغَوْثُ وَٱلرَّحْمَةُ ٱلْوَاسِعَةُ
A promise not false	وَعْداً غَيْرَ مَكْذُوبٍ
Peace be upon you when you stand	اَلسَّلَامُ عَلَيْكَ حِينَ تَقُومُ
Peace be upon you when you sit	اَلسَّلَامُ عَلَيْكَ حِينَ تَقْعُدُ
Peace be upon you when you read and explain	اَلسَّلَامُ عَلَيْكَ حِينَ تَقْرَأُ وَتُبَيِّنُ
Peace be upon you when you pray and supplicate	اَلسَّلَامُ عَلَيْكَ حِينَ تُصَلِّى وَتَقْنُتُ
Peace be upon you when you bow and prostrate	اَلسَّلَامُ عَلَيْكَ حِينَ تَرْكَعُ وَتَسْجُدُ
Peace be upon you when you profess monotheism and (God's) greatness	اَلسَّلَامُ عَلَيْكَ حِينَ تُهَلِّلُ وَتُكَبِّرُ
Peace be upon you when you praise and seek forgiveness	اَلسَّلَامُ عَلَيْكَ حِينَ تَحْمَدُ وَتَسْتَغْفِرُ
Peace be upon you when you begin and end your day	اَلسَّلَامُ عَلَيْكَ حِينَ تُصْبِحُ وَتُمْسِى
Peace be upon you in the night when it covers	اَلسَّلَامُ عَلَيْكَ فِى ٱللَّيْلِ إِذَا يَغْشَى
And the day when it appears	وَٱلنَّهَارِ إِذَا تَجَلَّى
Peace be upon you oh trusted Imam	اَلسَّلَامُ عَلَيْكَ أَيُّهَا ٱلْإِمَامُ ٱلْمَأْمُونُ
Peace be upon you oh preceding, the hoped for	اَلسَّلَامُ عَلَيْكَ أَيُّهَا ٱلْمُقَدَّمُ ٱلْمَأْمُولُ

Imam Mahdi (as)

Peace be upon you with encompassing peace	اَلسَّلَامُ عَلَيْكَ بِجَوَامِعِ ٱلسَّلَامِ
I call you to witness, oh my master	أُشْهِدُكَ يَا مَوْلَاىَ
That I bear witness that there is no god but Allah	أَنِّي أَشْهَدُ أَنْ لَا إِلٰهَ إِلَّا ٱللَّهُ
Alone, without partner	وَحْدَهُ لَا شَرِيكَ لَهُ
And that Muhammad is His servant and messenger	وَأَنَّ مُحَمَّداً عَبْدُهُ وَرَسُولُهُ
There is no beloved except him and his family	لَا حَبِيبَ إِلَّا هُوَ وَأَهْلُهُ
And I call you to witness, oh my master	وَأُشْهِدُكَ يَا مَوْلَاىَ
That Ali, commander of the faithful, is His proof	أَنَّ عَلِيّاً أَمِيرَ ٱلْمُؤْمِنِينَ حُجَّتُهُ
And Al-Hassan is His proof	وَٱلْحَسَنَ حُجَّتُهُ
And Al-Hussein is His proof	وَٱلْحُسَيْنَ حُجَّتُهُ
And Ali son of Al-Hussein is His proof	وَعَلِيَّ بْنَ ٱلْحُسَيْنِ حُجَّتُهُ
And Muhammad son of Ali is His proof	وَمُحَمَّدَ بْنَ عَلِيٍّ حُجَّتُهُ
And Ja'far son of Muhammad is His proof	وَجَعْفَرَ بْنَ مُحَمَّدٍ حُجَّتُهُ
And Musa son of Ja'far is His proof	وَمُوسَىٰ بْنَ جَعْفَرٍ حُجَّتُهُ
And Ali son of Musa is His proof	وَعَلِيَّ بْنَ مُوسَىٰ حُجَّتُهُ
And Muhammad son of Ali is His proof	وَمُحَمَّدَ بْنَ عَلِيٍّ حُجَّتُهُ
And Ali son of Muhammad is His proof	وَعَلِيَّ بْنَ مُحَمَّدٍ حُجَّتُهُ
And Al-Hasan son of Ali is His proof	وَٱلْحَسَنَ بْنَ عَلِيٍّ حُجَّتُهُ
And I bear witness that you are the proof of Allah	وَأَشْهَدُ أَنَّكَ حُجَّةُ ٱللَّهِ

You are all the first and the last	أَنْتُمُ الْأَوَّلُ وَالْآخِرُ
And that your return is truth, there is no doubt in it	وَأَنَّ رَجْعَتَكُمْ حَقٌّ لَا رَيْبَ فِيهَا
The day when "a soul's faith will not benefit it	يَوْمَ ﴿لَا يَنْفَعُ نَفْساً إِيمَانُهَا
If it had not believed before	لَمْ تَكُنْ آمَنَتْ مِنْ قَبْلُ
Or earned good through its faith" – Quran 6:158	أَوْ كَسَبَتْ فِي إِيمَانِهَا خَيْراً﴾
And that death is truth	وَأَنَّ الْمَوْتَ حَقٌّ
And that Nakir and Nakeer are truth	وَأَنَّ نَاكِراً وَنَكِيراً حَقٌّ
And I bear witness that the resurrection is truth	وَأَشْهَدُ أَنَّ النَّشْرَ حَقٌّ
And the raising (from graves) is truth	وَالْبَعْثَ حَقٌّ
And that the bridge (Sirat) is truth	وَأَنَّ الصِّرَاطَ حَقٌّ
And the watching place is truth	وَالْمِرْصَادَ حَقٌّ
And the scale is truth	وَالْمِيزَانَ حَقٌّ
And the gathering is truth	وَالْحَشْرَ حَقٌّ
And the reckoning is truth	وَالْحِسَابَ حَقٌّ
And Paradise and Hellfire are truth	وَالْجَنَّةَ وَالنَّارَ حَقٌّ
And the promise and threat about them are truth	وَالْوَعْدَ وَالْوَعِيدَ بِهِمَا حَقٌّ
Oh my master, wretched is the one who opposes you	يَا مَوْلَايَ شَقِيَ مَنْ خَالَفَكُمْ
And happy is the one who obeys you	وَسَعِدَ مَنْ أَطَاعَكُمْ
So bear witness to what I have called you to witness	فَاشْهَدْ عَلَى مَا أَشْهَدْتُكَ عَلَيْهِ

Imam Mahdi (as)

And I am a friend to you	وَأَنَا وَلِيٌّ لَكَ
Free from your enemy	بَرِيءٌ مِنْ عَدُوِّكَ
The truth is what you are pleased with	فَٱلْحَقُّ مَا رَضِيتُمُوهُ
And falsehood is what displeases you	وَٱلْبَاطِلُ مَا أَسْخَطْتُمُوهُ
And good is what you command	وَٱلْمَعْرُوفُ مَا أَمَرْتُمْ بِهِ
And evil is what you forbid	وَٱلْمُنْكَرُ مَا نَهَيْتُمْ عَنْهُ
So my soul believes in Allah	فَنَفْسِي مُؤْمِنَةٌ بِٱللَّهِ
Alone without partner	وَحْدَهُ لاَ شَرِيكَ لَهُ
And in His Messenger and in the commander of the faithful	وَبِرَسُولِهِ وَبِأَمِيرِ ٱلْمُؤْمِنِينَ
And in you, oh my master, your first and your last	وَبِكُمْ يَا مَوْلاَيَ أَوَّلِكُمْ وَآخِرِكُمْ
And my support is prepared for you	وَنُصْرَتِي مُعَدَّةٌ لَكُمْ
And my love is sincere for you	وَمَوَدَّتِي خَالِصَةٌ لَكُمْ
Amen, Amen	آمِين آمِين

Ziyarat Jamia Kabeera

قُل لَّا أَسْأَلُكُمْ عَلَيْهِ أَجْرًا إِلَّا ٱلْمَوَدَّةَ فِي ٱلْقُرْبَىٰ

Say "I do not ask you for any reward except love for my relatives"

Quran 42:23

This Ziyarah is one of our most authentic ahadith, with a very short chain of narrators going back to Imam Hadi (as). Imam Mahdi (afs) placed emphasis on this Ziyarah by name (Najm-us-Saqeb, p243). Its eloquence is undeniable and it is a summary of our beliefs.

You may begin by saying the Shahadah, followed by 100 "Allahu Akbar", then recite:

Peace be upon you oh Ahlul Bayt of Prophethood	اَلسَّلَامُ عَلَيْكُمْ يَا أَهْلَ بَيْتِ ٱلنُّبُوَّةِ
And the place of the message	وَمَوْضِعَ ٱلرِّسَالَةِ
And the frequented place of the angels	وَمُخْتَلَفَ ٱلْمَلَائِكَةِ
And the descent of revelation	وَمَهْبِطَ ٱلْوَحْيِ
And the essence of mercy	وَمَعْدِنَ ٱلرَّحْمَةِ
And the treasurers of knowledge	وَخُزَّانَ ٱلْعِلْمِ
And the pinnacle of forbearance	وَمُنْتَهَىٰ ٱلْحِلْمِ
And the roots of generosity	وَأُصُولَ ٱلْكَرَمِ
And the leaders of nations	وَقَادَةَ ٱلْأُمَمِ
And the guardians of blessings	وَأَوْلِيَاءَ ٱلنِّعَمِ
And the elements of the righteous	وَعَنَاصِرَ ٱلْأَبْرَارِ
And the pillars of the good	وَدَعَائِمَ ٱلْأَخْيَارِ
And the governors of the servants	وَسَاسَةَ ٱلْعِبَادِ
And the supports of the lands	وَأَرْكَانَ ٱلْبِلَادِ

And the doors of faith	وَأَبْوَابَ ٱلْإِيمَانِ
And the trustees of the Merciful	وَأُمَنَاءَ ٱلرَّحْمٰنِ
And the lineage of the prophets	وَسُلَالَةَ ٱلنَّبِيِّينَ
And the elite of the messengers	وَصَفْوَةَ ٱلْمُرْسَلِينَ
And the chosen household of the Lord of the worlds	وَعِتْرَةَ خِيَرَةِ رَبِّ ٱلْعَالَمِينَ
And the mercy of Allah and His blessings	وَرَحْمَةُ ٱللَّهِ وَبَرَكَاتُهُ
Peace be upon the Imams of guidance	اَلسَّلَامُ عَلَىٰ أَئِمَّةِ ٱلْهُدَىٰ
And the lamps in the darkness	وَمَصَابِيحِ ٱلدُّجَىٰ
And the banners of piety	وَأَعْلَامِ ٱلتُّقَىٰ
And the possessors of understanding	وَذَوِي ٱلنُّهَىٰ
And the endowed with intelligence	وَأُولِي ٱلْحِجَىٰ
And the refuge of mankind	وَكَهْفِ ٱلْوَرَىٰ
And the inheritors of the prophets	وَوَرَثَةِ ٱلْأَنْبِيَاءِ
And the highest example	وَٱلْمَثَلِ ٱلْأَعْلَىٰ
And the most excellent call	وَٱلدَّعْوَةِ ٱلْحُسْنَىٰ
And the Proofs of Allah upon the people of the world	وَحُجَجِ ٱللَّهِ عَلَىٰ أَهْلِ ٱلدُّنْيَا
And the Hereafter and the First	وَٱلْآخِرَةِ وَٱلْأُولَىٰ
And the mercy of Allah and His blessings	وَرَحْمَةُ ٱللَّهِ وَبَرَكَاتُهُ
Peace be upon the places of recognising Allah	اَلسَّلَامُ عَلَىٰ مَحَالِّ مَعْرِفَةِ ٱللَّهِ
And the dwellings of Allah's blessing	وَمَسَاكِنِ بَرَكَةِ ٱللَّهِ

And the essences of Allah's wisdom	وَمَعَادِنِ حِكْمَةِ ٱللَّهِ
And the guardians of Allah's secret	وَحَفَظَةِ سِرِّ ٱللَّهِ
And the bearers of Allah's Book	وَحَمَلَةِ كِتَابِ ٱللَّهِ
And the successors of the Prophet of Allah	وَأَوْصِيَاءِ نَبِيِّ ٱللَّهِ
And the progeny of the Messenger of Allah	وَذُرِّيَّةِ رَسُولِ ٱللَّهِ
May Allah's blessings be upon him and his family	صَلَّى ٱللَّهُ عَلَيْهِ وَآلِهِ
And the mercy of Allah and His blessings	وَرَحْمَةُ ٱللَّهِ وَبَرَكَاتُهُ
Peace be upon the callers to Allah	ٱلسَّلَامُ عَلَى ٱلدُّعَاةِ إِلَى ٱللَّهِ
And the indicators to Allah's satisfaction	وَٱلْأَدِلَّاءِ عَلَى مَرْضَاتِ ٱللَّهِ
And those steadfast in the command of Allah	وَٱلْمُسْتَقِرِّينَ فِي أَمْرِ ٱللَّهِ
And those complete in love of Allah	وَٱلتَّامِّينَ فِي مَحَبَّةِ ٱللَّهِ
And the sincere in Allah's oneness	وَٱلْمُخْلِصِينَ فِي تَوْحِيدِ ٱللَّهِ
And those manifesting Allah's command and prohibition	وَٱلْمُظْهِرِينَ لِأَمْرِ ٱللَّهِ وَنَهْيِهِ
And His honoured servants	وَعِبَادِهِ ٱلْمُكْرَمِينَ
Who do not precede Him in speech	ٱلَّذِينَ لَا يَسْبِقُونَهُ بِٱلْقَوْلِ
And who act by His command	وَهُمْ بِأَمْرِهِ يَعْمَلُونَ
And the mercy of Allah and His blessings	وَرَحْمَةُ ٱللَّهِ وَبَرَكَاتُهُ
Peace be upon the preaching Imams	ٱلسَّلَامُ عَلَى ٱلْأَئِمَّةِ ٱلدُّعَاةِ
And the guiding leaders	وَٱلْقَادَةِ ٱلْهُدَاةِ

Ziyarat Jamia Kabeera

And the ruling chiefs	وَٱلسَّادَةِ ٱلْوُلَاةِ
And the protecting defenders	وَٱلذَّادَةِ ٱلْحُمَاةِ
And the people of remembrance	وَأَهْلِ ٱلذِّكْرِ
And possessors of command	وَأُولِي ٱلْأَمْرِ
And the remainder of Allah and His well chosen	وَبَقِيَّةِ ٱللَّهِ وَخِيَرَتِهِ
And His party and the repository of His knowledge	وَحِزْبِهِ وَعَيْبَةِ عِلْمِهِ
And His proof and His path	وَحُجَّتِهِ وَصِرَاطِهِ
And His light and His evidence	وَنُورِهِ وَبُرْهَانِهِ
And the mercy of Allah and His blessings	وَرَحْمَةُ ٱللَّهِ وَبَرَكَاتُهُ
I bear witness that there is no god but Allah	أَشْهَدُ أَنْ لَا إِلٰهَ إِلَّا ٱللَّهُ
Alone, no partner with Him	وَحْدَهُ لَا شَرِيكَ لَهُ
As Allah testified for Himself	كَمَا شَهِدَ ٱللَّهُ لِنَفْسِهِ
And His angels testified for Him	وَشَهِدَتْ لَهُ مَلَائِكَتُهُ
And possessors of knowledge among His creation	وَأُولُو ٱلْعِلْمِ مِنْ خَلْقِهِ
There is no god but He, the Mighty, the Wise	لَا إِلٰهَ إِلَّا هُوَ ٱلْعَزِيزُ ٱلْحَكِيمُ
And I bear witness that Muhammad is His chosen servant	وَأَشْهَدُ أَنَّ مُحَمَّداً عَبْدُهُ ٱلْمُنْتَجَبُ
And His approved messenger	وَرَسُولُهُ ٱلْمُرْتَضَى
He sent him with guidance and the religion of truth	أَرْسَلَهُ بِٱلْهُدَىٰ وَدِينِ ٱلْحَقِّ
To make it prevail over all religions	لِيُظْهِرَهُ عَلَىٰ ٱلدِّينِ كُلِّهِ

Continuous Calling

Even if the polytheists dislike it	وَلَوْ كَرِهَ ٱلْمُشْرِكُونَ
And I bear witness that you are the rightly guided Imams	وَأَشْهَدُ أَنَّكُمُ ٱلْأَئِمَّةُ ٱلرَّاشِدُونَ
The guided, the infallible	ٱلْمَهْدِيُّونَ ٱلْمَعْصُومُونَ
The honoured, the brought close	ٱلْمُكَرَّمُونَ ٱلْمُقَرَّبُونَ
The pious, the truthful	ٱلْمُتَّقُونَ ٱلصَّادِقُونَ
The chosen, obedient to Allah	ٱلْمُصْطَفَوْنَ ٱلْمُطِيعُونَ لِلَّهِ
The establishers by His command	ٱلْقَوَّامُونَ بِأَمْرِهِ
The agents by His will	ٱلْعَامِلُونَ بِإِرَادَتِهِ
Victorious in His honouring	ٱلْفَائِزُونَ بِكَرَامَتِهِ
He chose you through His knowledge	إِصْطَفَاكُمْ بِعِلْمِهِ
And approved you for His unseen	وَٱرْتَضَاكُمْ لِغَيْبِهِ
And chose you for His secret	وَٱخْتَارَكُمْ لِسِرِّهِ
And picked you by His power	وَٱجْتَبَاكُمْ بِقُدْرَتِهِ
And honoured you with His guidance	وَأَعَزَّكُمْ بِهُدَاهُ
And distinguished you with His evidence	وَخَصَّكُمْ بِبُرْهَانِهِ
And chose you for His light	وَٱنْتَجَبَكُمْ لِنُورِهِ
And supported you with His spirit	وَأَيَّدَكُمْ بِرُوحِهِ
And was pleased with you as successors in His Earth	وَرَضِيَكُمْ خُلَفَاءَ فِي أَرْضِهِ
And proofs over His creation	وَحُجَجاً عَلَىٰ بَرِيَّتِهِ
And supporters of His religion	وَأَنْصَاراً لِدِينِهِ
And guardians of His secret	وَحَفَظَةً لِسِرِّهِ

And treasurers of His knowledge	وَخَزَنَةً لِعِلْمِهِ
And repositories of His wisdom	وَمُسْتَوْدَعاً لِحِكْمَتِهِ
And interpreters of His revelation	وَتَرَاجِمَةً لِوَحْيِهِ
And pillars of His Oneness	وَأَرْكَاناً لِتَوْحِيدِهِ
And witnesses over His creation	وَشُهَدَاءَ عَلَىٰ خَلْقِهِ
And signs for His servants	وَأَعْلَاماً لِعِبَادِهِ
And beacons in His lands	وَمَنَاراً فِي بِلَادِهِ
And indicators to His path	وَأَدِلَّاءَ عَلَىٰ صِرَاطِهِ
Allah has protected you against slips	عَصَمَكُمُ ٱللَّهُ مِنَ ٱلزَّلَلِ
And secured you from corruption	وَآمَنَكُمْ مِنَ ٱلْفِتَنِ
And purified you from impurity	وَطَهَّرَكُمْ مِنَ ٱلدَّنَسِ
And removed from you uncleanliness	وَأَذْهَبَ عَنْكُمُ ٱلرِّجْسَ
And purified you a thorough purification	وَطَهَّرَكُمْ تَطْهِيراً
So you magnified His majesty	فَعَظَّمْتُمْ جَلَالَهُ
And exalted His status	وَأَكْبَرْتُمْ شَأْنَهُ
And honoured His generosity	وَمَجَّدْتُمْ كَرَمَهُ
And continued His remembrance	وَأَدَمْتُمْ ذِكْرَهُ
And confirmed His covenant	وَوَكَّدْتُمْ مِيثَاقَهُ
And made firm the bond of His obedience	وَأَحْكَمْتُمْ عَقْدَ طَاعَتِهِ
And were sincere to Him in secret and in public	وَنَصَحْتُمْ لَهُ فِي ٱلسِّرِّ وَٱلْعَلَانِيَةِ
And called to His path	وَدَعَوْتُمْ إِلَىٰ سَبِيلِهِ

With wisdom and excellent advice	بِٱلْحِكْمَةِ وَٱلْمَوْعِظَةِ ٱلْحَسَنَةِ
And sacrificed yourselves in His satisfaction	وَبَذَلْتُمْ أَنْفُسَكُمْ فِي مَرْضَاتِهِ
And you were patient with what afflicted you in His path	وَصَبَرْتُمْ عَلَىٰ مَا أَصَابَكُمْ فِي جَنْبِهِ
And you established prayer	وَأَقَمْتُمُ ٱلصَّلَاةَ
And gave charity	وَآتَيْتُمُ ٱلزَّكَاةَ
And commanded good	وَأَمَرْتُمْ بِٱلْمَعْرُوفِ
And forbade evil	وَنَهَيْتُمْ عَنِ ٱلْمُنْكَرِ
And struggled for Allah, true to His struggle	وَجَاهَدْتُمْ فِي ٱللَّهِ حَقَّ جِهَادِهِ
Until you proclaimed His call	حَتَّىٰ أَعْلَنْتُمْ دَعْوَتَهُ
And clarified His obligations	وَبَيَّنْتُمْ فَرَائِضَهُ
And established His limits	وَأَقَمْتُمْ حُدُودَهُ
And spread the laws of His rulings	وَنَشَرْتُمْ شَرَائِعَ أَحْكَامِهِ
And enacted His Sunnah (way)	وَسَنَنْتُمْ سُنَّتَهُ
And in that, you attained His pleasure	وَصِرْتُمْ فِي ذَٰلِكَ مِنْهُ إِلَى ٱلرِّضَا
And submitted to His decree	وَسَلَّمْتُمْ لَهُ ٱلْقَضَاءَ
And confirmed His messengers who passed before	وَصَدَّقْتُمْ مِنْ رُسُلِهِ مَنْ مَضَىٰ
So the one who turns away from you is a heretic	فَٱلرَّاغِبُ عَنْكُمْ مَارِقٌ
And the one who adheres to you is joined	وَٱللَّازِمُ لَكُمْ لَاحِقٌ
And the one who falls short in your right perishes	وَٱلْمُقَصِّرُ فِي حَقِّكُمْ زَاهِقٌ
And the truth is with you and in you	وَٱلْحَقُّ مَعَكُمْ وَفِيكُمْ

Ziyarat Jamia Kabeera

And from you and to you	وَمِنْكُمْ وَإِلَيْكُمْ
And you are its people and its essence	وَأَنْتُمْ أَهْلُهُ وَمَعْدِنُهُ
And the inheritance of prophethood is with you	وَمِيرَاثُ ٱلنُّبُوَّةِ عِنْدَكُمْ
And the return of creation is to you	وَإِيَابُ ٱلْخَلْقِ إِلَيْكُمْ
And their accounting is upon you	وَحِسَابُهُمْ عَلَيْكُمْ
And the decisive word is with you	وَفَصْلُ ٱلْخِطَابِ عِنْدَكُمْ
And Allah's signs are with you	وَآيَاتُ ٱللَّهِ لَدَيْكُمْ
And His resolves are in you	وَعَزَائِمُهُ فِيكُمْ
And His light and proof are with you	وَنُورُهُ وَبُرْهَانُهُ عِنْدَكُمْ
And His command is to you	وَأَمْرُهُ إِلَيْكُمْ
Whoever befriends you has befriended Allah	مَنْ وَالَاكُمْ فَقَدْ وَالَى ٱللَّهَ
And whoever shows enmity to you has shown enmity to Allah	وَمَنْ عَادَاكُمْ فَقَدْ عَادَى ٱللَّهَ
And whoever loves you has loved Allah	وَمَنْ أَحَبَّكُمْ فَقَدْ أَحَبَّ ٱللَّهَ
And whoever hates you has hated Allah	وَمَنْ أَبْغَضَكُمْ فَقَدْ أَبْغَضَ ٱللَّهَ
And whoever clings to you has clung to Allah	وَمَنِ ٱعْتَصَمَ بِكُمْ فَقَدِ ٱعْتَصَمَ بِٱللَّهِ
You are the most straight path	أَنْتُمُ ٱلصِّرَاطُ ٱلْأَقْوَمُ
And witnesses of the transient abode	وَشُهَدَاءُ دَارِ ٱلْفَنَاءِ
And intercessors of the eternal dwelling	وَشُفَعَاءُ دَارِ ٱلْبَقَاءِ
And the continuous mercy	وَٱلرَّحْمَةُ ٱلْمَوْصُولَةُ
And the treasured sign	وَٱلْآيَةُ ٱلْمَخْزُونَةُ

Continuous Calling

And the preserved trust	وَٱلْأَمَانَةُ ٱلْمَحْفُوظَةُ
And the gate through which people are tested	وَٱلْبَابُ ٱلْمُبْتَلَى بِهِ ٱلنَّاسُ
Whoever comes to you is saved	مَنْ أَتَاكُمْ نَجَا
And whoever does not come to you is destroyed	وَمَنْ لَمْ يَأْتِكُمْ هَلَكَ
To Allah you call	إِلَى ٱللَّهِ تَدْعُونَ
And upon Him you indicate	وَعَلَيْهِ تَدُلُّونَ
And in Him you believe	وَبِهِ تُؤْمِنُونَ
And to Him you submit	وَلَهُ تُسَلِّمُونَ
And by His command you act	وَبِأَمْرِهِ تَعْمَلُونَ
And to His path you intimately guide	وَإِلَى سَبِيلِهِ تُرْشِدُونَ
And by His word you judge	وَبِقَوْلِهِ تَحْكُمُونَ
Happy is he who befriends you	سَعَدَ مَنْ وَالَاكُمْ
And whoever opposes you perishes	وَهَلَكَ مَنْ عَادَاكُمْ
And disappointed is the one who denies you	وَخَابَ مَنْ جَحَدَكُمْ
And whoever parts from you is astray	وَضَلَّ مَنْ فَارَقَكُمْ
And whoever clings to you succeeds	وَفَازَ مَنْ تَمَسَّكَ بِكُمْ
And whoever seeks refuge with you is secure	وَأَمِنَ مَنْ لَجَأَ إِلَيْكُمْ
And whoever believed you is safe	وَسَلِمَ مَنْ صَدَّقَكُمْ
And whoever clings to you is guided	وَهُدِيَ مَنِ ٱعْتَصَمَ بِكُمْ
Whoever follows you, Paradise is his abode	مَنِ ٱتَّبَعَكُمْ فَٱلْجَنَّةُ مَأْوَاهُ

Ziyarat Jamia Kabeera

And whoever opposes you, the Fire is his dwelling	وَمَنْ خَالَفَكُمْ فَٱلنَّارُ مَثْوَاهُ
And whoever denies you is a disbeliever	وَمَنْ جَحَدَكُمْ كَافِرٌ
And whoever wages war against you is a polytheist	وَمَنْ حَارَبَكُمْ مُشْرِكٌ
And whoever objects to you will be in the lowest depth of the hellfire	وَمَنْ رَدَّ عَلَيْكُمْ فِي أَسْفَلِ دَرْكٍ مِنَ ٱلْجَحِيمِ
I bear witness that this has been established for you in what passed	أَشْهَدُ أَنَّ هٰذَا سَابِقٌ لَكُمْ فِيمَا مَضَىٰ
And continues for you in what remains	وَجَارٍ لَكُمْ فِيمَا بَقِيَ
And that your spirits and your light	وَأَنَّ أَرْوَاحَكُمْ وَنُورَكُمْ
And your clay is one	وَطِينَتَكُمْ وَاحِدَةٌ
It is good and purified	طَابَتْ وَطَهُرَتْ
Some of it from some	بَعْضُهَا مِنْ بَعْضٍ
Allah created you as lights	خَلَقَكُمُ ٱللَّهُ أَنْوَاراً
And made you encircling His throne	فَجَعَلَكُمْ بِعَرْشِهِ مُحْدِقِينَ
Until He favoured us through you	حَتَّىٰ مَنَّ عَلَيْنَا بِكُمْ
And placed you "in houses	فَجَعَلَكُمْ ﴿فِي بُيُوتٍ
Allah permitted that they be raised	أَذِنَ ٱللَّهُ أَنْ تُرْفَعَ
And His name be mentioned in them" – Quran 24:36	وَيُذْكَرَ فِيهَا ٱسْمُهُ﴾
And made our call for blessings upon you	وَجَعَلَ صَلَوَاتِنَا عَلَيْكُمْ
And what He specified for us of your guardianship	وَمَا خَصَّنَا بِهِ مِنْ وِلَايَتِكُمْ

Continuous Calling

Goodness for our creation	طِيباً لِخَلْقِنَا
Purification for our souls	وَطَهَارَةً لِأَنْفُسِنَا
And a cleansing for us	وَتَزْكِيَةً لَنَا
And an atonement for our sins	وَكَفَّارَةً لِذُنُوبِنَا
So we became, with him, submitting by your grace	فَكُنَّا عِنْدَهُ مُسَلِّمِينَ بِفَضْلِكُمْ
And recognized by our belief in you	وَمَعْرُوفِينَ بِتَصْدِيقِنَا إِيَّاكُمْ
So Allah raised you to the most noble station of the honoured	فَبَلَغَ ٱللَّهُ بِكُمْ أَشْرَفَ مَحَلِّ ٱلْمُكَرَّمِينَ
And the highest ranks of the close	وَأَعْلَى مَنَازِلِ ٱلْمُقَرَّبِينَ
And the most elevated degrees of the messengers	وَأَرْفَعَ دَرَجَاتِ ٱلْمُرْسَلِينَ
Where no pursuer catches up to it	حَيْثُ لَا يَلْحَقُهُ لَاحِقٌ
And no surpasser surpasses it	وَلَا يَفُوقُهُ فَائِقٌ
And no proceeder proceeds it	وَلَا يَسْبِقُهُ سَابِقٌ
And no desirer desires reaching it	وَلَا يَطْمَعُ فِي إِدْرَاكِهِ طَامِعٌ
Until no close angel remains	حَتَّى لَا يَبْقَى مَلَكٌ مُقَرَّبٌ
And no sent prophet	وَلَا نَبِيٌّ مُرْسَلٌ
And no truthful one and no martyr	وَلَا صِدِّيقٌ وَلَا شَهِيدٌ
And no knowledgeable and no ignorant	وَلَا عَالِمٌ وَلَا جَاهِلٌ
And no lowly and no excellent	وَلَا دَنِيٌّ وَلَا فَاضِلٌ
And no righteous believer	وَلَا مُؤْمِنٌ صَالِحٌ
And no wicked sinner	وَلَا فَاجِرٌ طَالِحٌ

Ziyarat Jamia Kabeera

And no stubborn tyrant	وَلَا جَبَّارٍ عَنِيدٍ
And no rebellious devil	وَلَا شَيْطَانٍ مَرِيدٍ
And no creation that is between those a witness	وَلَا خَلْقٍ فِيمَا بَيْنَ ذَلِكَ شَهِيدٌ
Except that He made them recognize the majesty of your matter	إِلَّا عَرَّفَهُمْ جَلَالَةَ أَمْرِكُمْ
And the greatness of your standing	وَعِظَمَ خَطَرِكُمْ
The enormity of your affair	وَكِبَرَ شَأْنِكُمْ
And the perfection of your light	وَتَمَامَ نُورِكُمْ
And the truth of your status	وَصِدْقَ مَقَاعِدِكُمْ
And the firmness of your station	وَثَبَاتَ مَقَامِكُمْ
And the honour of your place and rank with Him	وَشَرَفَ مَحَلِّكُمْ وَمَنْزِلَتِكُمْ عِنْدَهُ
And your nobility with Him	وَكَرَامَتَكُمْ عَلَيْهِ
And your special status with Him	وَخَاصَّتَكُمْ لَدَيْهِ
And the closeness of your rank from Him	وَقُرْبَ مَنْزِلَتِكُمْ مِنْهُ
May my father and my mother	بِأَبِي أَنْتُمْ وَأُمِّي
My family and my wealth and my clan be sacrificed for you	وَأَهْلِي وَمَالِي وَأُسْرَتِي
I call Allah to witness and I call you to witness	أُشْهِدُ اللَّهَ وَأُشْهِدُكُمْ
That I am a believer in you and in what you believe in	أَنِّي مُؤْمِنٌ بِكُمْ وَبِمَا آمَنْتُمْ بِهِ
A disbeliever in your enemies and in what you disbelieved in	كَافِرٌ بِعَدُوِّكُمْ وَبِمَا كَفَرْتُمْ بِهِ
Aware of your matter	مُسْتَبْصِرٌ بِشَأْنِكُمْ

And in the misguidance of whoever opposes you	وَبِضَلَالَةِ مَنْ خَالَفَكُمْ
Loyal to you and to your allies	مُوَالٍ لَكُمْ وَلِأَوْلِيَائِكُمْ
Hating your enemies and opposing them	مُبْغِضٌ لِأَعْدَائِكُمْ وَمُعَادٍ لَهُمْ
At peace with whoever is at peace with you	سِلْمٌ لِمَنْ سَالَمَكُمْ
And at war with whoever wages war against you	وَحَرْبٌ لِمَنْ حَارَبَكُمْ
Confirming what you confirmed	مُحَقِّقٌ لِمَا حَقَّقْتُمْ
Nullifying what you nullified	مُبْطِلٌ لِمَا أَبْطَلْتُمْ
Obedient to you	مُطِيعٌ لَكُمْ
Recognizing your right	عَارِفٌ بِحَقِّكُمْ
Acknowledging your virtue	مُقِرٌّ بِفَضْلِكُمْ
Carrying your knowledge	مُحْتَمِلٌ لِعِلْمِكُمْ
Seeking refuge under your protection	مُحْتَجِبٌ بِذِمَّتِكُمْ
In recognition of you	مُعْتَرِفٌ بِكُمْ
Believing in your return	مُؤْمِنٌ بِإِيَابِكُمْ
Affirming your return	مُصَدِّقٌ بِرَجْعَتِكُمْ
Awaiting your command	مُنْتَظِرٌ لِأَمْرِكُمْ
Anticipating your governance	مُرْتَقِبٌ لِدَوْلَتِكُمْ
Taking by your sayings	آخِذٌ بِقَوْلِكُمْ
Acting by your command	عَامِلٌ بِأَمْرِكُمْ
Seeking shelter with you	مُسْتَجِيرٌ بِكُمْ
Visiting you	زَائِرٌ لَكُمْ

Ziyarat Jamia Kabeera

Clinging and taking refuge at your graves	لَائِذٌ عَائِذٌ بِقُبُورِكُمْ
Seeking intercession to Allah, Mighty and Majestic, through you	مُسْتَشْفِعٌ إِلَى اللهِ عَزَّ وَجَلَّ بِكُمْ
And seeking closeness to Him through you	وَمُتَقَرِّبٌ بِكُمْ إِلَيْهِ
And putting you forward before my requests	وَمُقَدِّمُكُمْ أَمَامَ طَلِبَتِي
And my needs and intentions	وَحَوَائِجِي وَإِرَادَتِي
In all my conditions and affairs	فِي كُلِّ أَحْوَالِي وَأُمُورِي
Believing in your secrets and your public affairs	مُؤْمِنٌ بِسِرِّكُمْ وَعَلَانِيَتِكُمْ
And your present and your hidden	وَشَاهِدِكُمْ وَغَائِبِكُمْ
And your first and last	وَأَوَّلِكُمْ وَآخِرِكُمْ
And delegating all of that to you	وَمُفَوِّضٌ فِي ذَلِكَ كُلِّهِ إِلَيْكُمْ
And submitting in it with you	وَمُسَلِّمٌ فِيهِ مَعَكُمْ
And my heart is submitted to you	وَقَلْبِي لَكُمْ مُسَلِّمٌ
And my opinion follows you	وَرَأْيِي لَكُمْ تَبَعٌ
And my support is prepared for you	وَنُصْرَتِي لَكُمْ مُعَدَّةٌ
Until Allah, the Exalted, revives His religion through you	حَتَّى يُحْيِيَ اللهُ تَعَالَى دِينَهُ بِكُمْ
And returns you in His days	وَيَرُدَّكُمْ فِي أَيَّامِهِ
And manifests you for His justice	وَيُظْهِرَكُمْ لِعَدْلِهِ
And establishes you in His earth	وَيُمَكِّنَكُمْ فِي أَرْضِهِ
So with you, with you	فَمَعَكُمْ مَعَكُمْ
Not with anyone other than you	لَا مَعَ غَيْرِكُمْ

Continuous Calling

I believe in you	آمَنْتُ بِكُمْ
And I have allied with your last ones as I have allied with your first ones	وَتَوَلَّيْتُ آخِرَكُمْ بِمَا تَوَلَّيْتُ بِهِ أَوَّلَكُمْ
And I disassociate to Allah, Mighty and Majestic	وَبَرِئْتُ إِلَى اللَّهِ عَزَّ وَجَلَّ
From your enemies	مِنْ أَعْدَائِكُمْ
And from idols and false gods	وَمِنَ الْجِبْتِ وَالطَّاغُوتِ
And the devils and their oppressive followers to you	وَالشَّيَاطِينِ وَحِزْبِهِمُ الظَّالِمِينَ لَكُمْ
The deniers of your rights	الْجَاحِدِينَ لِحَقِّكُمْ
And those who deviate from your guardianship	وَالْمَارِقِينَ مِنْ وِلَايَتِكُمْ
And the usurpers of your inheritance	وَالْغَاصِبِينَ لِإِرْثِكُمْ
Those who doubt you	الشَّاكِّينَ فِيكُمْ
Those deviating from you	الْمُنْحَرِفِينَ عَنْكُمْ
And from every unauthorized means other than you	وَمِنْ كُلِّ وَلِيجَةٍ دُونَكُمْ
And every obeyed besides you	وَكُلِّ مُطَاعٍ سِوَاكُمْ
And from the Imams who call to the fire	وَمِنَ الْأَئِمَّةِ الَّذِينَ يَدْعُونَ إِلَى النَّارِ
So may Allah make me steadfast forever as long as I live	فَثَبَّتَنِيَ اللَّهُ أَبَداً مَا حَيِيتُ
Upon loyalty to you	عَلَى مُوَالَاتِكُمْ
And love for you and your religion	وَمَحَبَّتِكُمْ وَدِينِكُمْ
And may He grant me success in your obedience	وَوَفَّقَنِي لِطَاعَتِكُمْ
And provide me with your intercession	وَرَزَقَنِي شَفَاعَتَكُمْ

And make me among the best of your followers	وَجَعَلَنِي مِنْ خِيَارِ مَوَالِيكُمْ
Those following what you called to	ٱلتَّابِعِينَ لِمَا دَعَوْتُمْ إِلَيْهِ
And make me among those who trace your footsteps	وَجَعَلَنِي مِمَّنْ يَقْتَصُّ آثَارَكُمْ
And traverse your path	وَيَسْلُكُ سَبِيلَكُمْ
And are guided by your guidance	وَيَهْتَدِي بِهُدَاكُمْ
And are gathered in your group	وَيُحْشَرُ فِي زُمْرَتِكُمْ
And return in your return	وَيَكِرُّ فِي رَجْعَتِكُمْ
And are empowered in your government	وَيُمَلَّكُ فِي دَوْلَتِكُمْ
And honoured in your well-being	وَيُشَرَّفُ فِي عَافِيَتِكُمْ
And is established in your days	وَيُمَكَّنُ فِي أَيَّامِكُمْ
And his eyes are delighted tomorrow by seeing you	وَتَقِرُّ عَيْنُهُ غَدًا بِرُؤْيَتِكُمْ
May my father and my mother	بِأَبِي أَنْتُمْ وَأُمِّي
My soul, my family, and my wealth be sacrificed for you	وَنَفْسِي وَأَهْلِي وَمَالِي
Whoever wants Allah begins with you	مَنْ أَرَادَ ٱللَّهَ بَدَأَ بِكُمْ
And whoever declares His oneness accepts from you	وَمَنْ وَحَّدَهُ قَبِلَ عَنْكُمْ
And whoever aims for Him is directed through you	وَمَنْ قَصَدَهُ تَوَجَّهَ بِكُمْ
My masters, I cannot count your praise	مَوَالِيَّ لَا أُحْصِي ثَنَاءَكُمْ
And I cannot reach your essence through praise	وَلَا أَبْلُغُ مِنَ ٱلْمَدْحِ كُنْهَكُمْ
And I cannot describe your worth	وَمِنَ ٱلْوَصْفِ قَدْرَكُمْ

And you are the light of the chosen	وَأَنْتُمْ نُورُ الْأَخْيَارِ
And the guides of the righteous	وَهُدَاةُ الْأَبْرَارِ
And the Proofs of the Almighty	وَحُجَجُ الْجَبَّارِ
Through you, Allah opened	بِكُمْ فَتَحَ اللَّهُ
And through you, He concludes	وَبِكُمْ يَخْتِمُ
And through you, He sends down rain	وَبِكُمْ يُنَزِّلُ الْغَيْثَ
And through you, He prevents the sky from falling on the earth except by His permission	وَبِكُمْ يُمْسِكُ السَّمَاءَ أَنْ تَقَعَ عَلَى الْأَرْضِ إِلَّا بِإِذْنِهِ
And through you, He relieves distress	وَبِكُمْ يُنَفِّسُ الْهَمَّ
And He removes affliction	وَيَكْشِفُ الضُّرَّ
And with you is what His messengers were sent down with	وَعِنْدَكُمْ مَا نَزَلَتْ بِهِ رُسُلُهُ
And His angels descended with it	وَهَبَطَتْ بِهِ مَلَائِكَتُهُ
And to your grandfather was sent the Trustworthy Spirit	وَإِلَى جَدِّكُمْ بُعِثَ الرُّوحُ الْأَمِينُ
Allah has given you what He has not given anyone from the worlds	آتَاكُمُ اللَّهُ مَا لَمْ يُؤْتِ أَحَداً مِنَ الْعَالَمِينَ
Every noble one has lowered himself for your nobility	طَأْطَأَ كُلُّ شَرِيفٍ لِشَرَفِكُمْ
Every arrogant one has yielded to your obedience	وَبَخَعَ كُلُّ مُتَكَبِّرٍ لِطَاعَتِكُمْ
And every tyrant has submitted to your grace	وَخَضَعَ كُلُّ جَبَّارٍ لِفَضْلِكُمْ
And everything is humbled to you	وَذَلَّ كُلُّ شَيْءٍ لَكُمْ
And the earth has shone with your light	وَأَشْرَقَتِ الْأَرْضُ بِنُورِكُمْ

Ziyarat Jamia Kabeera

And the successful ones have succeeded through your guardianship	وَفَازَ ٱلْفَائِزُونَ بِوِلَايَتِكُمْ
Through you, the path to divine pleasure is taken	بِكُمْ يُسْلَكُ إِلَى ٱلرِّضْوَانِ
And upon whoever denied your guardianship is the wrath of the Merciful	وَعَلَى مَنْ جَحَدَ وِلَايَتَكُمْ غَضَبُ ٱلرَّحْمٰنِ
May my father and my mother	بِأَبِي أَنْتُمْ وَأُمِّي
My soul, my family, and my wealth be sacrificed for you	وَنَفْسِي وَأَهْلِي وَمَالِي
Your remembrance is among those who remember	ذِكْرُكُمْ فِي ٱلذَّاكِرِينَ
And your names among the names	وَأَسْمَاؤُكُمْ فِي ٱلْأَسْمَاءِ
And your bodies among the bodies	وَأَجْسَادُكُمْ فِي ٱلْأَجْسَادِ
And your spirits among the spirits	وَأَرْوَاحُكُمْ فِي ٱلْأَرْوَاحِ
And your souls among the souls	وَأَنْفُسُكُمْ فِي ٱلنُّفُوسِ
And your traces among the traces	وَآثَارُكُمْ فِي ٱلْآثَارِ
And your graves among the graves	وَقُبُورُكُمْ فِي ٱلْقُبُورِ
So how sweet are your names	فَمَا أَحْلَى أَسْمَاءَكُمْ
And how noble are your souls	وَأَكْرَمَ أَنْفُسَكُمْ
And how great is your affair	وَأَعْظَمَ شَأْنَكُمْ
And how majestic is your standing	وَأَجَلَّ خَطَرَكُمْ
And how fulfilled is your covenant	وَأَوْفَى عَهْدَكُمْ
And how truthful is your promise	وَأَصْدَقَ وَعْدَكُمْ
Your words are light	كَلَامُكُمْ نُورٌ

Continuous Calling

And your commands are righteousness	وَأَمْرُكُمْ رُشْدٌ
And your advice is piety	وَوَصِيَّتُكُمُ التَّقْوَى
And your actions are goodness	وَفِعْلُكُمُ الْخَيْرُ
And your habit is excellence	وَعَادَتُكُمُ الْإِحْسَانُ
And your nature is generosity	وَسَجِيَّتُكُمُ الْكَرَمُ
And your affair is truth	وَشَأْنُكُمُ الْحَقُّ
And truthfulness and kindness	وَالصِّدْقُ وَالرِّفْقُ
And your word is judgment and decree	وَقَوْلُكُمْ حُكْمٌ وَحَتْمٌ
And your opinion is knowledge, forbearance, and resolve	وَرَأْيُكُمْ عِلْمٌ وَحِلْمٌ وَحَزْمٌ
If goodness is mentioned, you are its beginning	إِنْ ذُكِرَ الْخَيْرُ كُنْتُمْ أَوَّلَهُ
And its root and its branch	وَأَصْلَهُ وَفَرْعَهُ
And its essence, its refuge, and its end	وَمَعْدِنَهُ وَمَأْوَاهُ وَمُنْتَهَاهُ
May my father, my mother, and my soul be sacrificed for you	بِأَبِي أَنْتُمْ وَأُمِّي وَنَفْسِي
How can I describe the beauty of your praise?	كَيْفَ أَصِفُ حُسْنَ ثَنَائِكُمْ
And count the beauty of your trials?	وَأُحْصِي جَمِيلَ بَلَائِكُمْ
And through you, Allah brought us out of humiliation	وَبِكُمْ أَخْرَجَنَا اللَّهُ مِنَ الذُّلِّ
And relieved from us the depths of distress	وَفَرَّجَ عَنَّا غَمَرَاتِ الْكُرُوبِ
And rescued us from the cliff edge of destruction	وَأَنْقَذَنَا مِنْ شَفَا جُرُفِ الْهَلَكَاتِ
And from the Fire	وَمِنَ النَّارِ

May my father, my mother, and my soul be sacrificed for you	بِأَبِي أَنْتُمْ وَأُمِّي وَنَفْسِي
Through loyalty to you, Allah taught us the landmarks of our religion	بِمُوَالَاتِكُمْ عَلَّمَنَا ٱللَّهُ مَعَالِمَ دِينِنَا
And He rectified what was corrupted of our worldly life	وَأَصْلَحَ مَا كَانَ فَسَدَ مِنْ دُنْيَانَا
And through allegiance to you, the word was completed	وَبِمُوَالَاتِكُمْ تَمَّتِ ٱلْكَلِمَةُ
And the blessing became great	وَعَظُمَتِ ٱلنِّعْمَةُ
And the division was unified	وَائْتَلَفَتِ ٱلْفُرْقَةُ
And through allegiance to you, the obligatory obedience is accepted	وَبِمُوَالَاتِكُمْ تُقْبَلُ ٱلطَّاعَةُ ٱلْمُفْتَرَضَةُ
And for you is the obligatory love	وَلَكُمُ ٱلْمَوَدَّةُ ٱلْوَاجِبَةُ
And the elevated ranks	وَٱلدَّرَجَاتُ ٱلرَّفِيعَةُ
And the praised station	وَٱلْمَقَامُ ٱلْمَحْمُودُ
And the known place with Allah, Mighty and Majestic	وَٱلْمَكَانُ ٱلْمَعْلُومُ عِنْدَ ٱللَّهِ عَزَّ وَجَلَّ
And the great prestige	وَٱلْجَاهُ ٱلْعَظِيمُ
And the immense affair	وَٱلشَّأْنُ ٱلْكَبِيرُ
And the accepted intercession	وَٱلشَّفَاعَةُ ٱلْمَقْبُولَةُ
Our Lord, we believe in what You sent down	رَبَّنَا آمَنَّا بِمَا أَنْزَلْتَ
And we followed the Messenger	وَٱتَّبَعْنَا ٱلرَّسُولَ
So write us among the witnesses	فَٱكْتُبْنَا مَعَ ٱلشَّاهِدِينَ
"Our Lord, do not deviate our hearts after You guided us	﴿رَبَّنَا لَا تُزِغْ قُلُوبَنَا بَعْدَ إِذْ هَدَيْتَنَا

Continuous Calling

And grant us mercy from Your presence	وَهَبْ لَنَا مِنْ لَدُنْكَ رَحْمَةً
Indeed, You are the Bestower" – Quran 3:8-9	إِنَّكَ أَنْتَ ٱلْوَهَّابُ﴾
Glory be to our Lord	سُبْحَانَ رَبِّنَا
Indeed, the promise of our Lord will surely be fulfilled	إِنْ كَانَ وَعْدُ رَبِّنَا لَمَفْعُولاً
Oh guardian (over the believers) of Allah	يَا وَلِيَّ ٱللَّهِ
Indeed, between me and Allah, Mighty and Majestic, are sins	إِنَّ بَيْنِي وَبَيْنَ ٱللَّهِ عَزَّ وَجَلَّ ذُنُوباً
None can address them except your pleasure	لَا يَأْتِي عَلَيْهَا إِلَّا رِضَاكُمْ
By the right of He who entrusted you with His secret	فَبِحَقِّ مَنِ ٱئْتَمَنَكُمْ عَلَىٰ سِرِّهِ
And appointed you as caretakers over His creation	وَٱسْتَرْعَاكُمْ أَمْرَ خَلْقِهِ
And connected your obedience to His obedience	وَقَرَنَ طَاعَتَكُمْ بِطَاعَتِهِ
Please ask forgiveness for my sins	لَمَّا ٱسْتَوْهَبْتُمْ ذُنُوبِي
And be my intercessors	وَكُنْتُمْ شُفَعَائِي
For indeed I am obedient to you	فَإِنِّي لَكُمْ مُطِيعٌ
Whoever obeys you has obeyed Allah	مَنْ أَطَاعَكُمْ فَقَدْ أَطَاعَ ٱللَّهَ
And whoever disobeys you has disobeyed Allah	وَمَنْ عَصَاكُمْ فَقَدْ عَصَى ٱللَّهَ
And whoever loves you has loved Allah	وَمَنْ أَحَبَّكُمْ فَقَدْ أَحَبَّ ٱللَّهَ
And whoever hates you has hated Allah	وَمَنْ أَبْغَضَكُمْ فَقَدْ أَبْغَضَ ٱللَّهَ
Oh Allah, if I found intercessors	اَللَّهُمَّ إِنِّي لَوْ وَجَدْتُ شُفَعَاءَ

Closer to You than Muhammad and his Ahlul Bayt	أَقْرَبَ إِلَيْكَ مِنْ مُحَمَّدٍ وَأَهْلِ بَيْتِهِ
The chosen, the Imams, the righteous	ٱلْأَخْيَارِ ٱلْأَئِمَّةِ ٱلْأَبْرَارِ
I would have made them my intercessors	لَجَعَلْتُهُمْ شُفَعَائِي
So by their right which You made obligatory upon Yourself	فَبِحَقِّهِمُ ٱلَّذِى أَوْجَبْتَ لَهُمْ عَلَيْكَ
I ask You to enter me among those who recognize them and their right	أَسْأَلُكَ أَنْ تُدْخِلَنِي فِي جُمْلَةِ ٱلْعَارِفِينَ بِهِمْ وَبِحَقِّهِمْ
And in the group of those granted mercy by their intercession	وَفِي زُمْرَةِ ٱلْمَرْحُومِينَ بِشَفَاعَتِهِمْ
Indeed, You are the Most Merciful of the merciful	إِنَّكَ أَرْحَمُ ٱلرَّاحِمِينَ
And may Allah send blessings upon Muhammad and his pure Household	وَصَلَّى ٱللَّهُ عَلَى مُحَمَّدٍ وَآلِهِ ٱلطَّاهِرِينَ
And grant abundant peace	وَسَلَّمَ تَسْلِيماً كَثِيراً
And Allah is sufficient for us and the best of guardians	وَحَسْبُنَا ٱللَّهُ وَنِعْمَ ٱلْوَكِيلُ

www.ingramcontent.com/pod-product-compliance
Lightning Source LLC
Chambersburg PA
CBHW020401080526
44584CB00014B/1129